THE **COMPLETE IDIOT'S GUIDE** TO

Social Media Marketing

Second Edition

by Jennifer Abernethy

ALPHA

A member of Penguin Group (USA) Inc.

This book is dedicated to all those who have dreams. Dreams to make a difference in the world. Dreams to grow their business and brands so that they can do more to contribute, share information, and help others.

ALPHA BOOKS

Published by the Penguin Group

Penguin Group (USA) Inc., 375 Hudson Street, New York, New York 10014, USA • Penguin Group (Canada), 90 Eglinton Avenue East, Suite 700, Toronto, Ontario M4P 2Y3, Canada (a division of Pearson Penguin Canada Inc.) • Penguin Books Ltd., 80 Strand, London WC2R 0RL, England • Penguin Ireland, 25 St. Stephen's Green, Dublin 2, Ireland (a division of Penguin Books Ltd.) • Penguin Group (Australia), 250 Camberwell Road, Camberwell, Victoria 3124, Australia (a division of Pearson Australia Group Pty. Ltd.) • Penguin Books India Pvt. Ltd., 11 Community Centre, Panchsheel Park, New Delhi—110 017, India • Penguin Group (NZ), 67 Apollo Drive, Rosedale, North Shore, Auckland 1311, New Zealand (a division of Pearson New Zealand Ltd.) • Penguin Books (South Africa) (Pty.) Ltd., 24 Sturdee Avenue, Rosebank, Johannesburg 2196, South Africa • Penguin Books Ltd., Registered Offices: 80 Strand, London WC2R 0RL, England

Copyright © 2012 by Jennifer Abernethy

International Standard Book Number: 978-1-61564-159-8
Library of Congress Catalog Card Number: 2011912286

14   13   12   8   7   6   5   4   3   2   1

Interpretation of the printing code: The rightmost number of the first series of numbers is the year of the book's printing; the rightmost number of the second series of numbers is the number of the book's printing. For example, a printing code of 12-1 shows that the first printing occurred in 2012.

Printed in the United States of America

Note: This publication contains the opinions and ideas of its author. It is intended to provide helpful and informative material on the subject matter covered. It is sold with the understanding that the author and publisher are not engaged in rendering professional services in the book. If the reader requires personal assistance or advice, a competent professional should be consulted.

The author and publisher specifically disclaim any responsibility for any liability, loss, or risk, personal or otherwise, which is incurred as a consequence, directly or indirectly, of the use and application of any of the contents of this book.

Most Alpha books are available at special quantity discounts for bulk purchases for sales promotions, premiums, fund-raising, or educational use. Special books, or book excerpts, can also be created to fit specific needs.

For details, write: Special Markets, Alpha Books, 375 Hudson Street, New York, NY 10014.

Publisher: *Marie Butler-Knight*

Associate Publisher: *Mike Sanders*

Executive Managing Editor: *Billy Fields*

Senior Acquisitions Editor: *Tom Stevens*

Development Editor: *Ginny Bess Munroe*

Senior Production Editor: *Janette Lynn*

Copy Editor: *Amy Borelli*

Cover Designer: *William Thomas*

Book Designers: *William Thomas, Rebecca Batchelor*

Indexer: *Brad Herriman*

Layout: *Brian Massey*

Senior Proofreader: *Laura Caddell*

Contents

Introduction

Overwhelmed by all this social media talk? Maybe you are feeling as if it's just too much and you will never understand it. Well, you are not alone; many people feel the same way. Here's some good news, though: this book was written just for you! Whether you know enough to be dangerous and want to learn more, or are just a beginner and want to join the social media revolution, I guarantee you will discover something new to help you with your social media marketing efforts. Ready to go? I raise my glass to your success!

How This Book Is Organized

To make this easy to read and not too complicated, you'll find tons of screen shots to help you navigate the social media websites. I've divided this book into five key parts:

Part 1, The World of Social Media and Social Networking, is a breakdown of what I refer to as the Big Seven in social media marketing. You get the lowdown on each of them, including how to get a good feel for the types of people using these platforms and why you need to strongly consider them for marketing you and your business. You will learn about having the right mind-set and why it's critical to your success on these social media platforms. You'll also come away with a good grip on the basics of what you need to get started.

Part 2, Let's Begin Marketing Your Business on Facebook, is where we roll up our sleeves and get you into that savvy social networker mind-set. You will learn how to create an amazing Facebook profile, learn about applications to use on Facebook, and get the details on how to customize your Facebook experience. And all this is done by taking you step by step through each process.

Part 3, Twitter, shows you what all the chirping buzz is about and why the world is suddenly all a-Twitter. In this part, you'll learn how to set up an amazing marketable Twitter profile. And when you're finished reading, it's my hope you will run (not walk) to your computer to set up your Twitter account and incorporate the amazing applications and tools. If you follow my recommendations, you will become a Twitterer worthy of millions of fans and followers.

Part 4, LinkedIn and Other Social Network Options, gives you so much more additional information to put into your social media strategy. You'll go from the professional networking site, LinkedIn, to examining the differences of MySpace and Google+. You'll also gain a better understanding of how online video and .tv are taking over the social media marketplace. This part provides the tools, the knowledge, and the comprehensive fundamentals of LinkedIn, a high-level look at MySpace and Google+, and an analysis of video marketing strategies. By the time you finish this part, you'll be ready for your online close-up.

Part 5, Streamlining and Expanding Your Program, shares with you the incredible tools and processes you can incorporate into an effective social media marketing strategy. After reading this part, you'll no longer feel overwhelmed as you add social media marketing to your day. You will learn ways to make this process easier to manage, and you'll even have fun implementing these techniques. This part also introduces more tools and strategies to help you streamline your social media marketing as you reach out to more prospects and clients and wow them.

Extras

To help you get the most out of this book, you'll find sidebars covering different facets of social media marketing. You'll find tips, tricks, and interesting facts to further educate and empower you and your team.

> **DEFINITION**
>
> Terms you need to know to navigate the world of social media.

> **TRY THIS**
>
> Simple and quick social media marketing ideas to try online.

> **NETIQUETTE**
>
> Tips that help you know what to do—and not to do—online to stay popular.

> **ONLINE CAUTION**
>
> These sidebars give you warnings about what to watch out for while engaging in social media.

> **DID YOU KNOW?**
>
> These are interesting statistics and projections about the world of social media marketing.

Note from the Author

In writing a book on a topic that is so rapidly changing, I was well aware that most social media programmers and designers are busy working and developing the next generations of tools. This means it is likely that some of the screen shots and functionality described in this book could be a bit different by the time the book's in your hands. I still trust that by reading and understanding the techniques and strategies that I recommend, you'll become a savvy social media marketer.

Acknowledgments

A virtual applause and tremendous thank you goes to a number of people who helped me put this book together and for the opportunity. First, again I want to thank an incredible coach and person, Anne Byrd, for calling me early one morning as I was walking out the door to vacation, and telling me that her literary agent was looking for someone with my expertise and that she had recommended me to her agent. Anne, thank you! I'd also like to thank Marilyn Allen, my literary agent, and the Penguin/Alpha team for signing me. I'm excited to share with the world this second edition!

I'd like to also especially thank Tom Stevens, who is a great acquisitions editor at Alpha. This book could not have happened without my personal editor and now Twitter friend, Damon Brown @BrownDamon on Twitter. You were such a great listening ear and source of motivation and expertise; thank you for your assistance and guidance when I needed you.

Heartfelt and sincere thanks to those peers and friends who have championed me along the way: my Two Mastermind groups, thank you ladies! Business Friend/mentor Judy Robinett in Utah @JudyRobinett on Twitter—thank you for all of the opportunity you have shared and given to me Judy! Friend and Mentor extraordinaire, Simon T. Bailey @BrilliantTweet. My brilliant friend and TV and Video Coach @RuthSherman, thank you! My Sales Lounge Insiders Club members that contributed ideas and their amazing enthusiasm—and all of my 2009–2011 alumni, I carry you all with me! Business colleagues and collaborators Frank Spencer @FrankSpencer on Twitter and Preston Andrew @Pandrew3 and @RuthSherman on Twitter. Gina Schreck and Lou Bortone for your expert industry guidance. Hugs to you! Shashi Bellamkonda @Shashib on Twitter. Thank you for always being so supportive! My Alley to the Valley peers, I'm loving this group!

Thanks to Dr. Michael Mercer and friends, Evelyn Heitman and Tina Hamet, for your incredible support. Dr. Fern Beu for always being there and watching all of this happen and being an inspiration and true pillar of support. Dr. Gary Frankel and the Thursday Gang—you guys are the best! To all my Twitter followers and fans on Facebook and LinkedIn who have always cheered me on. For book content expert assistance, a warm thank-you goes to Denise Wakeman (blog tips), Lesley Bohm (photography tips), Gina Schreck (tech advice), and Sam Horn (book marketing). Thanks to Daniel Davis of Tinkernut (technical advice), thanks to Ginny Munroe and Janette Lynn for your expert editorial help! A big Merci to High 5 to Ania Benyounes, my summer intern from Paris, who helped with the book. This book is for you to continue growing, building, and reaching your dreams. Make a difference! Lastly, all the readers who championed the first book and all the event planners that brought me in to speak in 2010 and 2011; a few standouts are the Shine event with Ali Brown, Bronx Tourism Office, Tory Johnson of Spark and Hustle, Black College Fund, and the National Speakers Association and Brilliance Weekend with Simon T. Bailey.

On a personal note, I would like to extend a sincere heartfelt thanks to my family—in particular, my partner in crime, my incredible creative designer husband, Michael Abernethy, who ran the household during the writing of this book and helps me tremendously behind the scenes at The Sales Lounge. And our amazing children, Natalie and Brayan, who are already savvy social networkers after watching me tweet, Facebook, video, and podcast over the past few years. Thank you for putting up with me writing away in 2011. To my parents, Eddie and Bing Edwards, and brothers, Eddie and John, and sisters-in-law, Linda and Gina. Thank you for being you!

Special Thanks to the Technical Reviewer

The Complete Idiot's Guide to Social Media Marketing, Second Edition, was reviewed by an expert who double-checked the accuracy of what you'll learn here, to help us ensure that this book gives you everything you need to know about social media marketing. Special thanks are extended to Vince Averello.

Trademarks

All terms mentioned in this book that are known to be or are suspected of being trademarks or service marks have been appropriately capitalized. Alpha Books and Penguin Group (USA) Inc. cannot attest to the accuracy of this information. Use of a term in this book should not be regarded as affecting the validity of any trademark or service mark.

The World of Social Media and Social Networking

Part

1

The concept of social media can be overwhelming to the novice or first-time participant. This part takes away the confusion and highlights the most popular social media sites and platforms. You learn in detail what they are, who uses them, and why they are important to consider for marketing your business.

The first part of this book also explores one of the key components to successful social media marketing: your mind-set. You are introduced to mind-set strategies to help you become a savvy social media marketer.

What Is All This Social Media Stuff, Anyway?

In This Chapter

- What is social media?
- The scoop on social networking
- The big seven social media sites
- Social media and its effect on business marketing

Everyone is talking about it. By now, you've at least heard or seen the term "social media," and that's most likely why you are reading this book. Big companies are getting involved with it, and entrepreneurs and business professionals are using it. Many people feel they *need* to use it, but they're not quite sure how to use it or exactly why they need to. If that is you, then you're not alone. And you're in the right place to find the answers you seek.

Why should you use social media? Well, if you are in business for yourself, it's something you must consider because social networking is free and millions of other business owners are using it. Because so many are using it, it is a great way to reach your prospects, customers, strategic partners, and the media to get information to grow and enhance your business.

In this chapter, we briefly explore the concepts of social media and social networking. By the end of this book, you will be a savvy social media marketer.

Social Media

Are you ready to learn why combining social media with your small business marketing efforts is worth your time? I know you aren't quite sure how to begin wrapping your mind around all this, but don't worry. I lay it all out for you and show you how to get started. First, let's get you on your way by looking deeper into just what social media is. Then you'll understand how that ties into social media networking and social media marketing.

A simple way to view social media is in layperson's terms: social media enable you to socialize through the Internet. The Internet is the "medium" through which this socializing is accomplished. So you're socializing via the Internet with your current clients, future prospects, and *business champions*. What makes it so effective? It's an interactive way to communicate.

DEFINITION

Business champions are people who will always give you a great reference and are high-powered networkers who will sing your praises. They can also serve as your strategic partners so that no matter who they are talking to, when the opportunity arises they will bring up your name. For example, if you are a real estate agent, build a circle with a loan officer, an interior decorator, an insurance agent, a house inspector, a banker, a painter, and so on. And, of course, this is a circle you create, so you'd also recommend them to your own network.

Social media has revolutionized the way entrepreneurs and small business owners market their businesses. To put these changes in perspective, let's take a brief walk through the past.

When people started a business in the late 1990s, they would build Flash websites. Everyone ran to web developers and asked for Flash, hoping to get a beautiful opening page with music, movement, and an integrated sound. And then you would click to open the website and see changing art or words on the screen. People thought if they invested in that new software development, their phone lines would ring off the hook. As it turned out, the web hosting sites just couldn't handle the speed of this technology back then, and consumers got frustrated at the long loading times on their computers.

Also in the 1990s, most small businesses would usually buy a yellow page ad or phone book listing and purchase ads in the local newspaper to become more visible. Perhaps they'd also distribute flyers, network, and have an open house at their business storefront. Maybe they'd find a local PR person who would help write some press releases. And if they were really savvy, they would buy some local radio spots.

Well, times have certainly changed. People aren't reading newspapers like they used to. The yellow pages are, for the most part, obsolete as far as entrepreneurs and small business owners are concerned, or people are opting for their "yellow page listing" to appear on the Internet only. Why? Because most people search the Internet before they use a telephone book. In fact, most 20-something adults use Google as their primary search engine for research. Nowadays, a small business eager for customers has to ramp up marketing efforts in a hurry. Entrepreneurs and business owners have to quickly tune in to how prospects (and your customers) are getting information, or your business will not succeed.

It is exciting to imagine the number of people you can reach today by going to your computer and simply logging on to several social media platforms that have millions of people participating on them, and then networking with them and getting the word out about your expertise and your business. It's really an entrepreneur and small business person's dream come true. Think about it: free platforms to meet, connect, and share with people who might be your future clients, customers, or business champions! It is also important to realize that your customers are most likely using social media (or will be soon). You want to be there, too, right along with your customers and potential clients.

DID YOU KNOW?

Back in 2007, social networking represented about 1 out of every 12 minutes spent online, while today it accounts for 1 out of every 6 minutes spent online.

Source: Comscore, June 2011 statistics

I often say that in a world where we are so connected with things like email, instant messaging, texting, Bluetooth wireless technology, cell phones, and social media, people are feeling more disconnected than ever before, because they find it hard to directly "reach" anyone and they want to feel a part of a community. *The more connected you can make your prospects and customers feel with you and your business, the more successful you are likely to become.* People want to do business with people who make them feel good about doing business with them.

Social media gives you, as a business owner, the platform to reach people directly and make them feel a part of your community online. At the same time, it also gives your prospects and customers a platform to engage with you and for you to get to know them. In the past, consumers talked about their purchasing experiences with their friends, family, and neighbors. Now, they are more likely to write about it in their blog or share their experience on one of the social media networks. Keep reading, and before long you will be a part of the conversation loop, too.

Social Networking

In the previous section, we took a trip to the recent past. Now, let's go much further back. How much further? Way back to the 1800s.

In the 1800s, networking was by word of mouth. This was the way small business owners and, in those days, socialites or those who wanted to raise their status in society got the word out about themselves and their services. After all, the phone wasn't invented until the 1870s. If you wanted to expand your status and grow your business and connections, you needed to network with the well-connected, affluent folks, such as those in high society.

During this time, "calling cards" were used. An individual would carry his card when he went out on a stroll. And he would leave a card (imprinted with his name on it) at the home of a specific "card receiver." If the receiver wasn't home, the individual would leave the card with the housekeeper or family member so the resident would know he had stopped by. Then, as the card receiver got to know this individual—and if they got along—the receiver would make appropriate introductions and acquaint the card holder with the receiver's circle of friends.

Now, back to the future—specifically, the late 1980s to the early 1990s, when AOL offered chat rooms with member communities and profiles. Soon, everyone was running to get a PC into their home so they could hear those glorious words: "You've got mail." People would spend time searching online AOL chat rooms in an attempt to find folks who had similar interests. Websites such as Classmates.com sprung up on the Internet; this particular site reconnected us with our high school peers, which jump-started socializing with old acquaintances online. At this point, online conversations were in full throttle.

Now, let's fast-forward. This time, the destination is the present, 2012. Many of us are getting too much email, and our email relentlessly follows us on our iPhones, Androids, BlackBerries, and texting devices. We can't even relax while watching TV because the people we are watching are asking us to join their Facebook fan page or follow them on Twitter. Then, when we go online, we see videos—live video streaming of people connecting through webinars and teleseminars.

People are also making goofy videos that are getting millions of viewers. These everyday online celebrities are popping up everywhere. Maybe even your average neighbor, Joe, has become a cyberstar. Maybe he did one of these silly videos a few months ago, and now he suddenly has thousands of Twitter followers and raving Facebook fans online. And you're shaking your head because you know Joe isn't exactly fan-worthy … or is he? That's the power of the Internet.

But wait, put on the brakes! Let's forget about the 1800s, the 1990s, and even Joe; just take a moment to appreciate the fact that social networking isn't new—really, it's just the delivery mechanism that's new. After you get to know social media marketing and networking, you will see that there are many similarities to old-fashioned Victorian-era networking. Today's social networking simply involves different mediums in which to leave one's calling card.

The Big Seven

The social media platforms are evolving at such a quick rate that it's hard to know which services will be a "must-have" in your marketing arsenal by the time we go to print with this book. I've seen one list that showed more than 150 social media platforms.

However, my guess is that the top seven I'm going to introduce you to won't be too different by the time this book is published. What you see listed here could have easily included more sites, but I've chosen seven that I think you, at the very least, need to become aware of. You should know from the start that each of these sites has its own "netiquette" rules and culture, and many allow you to incorporate a "status update" to keep your audience current with your goings-on. As you go through this book, we get into all these sites (and many others) in much greater detail. This will include listing the big do's and don'ts for growing your audience on each of these platforms.

Facebook

You can find Facebook at www.facebook.com. I refer to Facebook as "the television network of social media" because it skews far and wide, including people of every age, gender, socioeconomic background, and ethnicity.

Here are a few interesting Facebook facts:

- With over 800 million users, Facebook is now used by 1 in every 11 people on Earth. Additionally, more than 350 million active users currently access Facebook through their mobile devices. Have you gone mobile yet?

- The average income is $89,000. Surprised? Many still think of Facebook as a site for college students, because that's where the phenomenon started. However, now baby boomers use it for socializing *and* networking for business.

- While still using Facebook, college kids are also using other devices (such as mobile texting and video chat).

- Facebook has become the place to engage in business networking for 30- to 60-year-olds. In fact, 35 percent of the users are over 35.

- Entrepreneurs, small business owners, and independent professionals are using this site with a high level of sophistication.

- Each month, more business applications on Facebook are emerging. Over 350 million people access Facebook via their mobile phones. About half of all young people say they now get their news through Facebook.

Does this begin to paint a clearer picture of the possibilities of social media marketing? You can network, post a *status update*, have a fan page, grow your client list, and have all kinds of fun connecting with old colleagues and new friends, all while marketing your business and brand.

DEFINITION

A **status update** on a social media site answers the question: "What are you doing right now?" or "What is on your mind?" Think of your status update as your marketing message on Facebook or Twitter or LinkedIn. Now, don't take the question literally: savvy marketers will use the update to share expertise, instill trust and credibility, and drive traffic to their websites.

We cover Facebook more in Part 2 of this book, but for now just keep in mind that it works well with numerous platforms, such as LinkedIn, Twitter, blogs, and podcasts.

Here's what the Facebook login page looks like.

Twitter

You can find Twitter on www.twitter.com. I call Twitter the "online cocktail party." Twitter is another incredibly popular place to shout out to the world your expertise and how you are different from other businesses. All types of organizations, companies, entrepreneurs, and independent professionals are using this social media site to do amazing things with their businesses. Demographics are hard to confirm, but 33 to 60 years old is the basic age range, with females slightly outnumbering males.

After you experience Twitter's potential and learn a few applications (we'll cover Twitter starting with Chapter 8), you will find this to be another fantastic tool to broadcast your message to your business prospects and fans. You really have to experience Twitter, and after you try it, you will understand how this popular platform works.

Here's the Twitter login screen.

LinkedIn

You find LinkedIn at www.linkedin.com. I call this "the cable channel of social media." Here are some facts about LinkedIn:

- LinkedIn has a white-collar audience. Executives from every Fortune 500 company are members.

- LinkedIn has approximately 101 million users.

- The average age is 49, and the average income is $109,000.

LinkedIn is a bit more serious than the other sites, but if you want to become a savvy marketer, you must include this in your marketing toolbox. It's a definite must if you want to network with business executives, C-level executives (for example, CEOs and CFOs), Fortune 500 executives, and other global professionals. Entrepreneurs and small business owners network here and often benefit from having a profile on LinkedIn. And there is much more to this site than just serving as an electronic Rolodex.

In fact, the LinkedIn team appears to be working on adding more interactivity to the platform by incorporating more *sticky* applications to the site to make it more fun and engaging for the users.

DEFINITION

Sticky refers to a social media site where one can easily write, post, or paste information on the page and then replace it with something else. As of now, the trend is the more sticky the site is, the more engaging and popular the site becomes. Facebook, for example, is extremely sticky because you can frequently replace your status update with something new.

This is the LinkedIn login screen.

YouTube and Online Video

Video marketing is quickly becoming a must-do for businesses. With video phones and small handheld video cameras made specifically for the Internet, just about anyone these days can be a producer. The great news is that you don't have to have a degree in acting or take Film 101 to participate.

In fact, trends are that while slick, well-rehearsed videos do work, viewers want to see the real you in an authentic and transparent way. People love the immediacy of getting to see and hear you. It's okay for the camera to move a bit and your words don't have to be read off a cue card. You only have to be yourself. It's time to tear down those walls to your business ... let people experience the day in the life of the professional "you."

With over two billion views per day on YouTube (that figure is cited in the July 2011 YouTube blog), you can see that video is extremely popular and by all signs is here to stay. There are entrepreneurs and business owners uploading speaking engagements, videos of their seminars, client testimonials, and live streaming from events. There are even many who are just "talking" to the camera and are attracting a loyal following to their businesses by just being visible and interesting to listen to.

In later chapters, you will learn more about some online strategies and get additional tips to support you in your online video marketing efforts. Although some might be shy about putting themselves out there on the Internet, studies show that people want to watch online videos. ComScore, a digital media research firm, cites the following statistics for May 2011:

- Over 176 million Internet users watched at least one online video.

- The average viewer logged in 15.9 video hours.

- Of the 81.6 percent of the U.S. Internet audience viewing online video, the largest majority used YouTube.

- YouTube had 147.2 million unique viewers, 2.17 billion viewing sessions, and an average of 311 minutes spent per viewer on the site. That's an average of 5 hours spent per view.

For the entrepreneur or small business owner, getting started with online video can seem a bit daunting. But don't fret. Later in this book, you will learn about sites to bookmark where you can publish your videos, products you need to begin shooting video, and, most importantly, the right mind-set and strategy you need to begin video marketing for your business. Who knows? You might just become the next Internet star.

Blogs

A *blog* is a contraction of the word "weblog." A blog is usually maintained by an individual who makes regular posts of commentary, descriptions of events, or other material such as graphics or video. Entries are commonly displayed in the reverse chronological order—that is, the most current post is at the top of the blog. The verb "to blog" means you maintain or add content to your blog.

Blogs are a great way to build a following, share your expertise, and get better at communicating with your readers and followers. Although blogs are not a must-have, most regular bloggers say the benefits are tremendous, not only to the business but for the writer as well. Many different types of blogs exist, and wonderful applications are available to incorporate into your blog to further inspire and educate your readers.

Blogs can help your business bottom line, and it can drive readers to your website and ultimately to your phone or online shopping cart (the modern-day cash register), or even to your brick-and-mortar business storefront. These days, new blogs are incorporating other components of social media marketing, such as Twitter, Facebook, and video. We review what you can do with blogs in Chapter 16.

Ning

You can find Ning at www.ning.com. This site enables users to create their own social network. It is the world's largest platform for creating social websites. Top organizers, marketers, influencers, and activists use Ning to create an online destination for their clients, followers, and members. Imagine having a platform to send information back and forth—all within one portal. As of July 2011, more than 1,852,000 social networks have been created using Ning, which has more than 43 million registered members. The site's popularity is expanding so quickly that, as of this writing, more than 5,000 new Ning networks are created *each day*. Members are from all walks of life—from dog owners to activists to Hollywood types. And they all use it to create a social destination for their followers, and you can, too.

The Ning login page.

Google+

As of this writing, Google+ has over 40 million registered users and is climbing quickly. It is a social networking site and many like the clean look and professional way it displays user information. Google+ users currently are predominantly male but female users are beginning to gain traction. While the site is no where near the size of Twitter or Facebook in terms of users, it is not one to be ignored. A good practice would be to get on the site and create a profile to at least be seen on the site. As more features integrate into the site it is destined to become more popular. In the meantime, Google+ has influenced Facebook to rethink its platform and therefore Facebook launched many changes in the Fall of 2011.

TRY THIS

To avoid feeling overwhelmed by all these social media choices, take a deep breath and keep reading. When you finish this book, just decide which social media platform you'd like to explore first. You don't have to jump into all of these at once. Take your time and get comfortable.

Social Media Is Impacting Marketing Strategies

Social media is an incredible way to market your business, your cause, and yourself. It's also a great way to connect, interact, teach, help, deliver, inspire, and engage with your customers, prospects, members, friends, advocates, and business champions. Social media is still in its infancy, but it's already changing the face of business marketing and personal branding and communication. Most experts agree that the potential and the impact of social media marketing are extraordinary.

The Least You Need to Know

- Social media is not just a trend, so it's worth your time to become familiar with its powerful potential.
- Social media refers to the mediums that people use to socialize on the Internet.
- Social media networking is the process by which people network with those they know and those they are meeting for the first time on social media sites.
- Although hundreds of social media sites exist, you should familiarize yourself with the handful of popular sites that seem to have the most staying power.
- Although social media marketing and networking are still in the relatively early stages, they will continue to evolve, and you want to be sure you're included.

The Right Mind-Set

In This Chapter

- Having the right mind-set
- Investing your time
- Networking online
- Building celebrity status
- Protecting your business reputation

What do you think is the most important aspect of successful social media marketing? Well, it isn't having the know-how to effectively use all of the available platforms. Sure, it helps, but that's something just about everyone can learn. You'll find that the most important aspect to successful social media marketing is having the right mind-set.

Think about this: there are millions of people on Facebook, Twitter, and LinkedIn, but only a few thousand are actually using it to its fullest potential. In this chapter, you'll learn what it means to have the right mind-set. When that happens, you'll become one of the few who use social media marketing to its fullest potential.

Attracting Clients

I know from my own social media programs that the people who are going to ultimately be successful using the platforms come with …

- An open mind.
- A positive attitude and a willingness to listen.
- A determination to learn.

It's natural to worry about learning a new way to market your business. Change can be stressful. But try to avoid starting out with thoughts like the following on your mind:

- "I just don't get it. I don't care if someone just purchased a cup of coffee. I really don't think this will help me."

- "I really don't have time for this."

- "If someone doesn't buy from me within the first month, forget it."

If you enter into social media marketing with one or more of these negative thoughts, then your social media efforts just won't work. You'll have a hard time making a commitment to master the techniques in this book.

However, start out with the right mind-set and you'll be amazed at what you accomplish! So what's the right mind-set? It's a combination of things. Keep reading and you'll get a few ideas about how to get off on the right foot in social media.

Keep an Open Mind

Most early adaptors to Facebook or Twitter didn't know how it would impact their businesses. Yet today, those same people are now successful social media or what is now often called "social business" marketers and are gaining thousands of followers and champions for their businesses. By keeping an open mind, early social media adaptors found that people from all over the country and the world referred their businesses to their own networks.

Early adaptors also didn't know how many strategic alliances they would make or how many products they would sell. However, they had a hunch that social media would pay off, and so they kept an open mind. They reached out to people and treated them with respect. They offered great customer service and follow up—and violà!—they ended up with raving fans and followers.

Be Yourself

You are probably wondering how you can stand out in a crowd of millions. Is it possible? After all, you might think you aren't the most outgoing person out there. Here's the good news: you don't have to be an extrovert! In fact, many introverts actually like social media because they can write easily and network online, and it's more comfortable for them. And for the extroverts, well, they just love this stuff, and it enables them to communicate in another way to potentially millions of people.

How do you stand out on a platform that has tens of millions of people? Believe it or not, the secret is to just be yourself. That's what participants in social media look for. They are seeking a new voice and a unique perspective. If you begin copying someone else's style, that won't feel right to you. And you won't keep up your efforts to participate because it will be too much of a struggle. Be yourself and you'll find it easy to keep engaging in social media. Express your thoughts—your way. Share links that *you* believe will be of interest to your audience, not links that everyone else is posting. Don't worry about the number of followers you have, just focus on quality. Follow those you want to follow and your unique voice and brand will begin to emerge.

Energy Attracts Followers

We've all had that consumer experience where we go to buy something in a store and an unenthusiastic clerk makes us wonder if we really want to buy the product after all. However, when you go to a store and the staff is helpful, you have the opposite reaction. When the staff asks you questions or wants to know if you need help with anything, you have a great customer experience. You feel important, right? And you feel good about buying the product.

It's really the law of attraction: good energy attracts people and, ultimately, followers. The same concept holds true on social media. If people find you friendly, engaging, and authentic, and they need what you have to offer, they will continue to read your posts. They might even go a step further and recommend you to their networks.

Know Your Ideal Client

Successful social media marketers who have the right mind-set also have a clear sense of who their ideal client is. As you begin to engage on social media platforms, a good practice is to write and converse as if you are talking to your future client base.

If you are having a hard time visualizing this, try this exercise: imagine that your ideal client is reading what you are posting. Then ask yourself some of these questions:

- Who is my ideal customer?
- What would they need to hear to make me a trusted expert in their mind?
- What are they looking for when seeking someone like me to work with or buy a product from?
- Why do they need what I have to offer?

- When searching for similar products and services to mine, what keywords would they typically use when searching online?

- What are your ideal clients really needing to know?

- What keywords would attract them to my business and where are they participating online?

Answering these questions now helps you later as you put together your social media strategy. As you write to your ideal client, be conscientious of your tone and what you are saying or posting. Although you want to be yourself, you also need to remember who you are talking to at the same time. By incorporating the previous ideas, you begin to attract the types of followers you want to attract, which, ultimately, should match the profile of your ideal customer.

Marketers used to use the "push" mentality. This means they would push their ideas or products in front of us so often that we would end up buying what they're selling. But now, savvy social media marketers use the "pull" or attraction mentality. You put out the right information with the right tone to the right types of users, and you begin to pull prospects and customers to your business. You or your offerings attract them, and they will become clients, followers, or champions of your business. Maybe even all three! And if you really hit the jackpot you may make a new lifelong friend.

Networking Online

Think of social media marketing as the largest and biggest networking event you can imagine. It's one that operates 24/7 and it's accessible to you anywhere, anytime, right at your fingertips. In a society where we are all busy and pulled in many directions (and watching our budgets), this really is an entrepreneur's dream.

NETIQUETTE

Just like you would do with in-person networking, don't try to sell people your products and services the first time you meet them online. Build rapport, earn credibility, and gain trust. Eventually, your business and brand will benefit from the supportive followers you build, and ultimately it will lead to sales.

By utilizing social media, you can now network not only with people from your town, but with people from other states and countries. You never know who your next customer will be or where your next referral source will come from, so treat everyone as a prospect or referral source.

As you begin your journey into social media, apply the following traditional networking strategies:

- Be interested in others versus worrying about being interesting.

- Don't constantly be in selling mode. Be social.

- Follow up consistently.

- Be helpful, give information, and bring great energy to conversations.

- A great networker stays involved, so don't just appear once or twice and then disappear.

Remember, just because your social media contact might not be a potential customer, he or she just might be connected to someone who *is* looking for your services. Treat everyone with courtesy and respect. You never know where your next client will come from.

Building a Network of Followers

One of the beneficial things about social media marketing is that you can build a great community of followers. This should clearly be one of your goals. Whether it's on Facebook, Twitter, your blog, or your YouTube video channel, new followers equal prospects. And prospects equal customers, customers equal referral partners, and referral partners lead to business champions.

Twenty percent of your core followers provide 80 percent of your business. Think of popular musical stars and where they'd be without their loyal fans. Their fan clubs serve as their base; it would be much more difficult to continue to sell out venue after venue without their base supporters. The musical star is loyal to his or her fans and that loyalty gets reciprocated.

This is similar to the way it works with social media. You will build your follower base over time. It won't happen overnight. Remember, you must build trust, they must like you (or at least your products and services), and they must have reasons to stay connected with you. In this book, you will learn strategies to keep people connected to you by incorporating a strategic plan using various social media platforms. You will then continue to grow and shift to maintain your "star appeal" with your followers and fans.

Building Online Celebrity Status

For many people, thinking of themselves as celebrity types is very uncomfortable. However, a unique phenomenon is happening on social media platforms. Every day, entrepreneurs and small business owners just like you, who are working from home or other locations, are garnering tens of thousands of followers and fans through social media marketing. In the past, you could not collect tens of thousands of followers without having huge marketing budgets or hiring a PR or ad agency to help spread the word about your business.

Do you feel self-conscious when you try to think of yourself as a star in your business? If so, try your best to get rid of this feeling. Get over it ... or G.O.I.! After all, if you don't think you are worth following or having others connect to you on LinkedIn or another social website, then no one else will. Good business owners roll out the red carpet for their clients and deliver exceptional customer service. Begin shifting your thinking to the fact that, like it or not, you are the star in your business. Tell yourself that no one does it quite like you do. The more confidence you project, the more people you'll attract to your blog or website. Sound good?

To begin creating your celebrity status, you have to show your readers that you have expertise in your area. In fact, you're not just another expert; you're the go-to person for what you do. Over time, you will build trust and your followers or blog readers will feel good about taking advice from you. How does this happen? Through your social media marketing, your followers will begin to develop an affinity for your brand and for you. This is how you build your celebrity-dom within the online social media universe.

> **TRY THIS**
>
> As you develop a following on various social media platforms, begin engaging in dialogue, whether it's through direct messaging on Twitter, or writing on a follower's wall on Facebook. Listen to what people are saying online and show your support. You are building trust. Focus on giving and acknowledging others.

Eventually, you begin to get testimonials from customers and clients. You guide your new clients to write online about the good experience they had with you and your business. Through writing online articles, sharing your expertise in your blog, participating on the top social media sites, and creating videos, you'll begin to elevate your online status.

I know it sounds a little overwhelming, but you'll learn how to do this quickly, and believe it or not, it will even feel natural. Remember this mantra: you are the expert in what you do, no one does it like you, and that's why they are following you. Are you ready for your close-up now? Say yes!

Guiding People to Your Business

You're already getting the picture that participating in social media for your business is a good thing. Meeting new people, finding old friends, and meeting strategic partners is a lot of fun, isn't it? However, at the end of the day, you are doing this to drive revenue to your business. To successfully "work" social media, you need to begin effectively networking and building your connections, just as you would do at live speaking events.

As we talked about in the previous section, sharing your expertise over time helps you build credibility and guides people toward your business or website. While participating online, one of your goals should be to build up your list of customers. You will see this repeated several times throughout the book, but it's worth repeating: your list is your gold mine. Don't ever forget that.

In the past, people would say, "I want to add you to my mailing list," and it meant, literally, the traditional mail that actually shows up in your mailbox (the one on the street, not on your PC). Today's social media marketers are building an email list of their followers and fans along with attaining a cell phone list of their followers for future "M Marketing" or mobile (cell phone) marketing.

DID YOU KNOW?

By gathering cell phone numbers of your customers and prospects, you will be ready for future mobile marketing to your followers via their cell phones. Start planning now! Many people are also already obtaining the .mobi domain for their business; this domain is for the mobile service. Mobile marketing is expected to be mainstream by the end of 2013.

From now on, in all of your marketing invite people to connect with you on Facebook, to follow you on Twitter, link with you on LinkedIn, and so on. After they are connected to you on these sites, invite them to get your newsletter or e-zine, subscribe to your blog, or look at your videos on your YouTube channel. This will drive more people to follow and connect with you, which in turn will guide people toward your business. The more people you have following you, the more people you are likely to have singing your praises and recommending you.

Remember, This Is Your Business Reputation

If I were your personal business sales stylist, I would sit you down and talk to you about your business reputation. This is a very important aspect of social media marketing. Everything that you write, tweet, podcast, video, respond to, or even say publicly is a reflection of your business and ultimately your business reputation. It might sound silly to even bring this up, but oftentimes on many social media platforms people get so caught up in the fast-paced typing and the quick responses, they often forget that after you hit that send button, it is on the Internet forever.

DID YOU KNOW?

Soon you will be measured on your digital clout or digital influence. People are going to decide, based on your digital influence and connections, if you are someone who truly is an expert at what you do and worth connecting to. Beginning to master this social media marketing now will help build your influence and clout in the future.

One story out there in the media is about a Twitter user who went on a job interview. When he left the building, he updated his Twitter status about how lame the interviewer was. Although he didn't mention the company's name, the company did a Google search on him and his Twitter status update (or tweet) appeared in the search findings. Needless to say, he did not get the job.

ONLINE CAUTION

There is a new segment of the legal industry beginning to appear: social media liability. Although it's a fairly new industry, it's good to think about your social media policy, particularly if you have more than one person representing your business online. Many businesses are developing social media policies and crisis communication plans to manage online defamation issues and personal liability.

Another mistake people make is writing about their political or religious views. Although some might think it's not doing much harm to comment on this political person or that particular religious holiday or issue, it might offend enough people that it could hurt your business. A word to the wise: stay away from politics and religion and any other sensitive topics. You wouldn't approach these in traditional networking settings, so avoid it online. Of course, you will find the diehard political consultants or advisers writing about political views, but that is what they do. Stay focused on topics that are of interest to your ideal client.

Another danger is not thinking before hitting the send button. You may read or hear something and feel strongly about it and immediately log on to a site, spill your guts, and hit send. In slightly few instances this can be fine; however, in the majority other cases, it is most definitely not okay. Remember what you post today stays on the Internet forever.

Fair warning: your social media entry just might pop up months or years later within a search engine (such as Google). You need to think about whether what you've written will help or hurt your business reputation. Facebook recently launched Facebook nostalgia where they are going back in time (say 3 years ago) and writing: "on this day in 2009 Jane Doe wrote: ...." Word to the wise. Keep it professional and be forewarned.

Some companies have hired people to help with *online reputation management (ORM)*, which is a new buzzword these days. As an entrepreneur or business owner, you might not be able to hire a reputation management team just yet, but you can manage your own online reputation by just becoming aware of what you are writing and posting on your social media sites.

It probably seems like a lot to think about, but maintaining the right mind-set will all come together for you as you read this book.

DEFINITION

Online reputation management (ORM) is the process of monitoring online references to a person, brand, company, product, or service with the objective of minimizing the damage of online negative feedback and defamation.

The Unwritten Rules of Engagement

Although social media is still in its early stages, some unofficial unwritten rules of engagement exist. Many people do not follow these rules, but the créme de la créme of marketers and networkers do. Remember that the following rules can shift a bit as the social media landscape evolves, but these are good, basic rules to adhere to as you enter the world of social media marketing.

- Never post anything negative about your competition, or anyone else for that matter.

- Don't post when you are angry.

- Do not spam, because sending unsolicited marketing to unsolicited prospects is considered electronic abuse.

- Do not sell continuously.

- Share your expertise and tips to help others.

- Build relationships and trust.

- Share success stories that will help people.

- Don't write ego-driven posts or promote a personal agenda.

- Really listen to what people are saying.

- Organically grow your list of followers using the tips in this book. Do not buy programs that will autofollow or auto connect you to thousands. Connect a person at a time.

- Don't over automate. Go onto the sites LIVE. You don't have to be updated 24/7 with automated programs that update on your behalf around the clock.

- Be your authentic self.

Looking Forward to Logging In

Two of the biggest objections people have before they even get started with social media marketing are that they just don't have time or they don't understand why they should start connecting to people they do not know. Here's a simple goal to start with: look forward to logging in to your social media platforms. Approach it without dread or fear.

This is where the mind-set again comes into play. All successful social media marketers look forward to logging in each day and reading the messages people wrote or seeing who their new followers are. To get yourself into the right mind-set, remember the following:

- This is efficient and inexpensive marketing.

- These social media platforms are marketing you and your business to potentially millions while you sleep.

- You never know who you are going to meet online that will change the destiny of your life and business for the better.

With all of these points in mind, you should look forward to logging in. Just keep the basic principals in mind: engage online regularly, tell everyone you know that you are now using social media platforms, and share your expertise. Before you know it, you'll be looking forward to logging in.

Some social media marketers who have built a large following have begun hiring either a virtual assistant, an intern, or an employee to help them with their social media efforts. We'll get into time management strategies later in the book, but imagine if you had so many followers and were gaining so much attention that you had to hire help to assist you in managing your social media. That would be a good thing, right? The more people who know about you, your expertise, and your business, the more likely your business will grow.

Investing Your Time

Although nearly all of the social media platforms are free, one cost does exist. That cost is your time. Business owners all know that time is money. However, the good news with social marketing is that now you're investing your time in something that can have substantial returns in the long run.

One mistake people make when they first get started with social media is thinking that the payoff is going to be immediate. They think that with a few Facebook postings or by starting a blog, business will start growing and loyal fans will start suddenly referring people to you.

You should know that this is not typically the case. It does take time to organically grow your online network of followers and fans. However, at a certain point, your network will expand faster and larger. When that happens, two followers grow into four, four grows to eight, eight to sixteen, and so on. Before you know it, you have 1,000 new connections.

A good strategy for beginning social media users is to invest 20 minutes in the morning and 20 minutes in the evening. Think of it as attending a networking event. First you log in to Facebook, then LinkedIn, and next Twitter. Eventually, your time spent on social media platforms will expand. As you become comfortable, make some weekly goals. For instance, perhaps once a week you'll update your blog and upload a new video.

For some, the time invested online using social media has allowed them to cut back on some in-person networking events. While I don't recommend you cut back entirely on in-person networking, participating online allows you to have a regular presence to share information about your business or to learn about what others are doing. The value is in the conversations and the relationships you are building.

The Least You Need to Know

- The right mind-set is one of the most important aspects you bring to social media marketing.
- Think of social media as networking with the world, and spend time each day networking by getting to know others and sharing your wisdom.
- Social media marketing enables you to build your network of business champions, future referrals, and strategic partners.
- Think before hitting send—everything you post on the Internet stays there forever and affects your business reputation.
- Follow the unwritten rules of social media and you can create online celebrity status for yourself.
- Be ready to invest some time, because growing your business doesn't happen overnight.

What You Need to Get Started

In This Chapter

- Examples of great headshots
- Using cameras and video cameras in your business
- Thinking about your business strategy
- Determining who your target audience is
- Using social media to communicate with new and existing customers

Okay, so you are reading this book and you are ready to get started. Are you wondering what to do first or where to begin? If you've talked to other people about this, you've probably discovered that everyone has a different idea about where to start or what you need to get going. It's a bit confusing, isn't it?

Honestly, there is no absolute correct answer as to exactly what you should do first. However, in this chapter, I'll suggest a few things that you should put at the top of your to-do list when building your social media marketing network. Are you ready? Okay, let's jump right in and talk about headshots first.

Your Headshot

Most social media platforms have a place for you to put your headshot—your profile picture. Other sites may ask you to upload your company logo or avatar. Which should you use? This is a question many ask. Here is the rule of thumb, consider using a logo if your company is a household brand, an association, or if you represent a social community cause or network.

A personal headshot (typically a picture of you from the chest up) is usually what most people go with, and in most instances a personal headshot is recommended. In fact, to be a savvy social media marketer, a headshot is required. As you begin connecting to people around the country and world, your headshot will be the image that reflects your brand and your business. Therefore, your headshot photo is extremely important.

If you can invest in a great personal photographer, be sure to tell him or her that you plan to use this for your social media marketing. Be sure to ask if the photographer has done headshots for this medium before, or if he or she is at least familiar with sites like Facebook, Twitter, and LinkedIn. Make sure to convey what kind of photo you are looking for, and that there is chemistry between you and the photographer so that your personality shines through.

ONLINE CAUTION

Social media identity theft is on the rise. Try to register your personal name (for example, John Doe) as a domain. Refrain from putting a lot of personal information such as home phone numbers, addresses, or a picture of your car with license plates on your social media platforms.

Also, Internet security experts recommend setting up a Google Alert (see www. google.com/alerts) for your personal name and your business name. The system will monitor the Internet for you and you'll get an email every time your name or business name is mentioned online. You'll want to do this to make sure someone isn't plagiarizing your thoughts or harming your online reputation. You will want to do this for reputation management more so than anything else. *Note:* Identity theft and white collar Internet crime is rare but it does happen. Eventually we will all be digitally connected so it's good to monitor who is saying what about you and your company.

What's your goal with your headshot? To ensure it accurately represents your personality and brand. The typical headshot with the swirly gray/black background is no longer required, and frankly, no longer desired. In fact, you will look dated if you use that type of photograph. Remember, it's 2012, and you are now embarking into the world of *Web 3.0:* social media marketing. This is your chance to stand out in a crowd of millions. Get creative with your photo, and let your personality shine through.

DEFINITION

Web 3.0 does not refer to a new type of any technical specifications for your computer, but rather it refers to the cumulative changes in the ways Internet users "use" the web. Interactivity, information sharing, and user-centered experiences are all part of the Web 3.0 evolution. While definitions of Web 3.0 differ, it's important to know we are in the middle of another shift.

The following are some tips to keep in mind when making decisions about your headshot:

- Have fun and be creative with your photo.

- There are no steadfast rules here.

- Laugh, tilt your head, use your hands, and bring your personality into the photo.

- Wear attractive clothing that either looks good on you or reflects your color scheme for your business.

- Solid colors work well and bright colors exude energy.

- Have your photo taken while holding one of your products.

- Use an action shot if appropriate. For example, one photographer I know had someone take a picture of her taking a picture—right away you know she is a photographer.

Your main focus should be on having the photo reflect what you want it to reflect. Whether you're an artist, writer, speaker, mompreneur, coach, or banker, have fun coming up with a photo that truly shows who you are. The latest trends prove that the social media audience likes not only out-of-the-box photos, but photos that reflect someone's true personality and business brand.

What's the bottom line? Don't be afraid to get creative. The whole idea is to attract people to you with the energy from the photo. You will see many people on social media sites with their headshots taken outdoors. The theory here is that you are bringing nature and life into a medium that is stagnant and one-dimensional.

If you don't have the funds to invest in a professional photographer, one way to get a good photo quickly is to go to your local mall and seek a family photo studio and get a decent headshot done in about an hour. In most cases, you can select the shots you want to keep and they will give it to you on a CD, and you can be on your way home.

However, if that isn't an option, at least have someone take a photo of you at your office, home, or outdoors. Many successful social media folks have great photos that were taken by friends.

Lorrie Morgan-Ferrero
www.redhotcopy.com

David Neagle
www.DavidNeagle.com

Cynthia de Lorenzi
www.Successinthecity.org

Kara Allen
www.KaraAllen.com

Mathew Stansfield
www.matthewstansfield.com

Anne Byrd
www.ihaveabooboo.com

Simon T. Bailey
www.simontbailey.com

Aly & Andrea
www.rockstarsrock.com

Linda Messina
www.mygenchan.com

Take a look at these headshots to get an idea of what works.

And keep in mind, too, that you will be updating and changing your photo from time to time.

So get your photo ready to upload on the social media sites and you can cross one thing off the top of your to-do list. More importantly, by getting the photo done, you are on your way to getting started with your social media marketing.

> **DID YOU KNOW?**
>
> Many savvy social media marketers are using bright color backgrounds in their photos to stand out on sites like Twitter and Facebook. Red, turqoise, white, yellow, and orange are popular as they pop off the page.

Your Virtual Business Suitcase

Social media marketing is a great way to socialize and network with friends and prospects, but again, you must remember that you're there to promote your expertise, too. So what should you have packed in your virtual suitcase?

Here are some business "supplies" you need to have in your virtual suitcase before you begin your first day of social media marketing:

- A .jpg or .gif version of your business logo.

- A website address or URL. If you do not currently have a website domain (for instance, www.nameofyourbusiness.com), register the domain of your business before you get started. You will want to do this before others see your name and claim it as their own.

- Your business address and phone number. *Note:* if you run a home-based business, a good practice would be to not post your address.

- If you conduct business via cell phone, have that number ready to put on your site as well.

- A digital camera should become your new best marketing friend. Make sure you can easily download photos to the Internet. Carry it everywhere. You are now a marketer of your business and brand.

- A video camera that allows you to upload easily to the Internet. I'm hearing great things about the Kodak PlayTouch HD camera. Remember, you are the marketing star now. Your digital camera and video are your other new best marketing friends.

ONLINE CAUTION

Don't ask your young teenage niece or nephew to set up or manage your marketing for you. While they are quick on the keyboard, they typically don't understand how to market a business on social media.

At this point, don't worry about where to place information on your website. In later chapters, you will learn how to place your website information on the social media sites.

Your Business Strategy

When starting social media marketing, it's easy to get caught up in the fun of finding old friends (or being the one who's found!). It's also fun seeing how many new followers and friend requests you get on a daily basis. However, in a medium where early adaptors weren't quite sure how social media would affect their businesses, recent adaptors have an advantage. You are going into social media with at least a basic business strategy.

Setting Goals

First, you want to have some clear goals in mind. Look at what your peers are doing. Look at your competition. Then, do things differently. Put your own spin on your marketing. Remember, you want to stand out and be different. However, it's also important to be genuinely authentic in your approach.

As you get more involved with several social media platforms, you want to ensure your message is consistent across all platforms. Otherwise, your message will be interpreted differently on different sites. That wouldn't be very effective, would it?

Perhaps your initial strategy would be to drive traffic to your website. Let's examine a few different ways you can do that. You'll want to market the benefits of visiting your website in all of your posts. Or maybe you should offer a special that is only available on your website, so that all of your social media marketing is guiding people in that direction.

Or maybe you want people to read your blog. If this is the case, you will want to talk about your blog in the majority of your posts and messaging, along with providing links to your blog and recent entries. Maybe your goal is to build your golden list.

(And it should be a goal!) If this is the case, your message should talk about the benefits of being on your list: you will give them advanced notice of sales and special events, and allow them to garner VIP status in your business.

Maybe you just simply want another way to build relationships with your current clients and new prospects; this is a great strategy. By doing this, you engage in more two-way conversations with your clients and prospects using social media platforms. It gives you an opportunity to listen more and understand what your clients and prospects are thinking about.

Do you get the idea now? By engaging in social media, you can create forums or message boards to have discussions and dialogue with your network. All you have to do is pick the direction that is right for you and your business. This is just a small sampling of great strategies you can use with social media marketing. We'll cover strategies in more detail later in the book.

For now, here are some good questions to ask yourself as you begin getting involved and setting goals:

- Why am I engaging in social media? Is it that I just want to learn the technology, or do I want it to try to drive traffic to my website or business or blog? Do I simply want to get the phones ringing?

- What message do I want to send to my customers and prospects?

- Do I want to handle this or will I delegate the social media marketing to someone else in my business?

- What types of people do I want to attract to my business?

- What is the profile of my ideal customer?

- Am I willing to participate daily, or at least regularly?

- Will I begin asking clients if they are using social media? (Say yes.) How will I collect that information?

- Do I want to try to drive readers to my blog, website, or YouTube channel?

- Should I feature a client or product of the week or day? Or maybe provide a tip for the day?

- Do I just want to get on the top social media platforms, or am I ready to create an entire social media strategy using a blog, Twitter, Facebook, LinkedIn, video, and other social media?

Yes, the previous list is a lot of questions, but you really do need to narrow down your focus. At the beginning of the chapter, I said there is no right or wrong answer when it comes to effective social media business strategy. That's true, but if you consider the previous list of questions, you will narrow your approach. If you begin social media marketing by randomly creating your accounts and occasionally posting comments, it isn't going to get you where you want to be. If you make it completely centered around you and your business, that won't work, either. Social media is about participation; it should be a nice give and take.

Also, make sure you're not setting your expectations too high. I've said it before but it bears repeating: social media is not immediate access to millions of people who will gladly spend millions of dollars on your business. The potential is there, for sure, but set reasonable goals for your social media marketing so you don't get disappointed early in the process.

And rest assured, by answering the list of questions above, you'll have a good initial strategy in place. It will help you know that you are on the right path for your business and to achieve your strategic goals. Over time, your plan and marketing strategy will continue to evolve, just as the social media networks and consumer-buying patterns evolve.

Know Your Target Audience

As with traditional marketing, successful social media marketing requires you to know your target audience. This might seem like a no-brainer, but some people do start businesses without a clear image of who they're selling to.

Even for the entrepreneur and small business owner, clarifying who needs your product or service and who wants it are key. To help you home in on your target market, answer these questions:

- Are your customers or readers men or women? Or both?

- What age group are you targeting?

- What are their income levels?

- Where do they live?

- Where are they when they go online—are they at home or in a corporate office?

After you answer these questions, you'll have a good feel for your customers. As you get into social media marketing, you will be seen and heard within the forums and sites where your target audience is participating. And on the flip side, you'll know in a hurry if you're participating on a site that doesn't fit your target market. By knowing who your customer is, you save time and market your brand more efficiently.

Gaining New Customers

Millions of people have been flocking toward social media marketing for business to meet new people, network with new and current prospects, and share their expertise. One of the big outcomes of this might be that you will gain new customers.

However, I cautioned you in the last section about having unreasonable expectations. Don't make the mistake of thinking this will happen overnight. When you first begin, remember that it's a social situation, even though it's online. Take your time and get comfortable with how the sites work.

If you follow proper netiquette while participating, you will meet more new people from around the country (and globe) than you would have traditionally met had you not used social media. You'll begin to feel a momentum in your business, perhaps a momentum that's been missing. Realtors, for instance, join social media to network with their past clients, but they're also finding new ones. Recruiters use social media to post job openings, and they find people to fill the jobs.

Those who are involved in nontraditional areas are also using social media to find new clients. Artists, for example, share their photographs and artwork, often finding buyers for their work. Like all entrepreneurs and freelancers on social media platforms, they are practicing the art of patient persistence. By participating in social media, your name will be in front of hundreds, thousands—and, perhaps, eventually millions.

After you take the plunge into social media marketing, you will remind people you encounter on these sites of what you do and who you are, and you'll connect to them on a regular basis. If you are offering a product or service that resonates with people, they might become your new customers or strong referral sources.

TRY THIS

Show your clients how much you appreciate their talents and how happy you are when their lives are going well. For instance, when a client is promoted or runs a marathon, you can cheer him or her on using social media platforms.

Talking to Existing Customers

Simply wanting to use social media as another medium to communicate with your existing customers is a great business strategy. Today, after they leave your store or office or after you conduct a phone meeting with them, you can share your positive experience with them online. You can also share some new information to help guide them back to your store or your website.

Throughout this book, you also learn many ways to talk to your existing customers, such as polling them electronically or surveying them online using various social media platforms. You can send a video message to them, post photographs, and interview them on a podcast or on Internet radio. Perhaps you can feature them on your Facebook page or in your e-zine or newsletter. When customers purchase products from you, send them a message on Twitter and ask how they like the products. After obtaining their reviews, then you can post the written testimonials. Better yet, after customers buy your product or service, ask them for permission to record a video testimonial and then publish it to your social media sites. It's one thing for prospects to hear from you, but when they hear from your happy customers, that's powerful! You can even record a video message from them as you hand them the product.

Do you see how much you can do with social media? You are a social media marketer now, so you get to be creative. The more you strengthen your relationships with your existing customers, the better you and your business will become.

Going Viral

In the days before social media, the business world relied on word-of-mouth advertising. Now, essentially the same thing happens with social media—virtually. No, really. It's called *viral marketing*. It's done on the Internet and on a large scale; you can watch your message spread like wildfire. Many industry insiders call this "social shopping."

 DEFINITION

Viral marketing is a marketing technique that encourages users to pass a marketing message to other users or websites, which can create an exponential growth in the number of people who see the message.

Today, with a few simple keystrokes from your clients, friends, followers, and online fans, your message can quickly and virally go out to worldwide networks. They can quote you, forward what you wrote, or retweet what you tweeted (you will learn about this in Part 3 when we discuss Twitter).

Your followers can also comment on your video or podcast. They might hit the Share button on some sites (I'm sure you've seen those buttons on websites and blogs) to spread the word to their network of followers. It's amazing how quickly the word can get out. You know what else is amazing? That when you hit Send on something you write in your office, you send it around the world in a flash.

However, going viral can have a dark side. In June 2011, a teenage girl in Germany who forgot to mark her birthday invitation as "private" on Facebook fled her own party when more than 1,500 guests showed up. Around 100 police officers, some on horses, were needed to keep the crowd under control. That's an example of a social media posting going viral!

Going viral can be a good thing, but just be prepared for the results. Throughout this book, you'll find ways to create a viral marketing effort for your business using each of the social media platforms.

The Least You Need to Know

- You should have a good headshot to get started in social media.
- Be creative with your headshot, but be sure it works with the image you want to project for your business.
- If you can afford them, a good digital camera and a video camera are extremely useful for social media marketing.
- Carefully identify your target customers or readers.
- Social media is an effective way to obtain new customers, but it takes time to build momentum.

Let's Begin Marketing Your Business on Facebook

This part teaches you how to use Facebook in a step-by-step format. You see helpful screen shots and you learn how to use Facebook as a powerful networking and marketing tool for your business.

You also learn about powerful behind-the-scenes business applications and strategies to help you stand out in a crowd of millions. This part also gives you the inside scoop on what you need to have in your virtual business suitcase. And in the last chapter, you find instructions on additional marketing strategies and online netiquette so you will know what and what not to do online.

Facebook:
The Television Network
of Social Media

In This Chapter

- Facebook terms
- How to get started on Facebook
- How to build an amazing profile page
- Creative ways to add friends
- The one daily task you should do on Facebook

Although not everyone is using it, most people have heard of Facebook. Today, Facebook has more than 800 million active users, and more than 50 percent log on to Facebook at least once each day.

Facebook started out as a networking site for college students. Now, it's a worldwide household phenomenon. More than two thirds of the Facebook population is older than college age. The fastest-growing demographic? Those in the 55+ age group.

Introduction to Facebook Terms

Facebook has its own language. The following is a primer for you on terms you'll frequently come across while interacting on Facebook:

- **Wall.** The wall appears on every user's profile page. You can delete wall posts easily from your page if you do not like what you see (put your cursor to the right of the post and an X appears asking if you want to delete). If you are friends with someone, you can write on that person's wall. It's a great strategy for marketing; the Facebook culture loves the wall. The wall is now also referred to as a profile page or page.

- **View Activity or Activity Log.** By clicking on this, you can see all of your activity listed in sequential order.

- **Friends.** These are your Facebook friends that you have already added to your profile page. Some people accept only people they know. Others prefer to be what is termed "an open networker," meaning they accept just about anyone as a friend to expand their network and connections. People who keep their friend list open or who are "open networkers" believe that just about anyone can be a prospect or a good referral source or simply someone who is interesting to know.

- **Subscriber.** This is a person who subscribes to receive your updates but is not connected to you as a friend. Think of it as a reader of your updates. Your number of subscribers is now listed prominently on your profile. The new goal is to get as many subscribers as you can because they validate that your content is useful or likeable.

- **Profile or Cover Page.** This is your personal profile on Facebook. Think of it as an advertisement page for you and your expertise. It summarizes who you are, where you've been, and, more importantly, where you want to go.

- **Status or What's on your mind?** This is your chance to send targeted messages out to the world. Update this daily. This goes into friends' news feeds on Facebook. *This is one of the single most important tasks you can do on Facebook to grow your brand.*

- **News Feed.** Go to your home page by clicking **Home** and you will begin to see lists of New Stories, Recent Stories, and updates or stories from your friends and subscribers. This is referred to as the news feed.

- **Home.** When you get lost on Facebook … go home. Among many things your home page lists are your network's news feed, messages, events, pages you like, and "apps" that you have installed. This is a great place to just go back to, to review your Facebook landscape.

- **Chat.** In the lower-right part of your Facebook profile, you can chat live via instant messaging with people online.

- **Events.** Events range from open houses to seminars, classes, meetings, parties, book clubs, and gatherings, both virtual and in person. To create an event, go to your home page. On the left-hand side of your page, under Favorites, click **Events**. Then click **Create an Event**.

- **Post.** This is another term that is used for status update copy. You can post your update or you can write a post on a friend's wall.

- **Groups.** Create groups on Facebook to further build community around your business and brand. Join groups to further network and market your business. This feature is being phased out, but rumor has it if your group has 20 people or less, the group will continue to exist.

- **Link.** To create a live link, always put "http://" in front of the www to your website URL or website address. You can view links either you or your friends have posted by going to Apps and clicking **Links**.

- **Applications.** These are additional features that Facebook or third-party vendors have supplied to the Facebook platform. Currently a list of applications on Facebook (if you don't have any) is hard to find. I found this link http://apps.facebook.com/appslist/directory/Default.aspx?locale=en&section=top which lists thousands of Facebook applications. There are mostly games but look at the list. Over time as you discover apps on your own they will be listed in the left column on your home page.

- **Fan/Likes.** This term is still used widely in the social media space. Although now people cannot "fan" your business page on Facebook, they can "like" it. Anyone can become a fan or "like" a person, business, or brand on Facebook if they have a business page or "page" as they are now referred to. Once you become a fan, that page will automatically be listed under your info tab and be part of your profile.

- **Tag or Tagging.** When uploading a photo or writing a note using the Notes application, you are given an option to tag someone. This means that the person is in the photo or mentioned in the note. When you tag them, the Facebook system sends them a note letting them know they have been tagged in a photo or note. Also, Facebook will ask you to identify people in the photo and then ask if you want them tagged. Tagging is very popular on Facebook. It's not good Facebook etiquette to tag people who are not in the photo or note, because that is considered a form of spamming.

- **Spamming.** A term that is used across all social media marketing and refers to abusing social media channels for one's own interest or profit. This is something you should never do.

Creating a Powerful Personal Profile for Business

Again, I refer to Facebook as the television network because it has such broad demographics. Check this out: the age range is from 11 to 90, there are both male and female users, and there's a wide range of income levels. It's hard to nail down the exact income level of the average Facebook user, but one statistic places the average income at around $89,000 per year. I mentioned that the largest demographic is the 45+ user, but the largest-growing segment is women and men age 55 and up. In fact, many grandparents are getting onto Facebook to keep up with their baby-boomer children and grandchildren.

Here are some other interesting Facebook statistics (as of summer 2011) as noted within the Facebook statistics section on Facebook:

- The average user has 130 friends.

- Worldwide, users spend more than 700 billion minutes on Facebook each month.

- The average user connects to or likes an average of 80 business pages or Facebook events at one time.

- There are more than 30 billion pieces of content (web links, news stories, blog posts, photo albums, and so on) shared each month.

- 50 percent of Facebook users access via their mobile devices.

- More than 150 million active users access Facebook through their mobile devices.

How do you stand out in a crowd of tens of millions? It does seem daunting, but you can begin by creating an amazing personal Facebook profile for your business networking and marketing. Remember, Facebook users want to connect with real people.

To get started, log on to www.facebook.com. First, you enter your name (make sure you spell it correctly). Some women question if they should give their married name or maiden name. Most savvy marketers use their business name. Thus, if you use your married name in business, go with that. However, you might want to use both your maiden and married name with hopes that you will connect to former friends and acquaintances; that's okay, too—it's a personal choice.

Enter your information here

Login page for Facebook.

Next, enter your email address and create a password. Enter your sex (male or female) and your birthday (don't worry about showing your birthday; I'll show you how to hide it in the next section). Facebook asks for this to identify you from the other people in the world that share your same name. Make sure you fill the security check in the CAPTCHA screen.

Facebook will send you a confirmation link to your email inbox to verify that you have indeed opened an account. After you verify and click the link in your inbox, you are ready to begin networking on Facebook. Next, you are asked to enter information in a series of steps.

1. To avoid being overwhelmed right now, I strongly suggest skipping the step of searching for friends on Facebook. Take a look at the screen shot of this step and you'll see what I mean. Click **Skip this step** to move past this step.

Here's Step 1 on Facebook.

2. The next screen asks about profile information, including your high school, college, and current company. You can see Step 2 in the figure. It's up to you whether you fill out the name of your high school or college, but many networkers feel it is a good thing to do because it makes you relatable and helps to connect you with past friends and alumni. You definitely want to fill out the Employer information with the name of your business.

Here's Step 2 on Facebook.

3. Next, you will be asked to upload that all important photo of you and be asked to select people you know to add them as friends. I suggest skipping this step until you get your profile page completed.

Here's Step 3. Uploading your profile photo.

Now Facebook officially welcomes you. Congratulations!

With the new Facebook Timeline you should be invited to go through four steps. We want to get your profile banner to look something like this.

This is my completed Profile Cover Banner with the new version of Facebook.

Now to get yours complete you will need to go through roughly four steps.

1. **Add a Cover.** Facebook first wants you to select background art for your page. I have the pumpkins on mine for now, but you can put a picture of your office, your building, your product or logo as long as the photo is legally yours. Or you can purchase artwork online as long as you have the rights to it. So upload and add the cover. *Note:* you can always change this.

2. **About.** This is where you will update your work history and all about you. This is where you want to be a savvy marketer. Go through each section as noted in the next screen shot from my page and add info about you that you want to share with the world. In the **About You** section be sure to put your business phone number and other marketable information that will attract new prospects and followers.

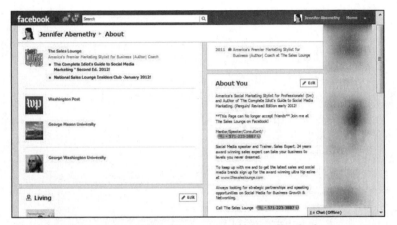

Here is my About You page on the new Facebook.

3. **Write a Status update.** In other words, fill in the section called "What's on your mind?" It is important to know that these updates will be archived as "stories" on Facebook as part of your historical timeline. So what goes on Facebook, stays on Facebook. Be strategic. Share a tip and be a resource by providing a link to something useful. You want to be known as someone with clout in this new digital age so share your information and watch the new subscribers come your way! In the future when you have a lot of updates, you can review your stories by clicking on the "timeline" on the right hand side of your screen or by viewing your activity.

Here is where you write a status update.

This is a screen shot of my tour of the new timeline and stories section.

The most important section within the About section is the **About You** section: tell the audience all about who you are and how you serve people. Don't be afraid to brag here and add contact information so that they can easily find your business phone number and email address. The other sections like Quotes, Where You Live, Relationships, and Political Views are not that important. Within the Basic info tab, I would recommend hiding the year of your birthday (so too much information isn't shared) and shying away from religious and political views so as not to scare potential customers away.

> **NETIQUETTE**
>
> For a Facebook business or public figure page or even your professional profile page where you'll be marketing your business and yourself as a professional, I recommend that you keep most of your shared information 80 percent business and 20 percent personal—just as you would in a professional environment. You don't want to come across as a robot, so feel free to share some personal information. Just keep in mind that this is business, so people want to get to know you professionally first.

This can be filled out or kept blank. However, if you've written a book, put that in. It's okay to let your personality shine through here.

Adding Your Photo or Headshot

The secret here is to put "you" in the messages and keep in mind that your ideal prospect may be reading this. Ask yourself, "What would make a possible customer want to further connect with me and get to know me and my business?" Adding a photo or a headshot can do just that.

How to Add Friends and Stand Out in a Crowd

Facebook is all about connections. Seeing the face of a new friend, renewing relationships with past friends, and finding new friends, prospects, and clients makes Facebook a terrific platform for connecting with others. However, some people think they just don't know that many people, or they think the ones they do know most likely aren't on Facebook. Think again, because you might be surprised as to whom you will find. Remember in the last chapter when we talked about mind-set and how that is your most important asset? Don't think you'll have problems finding friends, because most likely you won't.

Initially when you set up your profile, you might have added some of the suggested friends that were on that opening page and maybe not since I suggested you wait. Now you will want to find some more. A search box is in the top center of the page. Put your cursor in there and enter a name of a friend. Do you see your friend? Now you see why a good photo is important.

This is the drop-down menu of friend requests.

Many people might have the same name, so if you cannot see a photo, you might not be certain if that is the actual person you are searching for. *Note:* most experienced social media users are not willing to connect to people without a photo.

It won't take long for other Facebook users to notice you've arrived. You may already have a friend request, so go to the upper-left-hand corner next to the search bar and click the people icon. A box displays to the right of the photo asking if you want to confirm this friendship or ignore. *Note:* if you are not certain that the photo (or lack thereof) is a person you want to connect with, click the name and sneak a peak at the profile.

Let's say you know Miss X from the XYZ networking group. Search for her in the search bar at the top of the page. Click **Add Friend** once you find her. Remember, you want to stand out in a crowd of millions, so you should write a personal message. Once you add them as a friend, go to their Facebook page and say hello. Warning: don't leave your website or your latest marketing video. Just let them know you appreciate them reaching out and connecting and that you look forward to getting to know them! Otherwise you will be labeled a spammer.

ONLINE CAUTION

If you have some time and want to add a bunch of friends to your network on Facebook, only send out a small number of invites at a time, say 10 or so. If you go beyond that, they may see you as a spammer and suspend your account.

Obviously, if it's your neighbor next door, you won't need to be so formal, and write on their wall. But a savvy marketer will always sign with name and title, or name and website, or name and a tag line. Just by adding a personal message you will begin to stand out in a crowd. Remember, people want to feel like they matter and they want to be connected.

Congratulations! You have now set up an amazing profile, you've added some friends, and you have uploaded your photo and cover art. As time goes on, you will find people who want to add you as a friend or subscribe to your wonderful updates. A good tip for you, whenever you go to your home page, take a look in the upper-left corner for friend requests. Then, on the top bar, click **Find Friends**. You now should see another list of people with whom you can connect. Use your judgment about whom you want to connect with and whom you want to ignore.

For the most part, Facebook is today's equivalent of going to a convention and not knowing anyone in the room, and then, after a bit of time passes, several people ask you for your business card and you give it to them. I call it the world's largest trade-show with nearly 800 million people. The difference now is that instead of a business card, they are asking to connect to your virtual business profile. Most people add just about everyone, but others are not comfortable with that. Go with what you are comfortable with. If you choose to "ignore" someone who has friend requested you, they will not receive a notice telling them they have been ignored, but if they try to send you a message or look for you in their friend list they may figure it out.

Now let's get those friends feeling more connected to you and begin social media marketing.

What's on Your Mind?

The single most important task you can do on Facebook for effective social media marketing (aside from having a photo and good profile) is to update the "What's on your mind?" section at least once per day. Why? By doing this on a regular daily basis, people will get to know you and your expertise; it will also keep you in what experts call "top-of-mind awareness." They just won't be able to forget about you. They will grow to like you and then trust you. And people refer, recommend, and buy from people that they know, like, and trust.

How do you see the news feed? By clicking your **name** in the upper-right-hand corner you will go to your page. Look for your status update area on the left hand side. You should now see the words, "What's on your mind?" You are about to enter your status update as we discussed briefly earlier. As you begin connecting to friends, they will also enter their status update, which becomes part of the collective news feed as stories. You will see these stories on the home page as a story feed. As a new Facebook user, you most likely don't have much appearing on that page just yet. However, as you get more friends, that page will become populated under "Top Stories" and "Most Recent Stories" which is a real-time news feed of what's on everyone's mind. And remember, don't take this too literally.

The news feed is great for these things:

- Sharing tips and your expertise.

- Sharing websites and information with your target audience.

- Telling friends what's new with your business.

- Sharing a testimonial.

- Reporting about something exciting that is going to happen with your business.

- Networking and acknowledging your friends, clients, and prospects when appropriate.

Okay, you're ready. Enter your first "What's on your mind?" status update. Before long, you will start getting comments about what you've written.

The Least You Need to Know

- Facebook has a wide range of demographics, which means, most likely, your target audience is participating.

- A great photo and a completed profile will attract more people who want to connect with you.

- Get creative and use all areas of your profile to promote your expertise and your business.

- Your status update is the single most important way to stay active and keep your friends engaged on Facebook.

- Keep your shared information, including status updates, around 80 percent business and 20 percent personal.

Applications for Marketing on Facebook

Chapter

5

In This Chapter

- How to add photos to your Facebook page
- Using video as a marketing tool
- Why the Notes application is effective
- Creating Facebook events
- Birthdays on Facebook
- Marketing your blog

Now that you have a great Facebook profile, you're probably enjoying updating your status every day. You've probably also been busy adding new friends. Now, how about adding some great applications to your Facebook site to make your Facebook presence even more intriguing?

In this chapter, you learn what you need to know about Facebook applications. There are a lot of them, but only a few that you need to start with. In fact, I think you'll find that it's fun to explore these applications and find out what they can do for you and your business.

What Are Applications?

Think of applications as great tools that you can install onto your Facebook pages and profile. They help you reach out and connect in more unique ways. Where do you find the Applications menu?

Unfortunately, as of summer 2011, the menu doesn't exist any longer. The good news is that a new website, www.appbistro.com, lists the most popular "apps" on Facebook. Some are for a monthly fee, while others are for free. It will prompt you for permission to access your Facebook account (and they will give you some free apps for allowing them) so you can see all of the apps, or you can choose the just browsing option.

Here's how to install the AppBistro.com applications feature.

Click the icon and an applications window will open up just above the icon. Your list is simple at this point, but over time it can get long as you expand on the applications you are using. Literally thousands of applications exist on Facebook. Let's begin by looking at what is already installed for you.

Photos

The Photo application is for uploading photos and video. As a social media marketer, you will want to upload photos so your friends and soon-to-be fans will be able to share your experiences. As of July 2011, Facebook reports that more than 30 billion pieces of content are shared by members each month. The numbers are staggering, aren't they?

Okay, let's get started. If the Photo App is not listed on the left hand navigation bar on your home page under apps, type in PhotoApp in the search bar. Install PhotoApp. Click your **Photo**. Then click **+ Upload Photo**. Next, you'll see the following screen shot.

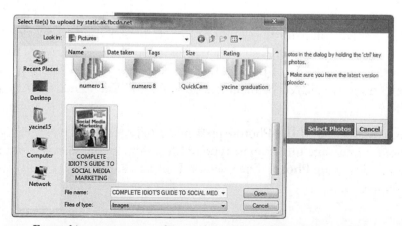

Here's where you upload photos and create a new photo album.

You can then name your album of photos or photo, give the location, and describe the photos. Next, decide who you want to see your photos. You can choose everyone, your networks and friends, friends of your friends, or only friends. Or you can customize the distribution of it to share with specific people.

DID YOU KNOW?

You want to be careful about posting photos of other people without their permission. A best practice is to get them to sign a release form, particularly if you are doing this for business.

Facebook then asks you **Who's in these photos?** so you can label them and notify friends in the pictures. I recommend you click **Skip Tagging Friends** in the photos—unless you have their permission to post. Next, you can add a description of the photo and share it.

From this screen, you can browse through your files and select photos.

After you click the **Upload Photos** button, you can add a caption to the photo (or photos) and identify people in the photo by clicking on them and adding their names. Then, click **Save Changes or Create Album**.

Your last option is to share the photo with someone—on Facebook. You can also add a message. Take a look at the next screen shot to see what I mean.

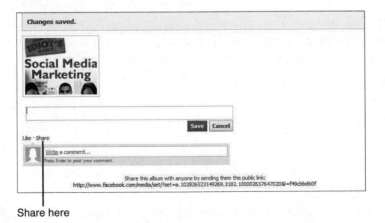

You can add captions on this screen.

Share here

You can share photos with Facebook friends.

ONLINE CAUTION

As of this writing, you can control the content and information you post on Facebook, and how it is shared, through your privacy and application settings. However, the "Internet Intellectual Property content" laws are always changing. Please keep checking back to privacy and IP content laws with your Internet attorney and on Facebook to stay within their legal guidelines.

Sharing Your Content and Information

You own all of the content and information you post on Facebook, and you can control how it is shared through your privacy and application settings. However, this is the first line in Facebook's legal guidelines:

> "You grant us a non-exclusive, transferable, sub-licensable, royalty-free, worldwide license to use any IP content that you post on or in connection with Facebook ('IP License'). This IP License ends when you delete your IP content or your account unless your content has been shared with others, and they have not deleted it."

This is another paragraph in the Facebook terms:

> "When you publish content or information using the 'everyone' setting, it means that you are allowing everyone, including people off of Facebook, to access and use that information, and to associate it with you (i.e., your name and profile picture)."

> **Note:** Facebook privacy settings continue to evolve. Be sure to check privacy settings from time to time at www.facebook.com/#!/terms.php. —Facebook's Statement of User Rights (April 2011)

Video

Video enables consumers to be entertained while also being informed. You might say this is "edutainment." Videos make your company's brand and services come alive. The Video application is already installed for you on Facebook. Here, you can share your videos, record videos from your computer, and upload and publish videos from your mobile (phone). Go back to the home page, then click **Photo**, which is on the left side of the screen just below the About button. Then you will have the option to Upload photo or video or Use Webcam. Click which ever you are going to do: **Upload Video** or **Record a Video**. Here's what you'll see.

*The Facebook Video upload screen can be found by clicking on **Photo**. The video box will then pop up.*

Many people spend time on Facebook, and as you get into video marketing, you will want to include Facebook as one of the major platforms for delivering your marketing message. You can either begin recording (you must have a computer with a webcam to do this) or you can upload a video as noted previously. Recording from your computer is very easy. No, really! Click **Photo** then **Use Webcam** and then the following screen will display.

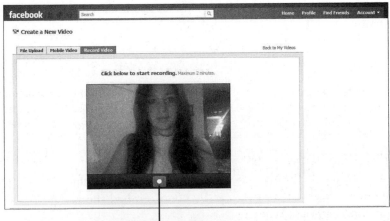

Simply click to record

You can start recording your own video on this screen.

Click **Allow** and then select your recording device (a mobile webcam, a computer webcam, or microphone for just recording audio). Then click **Close**. Your screen will show a video image of you. See yourself on the screen and click the white button to record. You will have a maximum of 20 minutes. *Note:* social media videos are most widely viewed when they are 2 minutes or less. Take a look at the next screen.

Here's how it looks when it's ready to edit or tag and share with friends.

Just like with the Photo application, Facebook asks who is in the video with you so you can tag them. You can title the video, put in a description, and decide who can see it. You will also notice Facebook asks you to choose a thumbnail. This is a photo icon that will appear next to your video when you email it out or post it on Facebook. You can put anything here—a photo, logo, and so on. When you click **Choose a Thumbnail**, you can browse your computer or use a screen shot from your video as the thumbnail.

NETIQUETTE

Don't tag people if they aren't in the video. You will be labeled as a spammer and lose the respect of those who take the time to open the video, thinking that they are in it. This goes with other applications as well, such as photos and notes.

You can then share the video on your profile or share it with specific Facebook friends, by clicking the **Share** button. You can do some slight editing to the video, delete the video, or, if you are technically savvy, embed the video to your other websites or social media platforms.

Notes

The Notes application on Facebook is another underutilized tool. Facebook Notes can help you share your expertise, continue to cultivate your following, and virally get your information out to the masses. From your home page, type in Notes in the search bar. Find the Notes application, you will see a box at the top that reads "Write a Note." Click **+ Write a New Note**. Here's what comes up on your screen.

On this screen, you can write a note about yourself or your business to share with your friends.

Here is your chance to write about a new service you are providing or to share your thoughts on an issue or problem. (Remember to keep politics and religion out of it.) Most importantly, write as if your ideal clients are reading it. What would they want to hear? What would interest them? Again, you can tag people that you mention in your note, but only if you mention them. You can also upload a photo or logo to go within your note.

At the bottom of this screen, you have options to save your note as a draft, preview your note, or republish your note to your profile. Once you are ready to publish, designate who will see it, and now your friends, clients, and prospects can comment on your note, and again, your name and voice is in front of them. You're really building relationships through your communication online!

If you begin importing notes from your blog, your Notes page will then include both notes typed on Facebook and posts from your blogs. Take a look at the following screen shot. Once here, you will click **Edit Import Settings**.

Use the Notes application to promote your business.

You are then directed to the following screen shot. You will need to enter your blog's website address in the text box. *Note:* it doesn't need to be your RSS feed, because Facebook magically posts your content for you. You have to check the disclaimer underneath the URL and then click **Start Importing**. We will discuss blogs later in Chapter 16, but it's good for you to know this is here.

From this screen, you can import your blog into your notes.

As a best practice, use the Notes application on a regular basis. Provide value, information, and entertainment, and your followers, friends, and fans will love it.

Events

Remember the days when a business owner had an event? It was typically an open house or a holiday gathering. Signs were posted at the office or store location, and a postcard or an invitation was sent through the mail. Perhaps the owner even made some phone calls. Today those rules still apply. And perhaps these gestures are even a bit refreshing because we don't get much in the mail anymore.

However, you can now post your event on Facebook. There are millions of events created each month on Facebook. It's a great place to post the event because it is another publicity avenue for your event.

What types of events are on Facebook? All kinds … in fact, for social media marketers, the possibilities are endless. There are events for open houses, wine tastings, book signings, group meetings, recitals, teleseminars, webinars, lectures, book launches, seminar holiday parties, classes, conference calls—the list goes on and on. To create an event, go to Apps and scroll up to Events. You will see upcoming events posted by other Facebook users, your friends' events, past events, and birthdays. You can search for Events App in the search bar or see if it's already populated on your home page on the left hand navigation bar under favorites.

This is the Events applications page on Facebook.

In the upper-right side of the screen, click **+ Create an Event**.

Use this screen to fill in the event's details.

You will fill out the following required information to post your event: event name, when, what, where, info about the event, and who's invited. Then click **Create Event**.

Next, you can upload a picture or logo and certify that you have the right to distribute the photo/logo. Then, consider the various options offered as shown in the following figure.

Remember, you are creating community, so get creative with what you and your invitees can do with this invite, both pre- and postevent. You can also decide if you want the event open (to anyone), closed (to invitees only), or secret (only those that you've invited or who are members of your group or fan page; we will get into fan pages later in the book).

Then, you can publish the event to appear on your home page and in the Events section. Lastly, you can invite friends who are on Facebook (or email friends who are not) and include a personal message.

You can show a guest list or hide it; allow guests to upload photos, videos, and links; or you can pass on these options.

You can choose Facebook friends to invite to your event.

From this screen, you can edit the guest list, cancel the event, message guests with event updates, print out your guest list, publish photos, add video, and include links. Ask your invitees to RSVP online. You can also add other information like parking details, bad weather plans, or other details that will make the event exciting. Try it for your next event. *Note:* don't depend on this as the only way to invite people, but do make it a part of your invite campaign.

Birthday Networking

Power Facebook users know that one of the best ways to network and market themselves is to be seen, heard, trusted, and liked. One of the networking techniques that many use is sending birthday wishes. On your home page on the right side, you will see a list of upcoming birthdays. Click the birthday person's name and write a birthday greeting on their wall. You can sign off with your company name, if you like. But most importantly, just take 5 minutes every day and see whose birthday it is. Go to their Facebook profile and write on their wall. It's a nice thing to do, and strategically, it's great PR for you and your company. Also, it feels good when you are on the recipient side, too.

Deals and Links

There are two additional applications that are populated into your applications menu as a first-time user: Links and Deals. The Links application is just what it says. Within your status update, you can post a link to a website, blog, or article. When you click the Links application, you can see all the links that your friends have posted, which is great for first-time users.

Social RSS

This is the most popular *RSS* reader application on Facebook. As a Facebook user, you can use this to add your blogs and live Twitter updates to your personal profile. As of July 2011, there were just under 521,000 monthly active users utilizing Social RSS.

DEFINITION

RSS stands for Real Simple Syndication, but sometimes it also means Rich Site Summary. It helps create website feeds that allow you to publish frequently updated texts, such as from blogs.

By adding this application, you can create a new box tab that appears at the top of your Facebook profile page. Or later on, when you learn how to create a Facebook fan page, you can have it appear there. Your articles will be posted automatically from your blog to your Facebook page by using this service.

The benefit of using this is that it keeps your content on your site fresh and updated and helps drive traffic to your website. To find this, go to the Search Bar and type in RSS and keep narrowing the results until you see RSS App. You'll see the following screen.

The main page for the Social RSS Facebook application.

Click **Social RSS** to add this application. Here's what you'll see.

You can read through this page to get more information on how you can best utilize this application for your business.

Networked Blogs

This is a fun application that promotes your blog and the blogs of your strategic partners, clients, and friends. Remember, social media is about promoting and marketing not only your own business, but those of others as well.

This application also does something else: it puts your blog onto a directory of blogs on Facebook. This enables your blog fans to promote your blog on their Facebook page, as well as other blogs they like to follow. To get this application, go to www. networkedblogs.com.

Here's the screen for the Networked Blogs application on Facebook.

Are you beginning to see how all your social media marketing is beginning to work together? Don't be overwhelmed. You can use some or all of these Facebook applications now, or wait until you are ready. The important thing is that you know they are there and available to you. This keeps you one step ahead of the competition and gives you multiple ways to network and market your business using social media.

As we go on throughout the book, and you learn more about the other social media sites like LinkedIn, Twitter, and YouTube, you will eventually want to incorporate them into your Facebook page. This is more advanced marketing, but after you create your presence on those sites you will want to upload the applications for YouTube Video Box, Twitter, and My LinkedIn Profile on Facebook. So hang in there! You are on your way to learning more fabulous ways to use social media marketing.

The Least You Need to Know

- Although there are tens of thousands of applications on Facebook, there are just a few that you really should know about and utilize for your business marketing on Facebook.

- Photos and videos are a great way to keep Facebook followers up-to-date and engaged with what you are doing with your business.

- Writing about your expertise using the Notes application on Facebook is a great way to keep your website content fresh and your readers connected to your business.

- Posting events and honoring your friends' birthdays are two good ways to keep your name and brand in front of your followers and those you network with on Facebook.

- Using the Social RSS application will help you promote your blog on Facebook.

- The Networked Blogs application places your blog in a directory, which allows Facebook users to promote your blog on their own Facebook pages.

Facebook Pages and Groups

In This Chapter

- Creating a fan page
- Great examples of fan pages
- Applications you can use on your fan page
- Why a Facebook group?
- How to attract raving fans

In this world of social media marketing, it seems everyone is becoming their own brand. And that's perfectly fine. You need to start thinking of yourself and your company as a brand.

And as with any good brand, you need to provide a place for your fans and followers to gather. With nearly 800 million people on one platform, Facebook fan pages which are now referred to also as business pages (or simply pages) and groups are a great place to start. Guess how many users join a Facebook fan page each day? Over 10 million! That's a lot of fans. Don't you think that some of these fans might as well be yours?

Choosing Fan Pages and Groups to Join

Before we jump into creating your own fan page or group, let's briefly discuss the strategy involved in joining other people's groups and fan pages. One of the strategies of savvy social media marketers is to create fan pages and groups on Facebook for their businesses. They also strategically join groups and become fans of their friends', prospects', and clients' businesses.

I was attending a social media conference a few years ago and one of the presenters shared a story about how his girlfriend wanted to go to Harvard for her MBA. Well, one of her strategies was to join the Harvard Business School fan page on both Facebook and LinkedIn (see Chapter 12). She began networking online with alumni and eventually talked with a member of the MBA candidate selection committee. The presenter ended the story by telling us that his girlfriend was now attending Harvard Business School. Obviously, she needed more than that connection to be accepted at Harvard, but oftentimes the people you know do make a difference.

Keep in mind that as people view your profile on Facebook, they will look at the groups you are in and the people or businesses you are fans of. It becomes a reflection of who you are, just as those networking groups and organizations that you join in your community and nationally do. This is the same thing; it's just printed on an Internet page and the group happens to be virtual. Think strategically about whom to follow and what groups to join.

You might follow someone simply because you admire the person and you are a true fan, and that's okay. But I caution those who become fans and join groups that might be fun from a personal viewpoint—sometimes these casual alliances don't look good from a business viewpoint. Remember, you are marketing your business and brand. Be authentic in your approach and aware of the image projected by the groups you are joining. I call this "conscious social media marketing." Always be sensitive to what you join, write, say, and do online, and all will be fine.

There are several ways to choose business pages to join. First, you can go to the search bar on the top of the page and type in the company name, a product, or a person's name, and see if their Facebook page pops up. Or, type Facebook Pages with their business name in the search bar to see a list of all the Facebook fan pages. Other sites I like are www.fanpagelist.com and www.thepagefinder.com; both are excellent sources of information on Facebook fan pages.

Popular pages are shown on the home page of Fan Page List, but you can also browse by type, such as politicians, celebrities, and organizations.

Do You Need a Fan Page, Business Page, or Group?

If you are not sure why you are creating a group or fan page, perhaps you should hold off until you experience more clarity. I'm told groups are really for 20 members or under, like a book club or social group. Remember, this is your chance to interact with current and potential customers, but you need to keep your message and brand consistent.

If you know you want to move forward with a fan page or group, take a few minutes to answer these questions before you create your page. It will help you focus on what your objectives are for your fan page or group:

- Who will monitor the page or group?

- Will your page be open, private, or secret?

- Will you commit to posting daily on the page and commenting on your page when others post messages?

- Will you want your fans to post their links and videos?

- Where will you promote your page or group—in your office, store, on your business cards, or in your email signature?

- What will be your goal when starting the group? Do you ultimately want to educate, inform, or meet people in person or together in a group?

- Will you create multiple administrators for your group or page? You have the ability to do that on Facebook.

- Will you begin discussion boards? Who will monitor the page, and how often?

> **DID YOU KNOW?**
>
> The term *fan page* is also now referred to as a "business page" or simply "page." It can be confusing! With the termination of the term "fan" on the pages along with the new term "like" on the pages, people refer to the pages differently. For the rest of this chapter however, we will refer to it as a page.

What's the bottom line? Think about your business strategy carefully. If it makes sense, go for it.

By creating a page or group on Facebook, you create a place where you can have a stronger interaction with people, as well as another community forum for them to engage with you. You can showcase products, services, business specials, news, updates, and events, all on one site. Take advantage of all the preinstalled applications, such as the Video, Photo, and Events applications, that are already there waiting for your marketing touch. Fans and group members are looking to stay connected to you, so reach out in different ways online. *Hint: in the back of the book or on The Sales Lounge.com I have a great tool to help you easily and inexpensively customize your page. Check it out!*

Creating Your Own Page

Your focus is now clear, and you're ready to create a page. For many of us, it might be uncomfortable to think of ourselves as so important that we need a page where people come to admire and comment about us. Who would have imagined that? After all, most of us don't have a lucrative recording or film contract, and we are not a household name (at least not yet, anyway). However, with social media marketing, you need to change your thinking. Remember what I said about mind-set? Your friends, best clients, and followers want a place to rally around you. Your business champions will be proud to say, "Yes I support you/your business!"

There are many benefits to setting up a page for your business. Here are a few big ones:

- You can build community with a fan/business page. Give people a reason to keep checking in. Have specials for fans and post videos on the pages. Poll them. Make fans feel as if they are part of your "club." This is great viral marketing because now all of the fan's friends will see your information. If they comment on your fan page, it will be noted on their page, too.

- Having fans and followers gives prospective clients confidence in you. It certainly won't hurt your business.

- The page has room for an unlimited number of fans, whereas your personal/ professional profile page is currently limited to 5,000. *Note:* this could change in the future.

- On your welcome page, you can poll your fans, post videos, have discussion boards, and have your blog feed into that page.

- The fan page enables you to listen to your fans and have a dialogue with them.

- Your fan page enables your fans to have star status by posting videos about your product and expressing their views.

- It's more free PR for your business and personal brand.

The Community Coffee Fan Page

Sometimes it helps to see an example, and we can all learn from those who've done it well. Look at the fun Community Coffee fan page in the screen shot on the next page.

Community Coffee has done a great job creating an interactive and engaging fan page. First, their bright logo occupies the photo space. They have used it to drive people to their website. Their fan page has energy combining engaging posts, photos, and a ton of interactivity. Finally, they boast a fan base of over 136,000 ... and growing daily!

The wall on the Community Coffee fan page.

Review all the page buttons on the left side column (going down) of the Community Coffee home page, and see how they market themselves. A fun one to look at is how they've incorporated recipes; this is a custom tab that was made with the help of a developer. The company also has buttons for events, birthday e-cards, recipes, contests, events, and so much more. It's really a great page!

Think about the creative ways in which Community Coffee engages fans by asking questions and sharing thoughts. Now think about what you can do for your business. You can do something similar with your fan page or create something altogether different. Let your fans experience what goes into operating your business. There is a reason why reality shows are so popular. People are intrigued by what is real. They want to know what happens behind the scenes. Take your fans with you on your journey. Remember, people want to feel part of something. It might as well be your community.

How to Set Up Your Fan Page

The easiest way to create a fan page is to log out and go to www.facebook.com. Look just below the signup area. See where it reads **Create a Page**. Click on that and you will see a selection of page types.

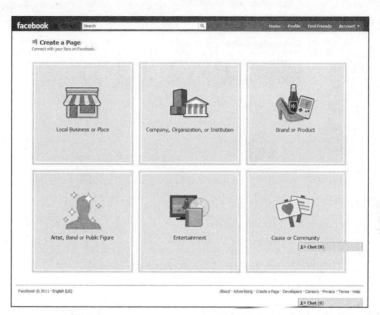

This is where you create your Facebook fan page.

You will most likely use the first icon to describe your page (unless you are a national celebrity, product, or public figure), so click it and select the type of business you own. If you don't see your type listed, just pick one or try to leave it blank if you can.

Following are the other steps for creating a fan page:

1. Agree to Facebook Page Terms. (Again, you might want to have your legal team review this, but note that it must be checked to continue with the process.) Facebook does this to confirm that it is indeed your business and that you're authorized to create the page.

2. Upload your logo or photo.

3. Invite some friends to join your page. Start with just a few invites, as you are still setting up your page.

4. Fill in basic information, like your website, and talk about the business in a few sentences. Also, pick a category of business.

5. Click **Create Page**. You should see the page like the one that follows.

This is a newly created fan page for The Sales Lounge.

6. Next click **Edit Page**. You will find this in the upper-right corner. Fill out this page as best you can with details about your business. Here's what you'll see on the screen.

After your page is created, fill in the details about your business.

7. Now, fill in the information that you deem appropriate, and then save it.

8. At the top left in the photo icon area, if there is still a question mark icon that displays instead of a photo or logo, scroll your cursor over the icon and the wording **Change Picture** will display. This is where you can upload your photo or logo.

9. There are many more customizable advanced features to add, but most are done with the help of a programmer. You can find the details on my blog site, as there are too many to cover here.

10. After your page is ready, update your "What's on your mind?" status.

Alert your friends that your fan page is up and ask them to write on your fan page wall. *Hint:* remember to become a fan of your own fan page. This way your fan page will appear on your individual profile page.

TRY THIS

Want to speak? Are you an author or national coach? Set up a page for you as a public figure on Facebook. Claim it! Build community around your own personal brand and page!

Your Page Strategy

It's important to think about how you want to run your page. Do you want to use it simply to communicate with fans? Do you want to have discussion boards? What types of photos will you upload? Do you want fans to review products and services for you? Will you place events on your page? Who will monitor your page?

Think about these questions so you can make strategic decisions about your page. And remember, as you get more fans, you will need to monitor it daily.

Applications for Your Fan Page

You can use many applications on your fan page. The ones I've listed in this section are just a few for you to consider. Just like your regular profile page, you have a wall with the information tabs on your page. With the page, you can also easily list events, run polls, and have fans post videos.

You can also add some of the other applications that were recommended for your pro-file in Chapter 5, such as Notes and Social RSS. The following are some additional fun applications that you can add when you are ready:

- **YouTube.** Have your favorite YouTube videos on your fan page. Later in the book, you will learn how to create your own YouTube channel.

- **My Google Calendar.** Have a calendar of events on your profile or fan page using Google Calendar. This is great for entrepreneurs, speakers, and those who have lots of public events.

- **Poll.** Remember the polling feature that we saw on the Community Coffee fan page? You can add that to your own page. Go to www.appbistro.com and search for "poll." Click on the poll icon and add the application. Next click on **Free** then install. It will ask you where you want to install it (what page) and click and it will be there!

There are a lot of things you can do to further develop your page. However, for our purposes here, we are working to get you started with the basics. When you're ready, you can move on to more advanced applications and marketing strategies.

Groups on Facebook

As of this writing, the Groups feature has been reconfigured. Groups aren't going away and are beneficial. To create a group, go to www.facebook.com/groups. Or click on home and then look at the left hand navigation side bar and see if you see groups. If so, click on it and at the top right hand side, it will read **Create a group**. Click on that.

People join groups because they share a common interest or cause with the group. Groups are currently private, so you can only be invited in by someone you know. There are groups ranging from sports teams and family reunions to traveling com-panions and garlic lovers. Some are also centered on an individual or a business.

Just like the pages, there are many reasons why you might want to create your own group:

- You want a small private online community to share information.

- You want to create one easy place on Facebook for this particular group of people to communicate.

- When people join your group, it's more viral marketing for your business.

- Creating a group enables you to further promote your business and brand presence on Facebook and offline as members will tell people they are a part of your group. You can create that community spirit within your group and share news, events, and discussions, and members will feel more connected if they should ever meet in person.

> **DID YOU KNOW?**
>
> Your page can have video, your Twitter stream, your photos, and your blog, as well as capture names and email addresses. It takes a savvy programmer, but it can be worth the effort!

Creating Your Own Group

Before jumping in to create your own group on Facebook, ask yourself some questions. Will this be a private group with weekly or monthly discussions? Will this just become a place to send messages out to a specific group of people? Do you want it to be a secret group, open group, or closed group? You have to be ready to manage the group, because it is a reflection of you, your business, and your brand.

First, go to www.facebook.com/groups. You should see a page similar to this. Or go to your home page in the left navigation column and find the words Create Groups and click on that.

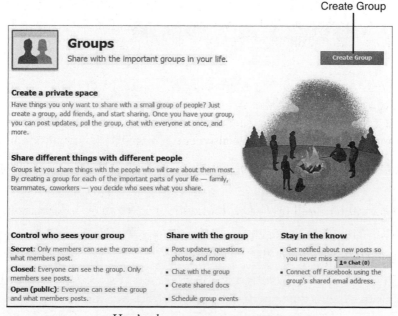

Here's where you create your group.

1. Enter your group's name and description.

2. Follow the online instructions. Click **Create Group**.

Here's where you enter your group's information.

3. The next screen displays the name of the group, its members, and whether it is a closed group, open group, or secret group.

You upload a photo or logo after you've created your group.

Remember to type in the hyperlink to your website (www.yourwebsitename.com).

Think strategically about which group option is best for you. For example, say you have a VIP club in your business. You might want to make that group or page secret or closed. Let's say you are a speaker and/or blogger and you want everyone to know about your group. If you want them to learn about your expertise and share experiences, then you might want to create an open group. Again, there are no rules here, just do what works for you. Don't be afraid to experiment; you can always change what you are doing if you don't find it's working for you and your business. That's the great thing about social media marketing. It's constantly evolving, so experimenting is acceptable and encouraged.

Raving Fans on Facebook

An interesting phenomenon has happened on Facebook and other social media sites. As mentioned earlier in the book, everyday people are developing a loyal following that is helping to market their business and brand worldwide; some even have *raving fans*. These marketers are doing a great job of initially introducing themselves—remember, this is a social platform, so instead of focusing only on selling, they are also introducing themselves and meeting others. They focus initially on adding friends and do so in an authentic, sincere way. Then, they make people feel good about connecting with them.

DEFINITION

A **raving fan** online is someone who essentially is proud to give you a virtual thumbs-up. They like what you do. They support you. They advocate your business and/or brand and are proud to say they are a fan to others!

You might know the saying, "People won't remember what you say, but they will remember how you made them feel." The same is true when using social media. Whether you are writing a personal note when adding someone as a friend, writing on his wall, or responding to a note he sent to your inbox, try to keep a positive tone and keep the focus on your prospective customer. Again, you are building your business. Eventually, you will want to begin taking it to the next level, which involves really engaging your friends and uncovering their wants and needs. You can do this with phone calls, polls, online questions about what they're looking for, and so on.

If you are adding many people locally, arrange to meet with a group of them. Get to know them; invite them to lunch or breakfast. You are now starting to take the networking to a different level. Another activity you can do is call five new Facebook friends on the phone each week. Get to know them and tell them you are glad you both connected. You will learn a lot about the person; he or she will feel good that you called, and you never know where the relationship will lead. This is a powerful strategy, but it takes work. Most successful people are not afraid of work, and that is why they are successful.

Another activity of successful social media marketers, which ultimately creates raving fans, is that they publicly (online) compliment others or they recommend others to their own network. Here's the point: don't simply make it about you. Help your friends grow their businesses. Share resources and publicly "shout out" online what great things your friends and colleagues are doing. This will go a long way with your friends. They will thank you and respect you for it.

Another strategy for creating raving fans is to feature perhaps a client or friend of the week on your Facebook profile page or fan page. People love to see their name in lights (whether they admit it or not). Feature fans' pet of the week because people love to post pictures of their pets!

Also, as you venture into video, you will want to have your friends in some videos. That not only promotes your business, but theirs as well. We will be talking a lot more about raving fans throughout the book as we introduce more social media sites and tools, so stay tuned.

The Least You Need to Know

- Think of yourself and your business as a brand and remember that everything you write, say, and do online reflects on your brand.
- Encourage your top clients and friends to support your fan page, but give them reasons to keep checking in (discounts, special information, etc.).
- Create a sticker, T-shirt, or mugs that say "I'm a fan of (your company)" so they can display their "fanship" outside of the Facebook site.
- Creating a group on Facebook is another way to build a community around your business. Facebook is always revamping this feature, but it has proven worthwhile for people who have used it.
- Successful social media marketers create raving fans for their businesses because they are great at promoting others and they make people feel good about networking with them.

More Facebook Marketing Strategies and Netiquette

In This Chapter

- Clever ways to keep your fans and followers happy
- Using proper "netiquette"
- Getting creative with video on Facebook
- Other "Stand out in a crowd of millions" tools!
- Making a Facebook marketing checklist

Now you have a multitude of fans, so your next challenge is to keep those fans happy. You don't want them to just join your page or your group and then disappear.

In the pages ahead, you'll learn some unique tips to help you maintain an enthusiastic fan base. You've already learned some marketing strategies for Facebook and now that you're ready, we'll kick it up a notch.

Keeping Your Fans Engaged

As you've learned by now, there are many ways for you to attract friends and followers. Are you still uncomfortable with having fans? Well, if you are, let me put this as gently as I can—it's time to get over it!

You become a fan of a baseball team because you admire what the team stands for, or maybe you admire the ability of a special player. You might not know him personally, but you are a fan. Now that you are on the worldwide platform of Facebook, you are now on center stage—even if it is only your profile page. You can attract and maintain fans who will be loyal to you, support you, and tell others about you and your business.

> **TRY THIS**
>
> Type in a different status update in "What's on your mind?" every day. Try asking a question or providing a tip. See if you begin getting more friend requests and comments on your page. Try it for a month to see what happens.

Here are some tips to keep your loyal fans happily engaged with you:

- Listen to your fans. What are they hungry for? What are they responding to? Run a poll. Pay attention when some of your posts get more responses than others. Fans love it when you ask them questions.

- Create a great customer experience online. For instance, follow up, be energetic, and keep the customer in mind with everything you post. Don't just post info about your business; post information that is relevant to the reader.

- It's okay to grow slowly. It's not a race to get the most followers. Think quality over quantity. It takes time.

- Post relevant links, and share useful data and statistics that will help your followers.

- Include people on your journey. Changing your office? Share the journey. Writing a book? Share the journey. Heading to a great conference? Share the journey. As I mentioned previously, reality shows are a big hit because people want to see the "real people." Now they want to see the "real you."

- Create events using Facebook, and choose settings to keep the event open. This allows friends to share the event with their own networks.

- Invite followers to get your newsletters or tell a bit about themselves on your fan page. Give them reasons to come back. Select a Fan of the Week or Fan of the Day.

- When people write on your wall or when you add them as a friend, treat them like a VIP guest to your business.

- Engage people. This is your outlet to millions of people. Host a live Q & A session on your fan page with you or one of your suppliers or experts. Record an interview with Skype.

- Get creative. Think of new and unique ways you can inspire your followers to participate in online conversations with your business. Invite them to send in videos, offer free webinars, or ask them to post on your blog. Use Facebook to drive them to your other marketing outlets, such as your website, blog, or YouTube channel.

- Post photos—but keep your image in mind. Don't post embarrassing or goofy photos, because people might not appreciate it. Always ask for permission first.

- Regularly congratulate and acknowledge people online. Feature your clients and prospects on your page by commenting on their success or on their status updates. Remember, everyone wants to be recognized.

- Everything you write can be picked up on the search engines tomorrow. Remember my advice about conscious social media marketing? Keep that in mind when posting on the Internet.

- If you don't like what someone is posting on your site and you are getting a bad feeling, block them. Go to **Account**, then **Privacy Settings**, then to **Block Lists**. Anyone you block will not be notified.

What Not to Do

Have you enjoyed reading the "Netiquette" sidebars throughout this book? People who are successful in social media marketing are people who respect and follow the unwritten rules of what works and what doesn't on social media platforms. Netiquette describes not only what's proper, but also what's improper on the Internet.

So, in the tradition of television's *What Not to Wear*, let's cover *what not to do* on social media platforms:

- Refrain from politics and religious rants. Let's expand that a bit: refrain from *all* rants.

- Do not write private messages to people on their wall. Send them via private email or their Facebook Message inbox. You can access their inbox right above the subscribers box on their profile page. Simply click on message and send.

- Do not begin selling your products or services as soon as someone adds you as a friend. It's a big turnoff on Facebook when people post their products or services on your wall just as soon as you meet them.

- Don't write when you are angry or have had too much to drink. Ever.

- Do not use the Notes feature to "tag" people who are supposedly referred to in the note when they really aren't mentioned at all. Many people do this thinking it will get their notes read, when in fact it turns people off.

- Don't post photos from the crazy private New Year's Eve party that your company hosted. Be aware of the messages you are sending to clients and prospective buyers.

- Just as in email, if you write in all caps, it appears as if you are yelling.

- Don't write negatively about the competition or about others in general. People surf around online and you never know who may come across your page or profile.

DID YOU KNOW?

Can you guess how many videos are uploaded each month on Facebook? There are 48 hours of video uploaded on YouTube every minute of the day. The Facebook stat just can't be verified. There are millions and millions! Video is huge on Facebook.

Video Ideas for Facebook

You can use the Kodak Mini video camera, the Canon Powershot SX10, or even your iPhone for wonderful videos on Facebook. All of these have built-in software that allows you to easily download the video and import it directly to Facebook and other social sites. However, if you have another video camera and you know how to download videos from it, that is fine, too.

The great thing about putting videos on Facebook is that it gives you the ability to share your message with potentially thousands, if not millions, of others. Let people meet the real you—let them see inside your business, meet your team and partners, and share your expertise.

Facebook makes it easy to share your video and make it viral. We get more into videos for social media in future chapters, but while we are examining Facebook, here are some ideas for you to try:

- Are you an expert in your industry? If so, give a 30-second tip each week.

- Having an open house or a holiday celebration with clients? Have the video camera ready and ask people about their thoughts regarding your business.

- Speaking at an event? Get some audience testimonials after your speech.

- Record some of your top clients talking about why they enjoy what they do *and* why they enjoy working with you.

- Take a group of your top clients/prospects to dinner. Ask them to share what they are looking for in their business. Help promote them in your video.

- Are you a Realtor? When you hand clients the keys to their new home, ask them to record their thoughts on video and then share it on your profile page.

- Are you a recruiter? Share interview tips each week. Keep it short and succinct.

- Do you have a pet? People love to meet your pet on Facebook. Oprah did that recently (and so did I), and people love it!

- Are you a writer? Share the top takeaways of an article you've published in a video. Include a link where friends can read it online, or tell them where they can find it in print.

- Have a new product? Give people a sneak peek when it arrives at your business. Smile as you take it out of the box. Remember, people want to see real situations.

- Are you a motivational coach? Share your tips of wisdom once a week with a motivational/inspirational message. This allows people to get a feel for who you are.

- Are you a florist/baker/artist? Share some of your dream creations on video each week or month. Bring the wow factor to your page. People love to "oooh" and "aaah" over great images.

- Are you an account rep/professional organizer/interior decorator? Share a tip or have a client give a testimonial, and then show before and after images.

The list can go on and on. The good news is, again, it doesn't need to be a slick Hollywood production. The more real and relevant the material is to your prospects, the better. Experiment and don't be afraid to show it on Facebook.

Later, I will show you how to take that video and put it online on other sites to drive people to your website, blog, Facebook fan page, and other social media sites. You just might be on your way to becoming the next social media celebrity.

The Marketplace Application on Facebook

The Marketplace application is a little gem of a find. It's not necessarily for everyone, but it's good for you to know what it can do in case you see a need for it in your marketing efforts.

The Marketplace application is what many are calling the "Craigslist of Facebook." To find it, go to the search bar at the top and type in **Marketplace App**. Then open the application and add it to your profile.

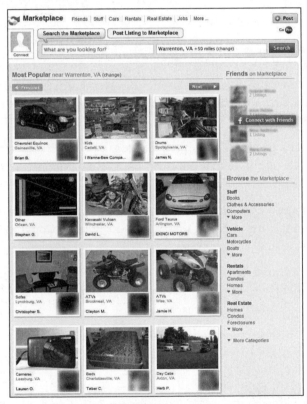

Facebook's Marketplace application.

As of this writing, there are millions of active monthly users of the Marketplace application. If you are a Realtor, the marketplace application is a great place to post a listing of a home or townhouse for sale or rent. If you are an auto dealer, you can list your cars for sale here. Do you sell or make children's clothes or furniture? Put it on the Marketplace. It's another avenue for you that is free and could, potentially, reach just the right buyer.

It's also useful if you need to hire someone or find a job. Looking to hire an intern? Put your listing in the jobs section on Marketplace. This is a good application for, in particular, Realtors or retail merchants who can sell individual products or solutions. You also might find something you need to buy here. *Hint:* it's a good place to find furniture for your office.

Savor Chat

This is not a Facebook application that is found on the Application menu, but it integrates directly with the Facebook platform, so it is worth mentioning. You can find it by going to www.savorchat.com.

Savor Chat enables you to create and host your own chat room. You can make your chat room public or private, send direct messages to individuals or group members, and invite your Facebook friends. It is perfect for networking and for meetings with Facebook friends who are currently online and those you want to join together in a separate forum for additional discussion.

It also enables you to have live discussions about projects or upcoming events. So it's a tool worth checking out. You can create your own branded virtual chat room and host your own meetings and discussions.

Once you've signed in, you can name your room, list the times your room is open, place it in a category, and save the room. You can also browse rooms that are currently set up and join in if they are open.

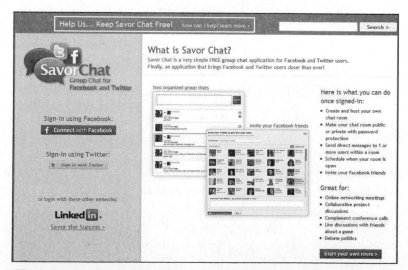

The home page for the Savor Chat: "Group Chat for Facebook and Twitter."

This is where you name your room on Savor Chat.

Get creative with your business on Savor Chat. Perhaps you can host an online monthly meetup, a business break, or a literary luncheon. What would your prospects or customers be interested in discussing? This is another online tool that merges your Facebook friends with a live text chat tool for engagement and interaction.

Facebook Marketing Checklist

You've learned a lot, haven't you? I don't want you to get overwhelmed, so let's take a breather and make up your official Facebook marketing checklist:

❐ Your dynamic headshot. Use one that reflects the best of you and your brand.

❐ Your amazing profile cover photo that you update regularly to feature you, your products and/or services, and/or your team. And a powerful About section with your website, phone number(s), and a description about what your business can do for people. Make it uniquely your own and say what you need and want to say. This is an advertisement for your business.

❐ Highlight your friends and fans on your profile by making them stand out in some creative way.

❐ A daily status update ("What's on your mind?") entry. This is key so that you will maintain energy around your page, you will appear in your friends' news feeds, and you are keeping top-of-mind awareness. Think of it as generating publicity for your brand every time you post. Status update ideas include listing or sharing a tip, letting friends know what you are working on, congratulating a client, announcing a new client partnership, posting a job or open house, letting people know about an upcoming event, announcing a new product, sharing news about your business, or giving a general business tip.

❐ Add friends and include a personal, genuine message. It's person to person marketing at this point.

❐ Think about creating a group on Facebook that would further bring together your clients and prospects in a meaningful way. Maybe it's a group for your VIP clients only.

❐ As a beginner, log on daily for 20 minutes, add friends, and post a greeting on a friend's wall.

❐ Check your inbox daily for messages. Respond with a note along with your name and website, name and business title, or phrase on what you can do for people.

Example: "Hi John, Thank you for the note. I look forward to your postings on Facebook. If I can do anything to assist you, please do not hesitate to call. Jennifer Abernethy, America's Sales Stylist for Business Professionals with The Sales Lounge"

❐ Go to the home page and look at upcoming birthdays. Clicking on the name will take you to his or her profile page. Write a greeting on the wall!

❐ Invest in a small handheld video camera or, if it is powerful enough, learn to use your smartphone's video function. Start posting videos on Facebook. Create a video marketing strategy on Facebook.

❐ Add the appropriate applications that will help your business become more visible, likeable, and relatable.

❐ Use the Events application as a way to virally grow your brand, whether you host your own event or RSVP to others. Come up with a catchy name for your event. Click the **Share** button and post it to your profile with a quick message. When you RSVP for someone else's event—whether it's a yes, no, or maybe—write on the wall with your name and website address with a short note. You never know who is going to stumble upon it and visit your site. Get creative and post a video on your Event page.

❐ Post a video RSVP to someone else's events. Go to your home page, search for events, find events that you want to RSVP for, open the page, look for the video section, and click **Upload Video**. It's that easy.

❐ Keep your mind-set positive. You never know where your social media marketing is going to take your business. Stay in it for the long haul.

So now you're practically a Facebook expert. The only thing left is to customize your settings and get everything just the way you want it. In the next chapter, you learn how to do just that.

The Least You Need to Know

- Treat your Facebook friends and followers as if they are the top VIPs in your business.

- The number one activity you can do on Facebook to build momentum and keep your fans engaged is to update the "What's on your mind?" status every day.

- Always follow the unwritten netiquette rules when interacting online.

- The video revolution has begun, so incorporate it into your social media marketing now.

- Try different strategies, such as the Marketplace or Savor Chat, and live Q & A sessions to engage your friends and fans.

Twitter

In this part, you learn why all the world is tweeting. Are you scratching your head and wondering what the fuss is about? You don't need to wonder any longer. This part introduces you to Twitter with step-by-step instructions and screen shots.

Not only will you learn how to create an amazing Twitter profile, but you'll also learn why this is a powerful social media tool. You also find out the do's and don'ts of Twitter culture, how to write great tweets, how to attract amazing followers, and all about TweetChats. When you have completed this part, you will be astounded at the newfound power at your digital fingertips that the Twitter applications offer you. The marketing strategies and recommendations you'll read about will help you build momentum and incorporate new ideas in your social media marketing strategy.

The Networking Cocktail Party of Social Media

In This Chapter

- The evolving world of Twitter
- Why you should join Twitter
- Understanding the language of Twitterers
- How Twitter can help your business
- Choosing the right user name

It's not surprising that *The New York Times* called Twitter "the fastest-growing phenomena on the Internet." Twitter has quickly become a part of our everyday media and social culture. So how did we get to this point? Twitter began in August 2006 as a microblogging site with the sole purpose of answering (in 140 characters or less) this question: What are you doing right now?

In 2006 and 2007, many people were posting items, called "tweets," such as "going to Starbucks," "watching television right now," or "looking forward to buying the new Mac laptop tomorrow." But initially, many users were turned off because there wasn't a clear explanation on the site about how to actually use it.

Since 2007, though, Twitter has become a valuable tool for entrepreneurs, artists, media personalities, reporters, and marketers. In this chapter, you'll learn why Twitter is a terrific way to market your business and services. You'll also learn about building strategic alliances, attracting raving and dedicated fans, the finer points of Twitter culture, and much more.

DID YOU KNOW?

By the end of 2011, it is estimated that there will be more than 500 million Twitter users, with an average age of 42. As of October 2011, Twitter users were sending 250 million tweets per day according to their CEO Dick Costolo and 100 million users were actively engaging on the site monthly. The most active days to tweet are Thursdays and Fridays.

The Twitter Culture

What used to be a place where you shared what you are doing "right now" in 140 characters (or less) has turned into a place of sharing tips, tricks, information, motivation, inspiration, and a whole lot of communication. It is a content-rich platform where power Twitterers are wonderful about sharing your name, following you while you promote your business, and, potentially, strategically partnering with you. Thirty percent of Twitter users earn 100K annually—and the number is climbing.

What do I mean by power Twitterers? They are a very motivated, enthusiastic group who are eager to share, learn, and network. However, they also want to add income to their bottom lines and make strong connections to advance their business forward.

You'll find many different types of people using Twitter—coaches, consultants, celebrities, corporate CEOs, artists, nutritionists, speakers, Realtors, recruiters, and entrepreneurs. You'll also find airline companies, restaurant chains, hotels, gas stations, tourism destinations, and media outlets such as radio, TV, and print.

This is the Twitter.com login screen.

To be successful and keep a loyal following, you must abide by the "unwritten rules" of Twitter culture. I'll touch on these rules throughout the book because they're so important, but in a nutshell, keep these Twitter tips in mind to get loyal followers, network, and grow your business:

- Share information.

- Care about other users.

- Provide value.

- Share your expertise.

- Be welcoming and generous.

- Be authentic.

- Do not over automate your tweets.

- Do not plagiarize or "Twagiarize."

- Do not spam.

- Have fun with it.

Keep these tips in mind and you'll be on your way to becoming a valuable member of the Twitter community.

 ONLINE CAUTION

One of the things you do not want to do is to constantly be in "sell" mode. Be interested in others and share your expertise, but don't constantly sell your services, particularly when you first begin using Twitter. Remember, this is "social," so be social and communicate with others.

Blocking People on Twitter

Unfortunately, there are spammers on Twitter who have a very disingenuous way of following and attracting folks. What's a spammer? Twitter recently released this list that describes who and what is considered spam:

- Following others to gain attention to your account or links.

- Creating several accounts to promote the same product or links.

- Sending large numbers of @reply messages that aren't really genuine replies. (@reply messages are personal replies to Twitter users; you'll learn more about @replies in the next few pages).

- Creating updates just so they show up in search results.

- Disguising links (similar to bait and switch; writing about one thing but linking to another).

- Developing a large number of users (relative to followers) who have blocked you.

If you block someone, you're saying that you don't want them following or contacting you. How do you block users? You'll find this by logging in to your Twitter account. Then go to the profile page of the person you want to block. Click their headshot or logo. This will display a drop-down menu. Click **Block**.

Why You Should Join Twitter

Although Twitter is a social networking site, it has also been called an information site and a "listening" site. There is so much great content on Twitter that's being passed around from tweeter to tweeter. Think of it as a giant cocktail party where people share tips, resources, links, videos, and inspirational quotes. If every true "cocktail party" was like that, everyone would want to attend, right? And no one would want to leave. That is the appeal of Twitter.

More often than not, it's not just *what* you know, but *who* you know. Twitter is an amazing resource for all-around networking and getting to know people from all over the world. In one day, you could have a conversation on Twitter with someone from Scotland, California, and Australia. The more people that you know and who know you, the more empowered you become with information, new ways of looking at things, and new ideas. You'll eventually find new champions for your business and even new customers!

Imagine that your competitors are on Twitter and they're experiencing amazing conversations, sharing their expertise, and making a lot of new connections. Wouldn't that make you feel a bit behind? Well, even if they aren't on Twitter today, chances are they will be soon. Here's your chance to be a leader in your industry!

As of this writing, Twitter has already merged into the mainstream television media, with reporters on CNN saying, "Follow me on Twitter." Piers Morgan has "real time *live* Tweets" going across the bottom of the screen during the middle of his show. You almost can't go to a conference without finding someone Twittering away in their seat.

> **DEFINITION**
>
> A **Twitter feed**, also referred to as a Twitter stream, is a stream of live Twitter updates scrolling horizontally or vertically on one's TV or computer screen.

In fact, at a technology conference, you're more likely to have conversations on Twitter than you are in person—even if you're both attending the same conference. Doesn't it now seem like the whole world is "a'tweeting"? If it isn't, it may soon be. Even the pope from the Vatican has joined along with the Dali Lama.

Okay, so let's get down to the details. How can Twitter help your business?

Twitter is an amazing tool for accomplishing the following:

- Producing great PR for your business
- Marketing your business
- Networking for your business and building relationships
- Driving traffic to your website
- Getting others to talk about your business to their followers
- Attracting and keeping loyal customers
- Asking your followers/customers questions
- Staying informed by reading what people are thinking

Twitter Terms You Need to Know

Twitter has an entirely new language, which has emerged as the short "sound-byte" chatter" within the Twitter culture. If you're new to Twitter, you might feel like you've entered *The Land of the Lost* when reading tweets like this: "Thanks for the RT on #followfriday see u at the Tweetup."

Here's the translation: Thank you for the retweet (sharing my tweet to your network and referencing me) on Follow Friday (the day that tweeters recommend people to follow). See you at the tweetup (also called a meetup—a physical location agreed upon on Twitter where the tweeters will meet).

NETIQUETTE

"Twagiarizing" is the act of posting someone else's tweet and not giving the original tweeter credit, similar to plagiarizing. So if you do post something that was written or originated by someone else, give them credit by incorporating their Twitter user name preceded by the @ symbol.

As Twitter folks merge their tweets into other social media sites such as Facebook, the Facebook "language" is also shifting as people update their Facebook status via Twitter. (I do not recommend this because they are two distinct platforms, but many do it to save time.)

Tweet example

This is an example of a tweet.

Don't worry; you'll be a savvy Twitterer in no time. To get you on your way, here are some terms that every Twitterer simply must know:

- **Tweet.** Commonly referred to as a status update. People use this to post links, share thoughts, and give information, all in 140 characters or less.

- **Retweet (RT).** An RT is the same as quoting someone on Twitter. Simply use RT @(person's user name). Example: RT @SalesLounge (then repeat the tweet). Some Applications such as TweetDeck (which we discuss later in Part 3) allow you to automatically RT with a push of a button. Cool, huh? An RT is the forwarding of a message out to your followers, which helps it become more viral. The fun part is when people start RT-ing what you write. Simply scroll over the tweet and you will see the Retweet icon pop up.

Here's a tweet that shows the retweet button (RT).

- **Hashtags.** This is simply a way to group or "tag" tweets together to be searched for later or followed by others interested in that topic or event. A hashtag is preceded by the # symbol and is usually made up of an acronym of letters for an event or cause (in parts of Europe, the # symbol is called a hashmark).

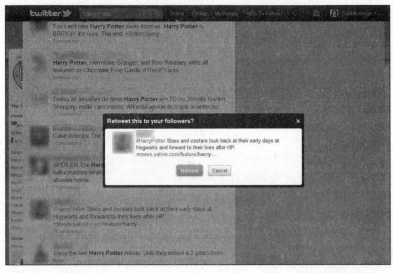

This is a tweet using a sample hashtag #HarryPotter.

DID YOU KNOW?

Hashtags help to create Trending Topics. Getting your network of followers to use your tag can help move it to a trending topic (but you must get a lot of followers to do that). Hashtags can be placed in the beginning or end of tweet.

- **Trending Topics.** This describes what the Twitter users are talking about most often. The Trending Topics are always changing, depending on what is happening in the news, entertainment, or online worlds. For instance, when the verdict was announced in the trial of Casey Anthony, the Florida mother accused of murdering her daughter, in the summer of 2011, #CaseyAnthony was a Trending Topic for days.

Trending Topics

Here's a screen shot of Trending Topics of which you can list by state, country, or world.

- **Followers.** These are the people who are "following" your tweets. They can be your potential friends, advocates, champions, business referrers, strategic partners, customers, and fans.

- **Peeps.** Another term in Twitter culture for your followers. Also referred to as Tweeps.

- **Updates.** Twitter keeps track of how many times you post a tweet. Your tweets are often referred to as updates.

- **Message.** This is your inbox on Twitter. *Note:* This was formerly called a Direct Message and many still refer to it as a direct message. A Message might only be seen by you and the sender, if sent privately, and it can be automated or individually typed and sent to you by someone on Twitter. If both parties are not following each other, they cannot message each other privately. Any messaging would be public until both parties are following each other.

- **#FollowFriday.** Each Friday, power Twitterers put the phrase #FollowFriday in front of user names of folks they want to recommend. #FF is also commonly used.

By recommending people to follow, you'll quickly become likeable in the Twitter culture. When someone from another network, city, or even country recommends you on Follow Friday, you know you're doing something right on Twitter. One of your goals should be to eventually be on the #FollowFriday list.

Follow Friday tweet

This is an example of a Follow Friday tweet.

- **Tweetup.** A term a Twitterer uses when she wants to meet in person.

- **Tweeting.** This is the act of posting a tweet.

- **Tweeps.** Another word for the people who follow you; same as peeps. It often refers, more generally, to the people (or tweeple) who participate on Twitter.

- **Twictionary.** An unofficial listing of Twitter terms. Find it at www.twictionary.com.

- **TweetChat.** There are hundreds of weekly #Tweetchats that have specific, timed conversations around a topic. #VideoBizChat, #SmallBizChat, #Speakchat, #Luxchat, and #LoungeChat are a few popular ones.

How Twitter Helps Your Business

When initially viewing the Twitter landscape, many entrepreneurs and business owners just cannot imagine how typing in 140 character comments on a site can help their businesses. If that's how you feel, you're not alone. My best advice is to look at this as a free networking and PR avenue for your business.

If your ongoing tweets make use of the Twitter tips that we've already talked about, you'll begin attracting new followers, and then some of their followers will start to follow you. There's a natural progression that occurs after you get those first followers.

Here's what usually happens next: after someone recommends you to his or her network, you will get even more followers. Your new followers simply tell their network how great your services or products are. Next, the tweeps in your new followers' network decide to check out your website. At that point, there's a good chance you'll land a new client or at least develop a solid prospect. All this takes time, of course.

Why don't you try this goal? Get five new people (tweeps) to follow you during your first week on Twitter. (Hey, that's five more than you had last week!) In the second week, you shoot for five more; then in the third week, you shoot for 10 more, then 20 more, and so on. All you need to focus on are a few tweeps at a time.

Okay, let's get into the nitty-gritty about how Twitter can help your business.

Creating a Tech-Savvy Image

In today's business world, you can't afford to look like a dinosaur. You want to be seen as an on-trend and in-the-know entrepreneur. In fact, some say if you aren't using Twitter, your business savvy might appear suspect to others. Conversely, after you're on Twitter, you'll look like a savvy techie (even if you aren't). You will be marketing yourself and your business while networking with the tech-savvy in crowds of tens of millions.

Communicating Information About Your Business

Twitter also helps you quickly send information out to your followers. Let's say you're speaking at an event, holding an open house, running a big special, or announcing a new client partnership. Or maybe you're closing your business early on Tuesday for some reason. Now you can send that message out with a few simple keystrokes and—voilá!—you're done.

Building Your List

Another Twitter benefit is that it can help you build your list. In the past years, the "list" referred to your mailing list. Today, it refers to your email list, but you can also gather office and home addresses as well. To the small business owner or entrepreneur, your list is your gold mine. You want to build a list with which you can regularly communicate with folks outside of Twitter and other social media platforms.

How does Twitter help you do this? By driving people to your website, where you invite them to sign up for your e-zine or newsletter. You'll learn what you need to know about e-zines and newsletters in Chapter 20.

Networking with Colleagues, Clients, and Prospects

Twitter is also a great place to build rapport with folks you've been networking with. Let's say you meet someone at a networking event. Find out if he or she is on Twitter. If so, tell him or her you'll become a follower. More than likely, people will follow you back and you'll begin building a rapport. You'll share your expertise, tips, and information with each other. This approach also builds credibility and, hopefully, likeability, which certainly helps every business owner.

More Ways Twitter Helps Your Business

You're a busy professional who wants to ensure that your social media choices give you a lot of bang for your buck. Here are a few more quick tips for ways to use Twitter:

- Use Twitter as a PR tool to promote your business as a great place to work or to do business with. Tweet something good about your employees or clients. This will give you not only happy employees and clients, but it just makes you look (and feel) good!

- Share interesting links or information about your industry to position yourself as a subject matter expert. Let's say you run ABC Catering. Instead of only tweeting about ABC, tweet about an article you've read that covers new trends in wedding cakes. This approach also shows you're willing to be a "sharing resource," which will ultimately expand your business reach.

- Create a sense of community around your business. Commenting on fellow entrepreneurs, business owners, clients, and followers will make them feel more attached to you and your business. We've talked about how networking can bring you new business and help you retain your clients. But if your tweets show genuine interest in others, this engenders a neighborhood feel.

- Create top-of-mind awareness for your brand. By tweeting each day, you will keep your name and business in front of people. When genuinely used, a daily tweet or two can be an incredible source of PR, marketing, and branding for you and your services. Companies pay a lot of money for advertising. Think of Twitter as a free way to get some advertising for your brand or company name.

- Learn what your community, customers, and market are looking for. When you read and have dialogue on Twitter, you'll know what your followers want and what they have to say. You'll learn things that will help you make decisions about the direction of your business.

- Invite your current clients and prospects to follow you on Twitter. They'll learn from you and you can follow them back, which will ultimately make you, your clients, and your prospects feel more connected.

> **ONLINE CAUTION**
>
> The Twitter culture does not like negativity. You can share your point of view, but refrain from name calling or pointing fingers. I've seen those that have done it … and the outcome is not pretty.

What's in a User Name?

Before creating your Twitter account, think about your Twitter user name—your "handle" or your call name. It's the word that will be placed directly below or next to your photo, or *avatar*. It can also be an instrumental part of your branding strategy.

> **DEFINITION**
>
> **Avatar** refers to the "personality" or image connected with the user name on a social media site such as Twitter. It can also be a computer's representation of one's self or alter ego on 3-D sites like Second Life. An avatar can also be your professional "headshot."

In fact, a great Twitter user name will be part of all of your marketing. It will go on your business cards, your email signature, your Facebook and LinkedIn pages, and your blog. So think carefully about it. Oh, one more thing—you have only 15 characters for your user name.

This requires thinking a little differently from what you're used to. When we all first got into computing, our user names weren't made public. We wrote them down and filed them away. Well, with Twitter, it's very different. Your user name on Twitter is very public.

So as you begin thinking about your strategy and why you want to use Twitter, carefully plan your Twitter user name to attract your target audience. There are also many ways your chosen user name can help you reach out to the people you want to follow you.

As you get more savvy on Twitter (which will happen faster than you can imagine), you'll learn that one way to find people is to type in an industry within the Find People tab on Twitter.

Here's an example: Say you want to find someone in sales or a sales expert. Well, if you type in the word "sales," using Find People, anyone with the word "sales" in their user name will pop up. Most people who use "sales" in their user name have something to do with sales. The same is true with the word "realtor" or "financial." So your user name could include the name of your industry.

Another way to find people is to search by their business name or actual name. Many people use their business name for their user name. When setting up your account, it's important to include your actual name so that people can find your Twitter profile.

TRY THIS

A fun way to create a great Twitter user name is to gather friends and associates, and brainstorm. Tell them you are creating your Twitter user name to align with your profession or your passion. Share your ideas and ask for theirs. Then gauge your friends' reactions to the various suggestions. (Remember, the maximum number of characters you can use to create your handle is 15.)

After you get a good name that draws a good reaction, claim it! You'll be amazed at how effective this brainstorming approach is and at how quickly you'll discover a great name to use on Twitter.

You might want to brand your own name, such as @JohnDoe. Or you may want to use the name of your business as your user name. That's also fine.

In the next three chapters, you'll learn about applications that will help you manage Twitter. Applications such as TweetDeck and TweetLater make Twitter easy to keep up with. What's my handle? I invite you to follow me @SalesLounge.

The Least You Need to Know

- Even if you don't immediately understand how it will ultimately help your business, get on Twitter and become involved in the conversations.
- Don't be in constant sell mode, because the Twitter culture hates spammers but loves givers of information and good energy.
- Participate in #FollowFriday, which involves recommending people (or peeps) to follow.
- Retweet someone when you can to show that you're part of a community, that you don't always have to take credit for everything, and that you're willing to give the spotlight to someone else.
- Think about your overall Twitter marketing and branding strategy when you select your user name and photo or avatar.

Creating a Twitter Profile

Chapter

9

In This Chapter

- What's a tweet?
- Making the best Twitter profile
- Finding people and following them
- Creating Messages, @Replies, and Trending Topics
- Applications to help your Twitter mobile experience

Remember what I said about first impressions? Well, they count on Twitter as well. From your engaging photograph to a nice short bio with a website link, creating an amazing Twitter profile will only add to your marketability in the culture of Twitterers.

Let's get your profile ready and get you meeting and tweeting like a pro. By the end of this chapter, you'll love how easy it can be to be a savvy social media marketer on Twitter.

Setting Up Your Twitter Profile

Let's get you started on Twitter. First, go to www.twitter.com, and you will see a page that looks like the following screen.

Sign up

*Click **Sign up** to get started on Twitter.*

Welcome to Twitter. It looks pretty basic, but inside is a happening social experience that you'll be glad you're a part of. Click the gold box that reads **Sign up**.

Here's where you sign up to participate on Twitter.

1. First, enter your business name or personal name for Full Name. Ensure you spell it correctly. Or click **Sign up**, and then enter your information.

2. In the next section you will see a field that reads Username. Remember a good user name is important because it will be your call name or handle. The Twitter world will come to know you by this name. Enter your user name, using up to 15 letter characters with no spaces.

3. Now, enter your password and email address. You'll be referring to this password and email address in the future when we merge Twitter with Facebook, so be sure you write it down.

4. Type in the security words that you see on the page (using capital letters and spacing as appropriate). If you cannot read the security words, click **Get two new words** or **Hear a set of words**.

5. When finished, click **Create my account**.

The full signup process is described at https://support.twitter.com/articles/100990-how-to-sign up-on-twitter.

You will next see a screen welcoming you to Twitter and showing you a sample tweet.

Sample Welcome page once inside Twitter.

ONLINE CAUTION

If there is a user name that really carries your brand, then grab it quickly. With so many joining Twitter each month, the most common surnames are going quickly. While you can always change your user name, it's good to think about long-term identity and branding when you are initially creating your user name. Think ahead, too, and create Twitter accounts for other business endeavors.

6. The next screen will suggest a few people to follow. Most likely these will be celebrities or national figures. You can choose to follow or at the bottom left of the page you can skip this step. *Note:* by now Twitter has most likely sent you a confirmation email, so check your email inbox.

If you want to follow celebrities, figureheads, and popular publications, here's where you can find them.

7. Twitter gives you a varied list of celebrities, figureheads, and popular publications to follow initially. Under the Search Bar tab on the top, type in a name and up will pop a Twitter stream of anyone who mentions that person and also most likely that person.

8. If you do want to follow a certain person, go ahead and click on their Twitter name. You've added some people to follow and you can see how they tweet.

9. Now click on your Twitter name or handle in the top-right corner. A drop-down menu displays. Click **Settings**. On the settings page, be sure to select your time zone. Next, click **Profile**.

This page is also important because you want your Twitter information page to look professional to attract and maintain followers.

Within the profile section, you need to upload a photo or logo in this box versus the white egg avatar that is automatically provided. This way you will appear as a legitimate Twitterer. Browse through your computer to upload your photograph or logo. Then click **Save** and follow these steps:

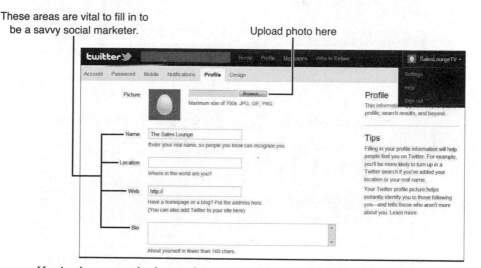

Here's where you upload your photo or your business logo and your important bio.

1. Select your location. You can put your town and state, state only, or just your country. Some people put their cell phone number here or something interesting like "wherever you would like me to be or global."

2. Put in your URL (or business website). *Note:* make sure you put "http://" in front of the "www" so it will be a live link to your website.

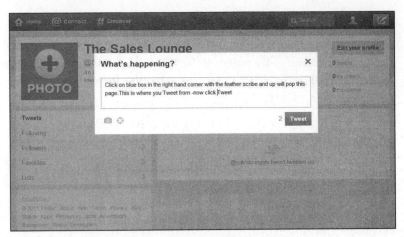

Here's where you type your tweet.

Here is what pops up when I search for President Obama. You can also see top images and top videos that have been shared on Twitter on President Obama.

3. An important step: In the Bio box, enter a one-line description of you, the business, or the group that is being represented. You can use a series of one-word adjectives in this area as well. Get creative.

Here are some examples of what others have put in this line:

- @SalesLounge America's Social Marketing Stylist / Million $$ Sales Expert. Speaker| Mentor |Consultant, Media Guest, Author: *Idiot's Guide to Social Media Marketing.* (Alpha Books)

- @Maryvandewiel Brand anthropologist + Dutch sea captain's daughter. Interprets clues for a living. Leads the NY Brand Lab workshops. Weekly radio show host. Incurable doodler.

- @NeenJames: Productivity Expert and Thought Leader, keynote speaker, author, fabulous shoe collector

- @FrankSpencer Professional Futurist, Strategic Foresight, Professional Speaker, Visionary, Social Innovation, Human Emergence, Transformational Development, Global Issues.

- @EddieRents @Eddierents: RentalPrenuer, Leasing Rental Expert, Owner RentalHousing.com, RoommateRentals.net, RoommateRentals. com, RentMatch.com, Marketing Expert, Positive Minded! :) http:// eddieedwards.com

4. After you click **Save**, go to the top left under your Twitter name and scroll down to Settings. Now click **Design**. You can change the colors of your background for your Twitter profile here. (We will get into custom Twitter backgrounds later, but if you're ready you can go to www.twitrbackgrounds. com or www.twitrounds.com.) Next, click **Save Changes**.

5. Now click **Profile** on the top bar and take a look at your page.

6. Congratulations! You now have a great-looking Twitter profile. For fun, click **Home** and type another tweet. Say, perhaps, "I'm just learning about Twitter and am ready to connect!"

Finding People on Twitter

You already have a few people you are following from the initial list that Twitter provided to you when you created your account. How do you find and follow other people? The easiest way initially is to sign in to your Twitter account and click **Search in the upper right half of your screen**. Type in someone's name. Here I've typed in mine. Now a list will pop up of everyone that shares that name.

Here's what you'll see:

Type in a name and see all the people that pop up and connect with the person you are looking for.

Now go to the Search bar on Twitter. Experiment with your searching or click **Advanced Search.** Or try typing in someone's name. If that person has a user name that's different from their real name, their name will pop up as long as they have listed their real name when they created their account. Here are several additional ways to search for people using this search page:

- Type the person's last name with no spaces in between first and last name, or try the last name only.

- Type the person's industry, such as dental, sales, or real estate.

- Type the name of the company where the person works.

- To follow major publications or TV networks, type *New York Times, USA Today,* CNN, BBC, or whatever you're looking for. Or, go to www.muckrack. com a great site for media outlets and people on Twitter.

- If necessary, go outside of Twitter and search on Google for the person or company name, and then add the + sign and the word Twitter. If the person has a Twitter account, it will show up here.

When the search results pop up, click the avatar or person's photo to check him or her out, read the bio, and then decide to follow or not. The system isn't perfect, so don't be discouraged if you can't find the person you are seeking. There are still other ways. *Note:* You can also find people by clicking the #Discover tab at the top of your Twitter page.

Another way to search for a topic or person is to go to www.search.twitter.com and type in the person, place, or subject you are looking for. For example, want to find out if someone is tweeting about the Hamptons? Type "The Hamptons." This search will find the keyword you are looking for within the tweet itself. Try typing in "PT Cruiser." All tweets will pop up that mention the words PT and/or Cruiser.

Check your industry. You can then decide whether or not to follow those people whose tweets pop up on screen. Remember the #followfriday that was mentioned in the previous chapter? Stay on www.search.twitter.com and type in #followfriday and see the names that populate the screen. Here's a fun one: stay on www.search.twitter.com and click **Advanced Search**. The Advanced Search page will appear.

If you are interested in locating people who are tweeting near your location or another worldwide location, you can do a search on that. Or type in "Airline Deals" in the first line and you will see tweets based on that subject (and most likely either find some great deals or find companies to follow that regularly publish great deals). I hope you can now see why they call Twitter a great informational tool, because there is so much information at your fingertips. We will get into more ways to find people as you continue to learn about more advanced applications.

DID YOU KNOW?

You can find the most popular tweeters at twitterholic.com. And www.tweetscan.com allows you to type in a Twitter user name and see who is mentioning that person in a tweet.

What's a Tweet?

Now that you have the basics set up on your Twitter profile page, let's review the types of tweets you should be thinking about. At first, you should just get a conversation going. Ask a question, offer a tip, and share your expertise while you are gaining followers. As you get more comfortable typing in the 140 character format and having your tweets become your company's voice on Twitter, you'll need to start taking your tweets to the next level.

First, you want to think about strategic tweets that people would love to retweet (RT) to their network. What would people like to share? Again, it doesn't matter if you're an interior decorator, recruiter, coach, plumber, tailor, writer, speaker, consultant, or accountant; anyone can write a tweet that is helpful to others. The goal here is to be retweeted around the Twitter network. When someone retweets you, it gives you credibility and tells you that you are writing something that is valuable. It might take several months before you are retweeted, but when you get your first one by someone somewhere else in the world, it can be rather exciting.

As mentioned in the previous chapter, another type of tweet you can do is to retweet someone else, particularly early on but also as you become more experienced. This does two things: it helps you fit into the Twitter culture and it spreads goodwill. You are sharing that person's Twitter handle and thoughts with your network, which is a good thing. Tweets you will see often are motivational or inspirational quotes. These are fine and well meaning, but these types of tweets are starting to lose popularity with the power Twitter crowd as of this writing. An occasional quote is fine, but as a best practice don't consistently tweet motivational, historical, or inspirational quotes. People want to read your thoughts, your insight, and your expertise, and by doing these types of tweets, your popularity will increase rapidly.

Another type of tweet that's common involves providing links. Again, these are good, but think strategically. Ideally, it's nice to mix it up a bit with links, personal commentary, tips, advice, retweets, and, of course, recommendations for #followfriday. The most popular mainstream tweeters combine information and entertainment. Therefore, they're providing infotainment to their followers.

Deciding When to Tweet

There is no correct answer to this, but because you're a beginner, it's good practice to tweet once first thing in the morning before 9 A.M. Tweet again around noon, and then again in the evening. Now, of course, if you are hosting an event or attending an event and want to tweet throughout the day to report what's happening at the event, that is an acceptable practice. Some people seem to tweet literally all the time. Some do this by automating the tweets, while others just love to tweet. There is no right or wrong—just try not to overtweet like so many of the automated Twitterers do. Many find this annoying, particularly if you are in constant selling mode and not relating to others. Do what works best for you. However, at the very least, tweet one time per day or, if you can, once in the morning and once at the day's end. And *always* remember to respond to others.

An interesting project to do after you have been tweeting for a little while is to go into your web hosting site and look at the AWStats, which will tell you where people are coming from to get to your site. Look at the days of the week and the times. See if there is a correlation with your tweets. If you do not know how to do this, ask your web master. If you do not have a web master, ask the company that is hosting your website if they have a dashboard or panel you have access to, in order to see how folks are finding your website.

TRY THIS

For several weeks or even months, try tweeting at different times of the day. See if you notice a difference in direct messages, retweets, or visits to your website. Ask a question and see if you get answers immediately, and whether participation is higher at certain times of the day. Wait until you get at least 500 followers, however, to test this out. The more followers you have, the easier it is to measure your results.

Home, Trending Topics, @Connect, #Discover, Messages, and @Replies

As you become more engaged with the Twitter community, you will begin to get Direct Messages or what is now called "Messages" from your followers. It is important to note that if someone is following you and you are *not* following them, they cannot send you a Direct Message. On your Twitter profile, go to the top of your screen and click **Messages** to see all of your Messages. You can write a message from here as well. See the following figure.

Here's the Direct Messages page on Twitter.

In the next chapter, you'll learn about TweetDeck, a platform that makes it even easier to see your Direct Messages. However, for now, put your cursor on the Person Icon on the top-right side of the Twitter home page. Tab down to Direct Message and open your messages and respond. Click on back to **Home**, you will see Trending Topics or what is now called **Trends**. These are the topics that are most commonly discussed at that moment on Twitter. Some companies, conferences, or marketing directors will try to get their "topic" to be a trend on Twitter. That simply means a lot of people are talking about their particular topic, which is giving them a lot of PR and marketing for their brand. Let's say there is a huge earthquake, it would become a trend on Twitter. Now you can set your trending topics to display global trends, country trends, or by state, by clicking on the **Change** button next to the word Trends. Next to **Home** you will see **@Connect**. **@Connect** allows you to quickly see all of your Twitter interactions and mentions at a glance. Once you get heavy into Twitter, this also is a great page to keep referring to. Next to the @Connect you will see the **#Discover** tab. There is a lot of information here. Here you can search for all things people, places, and things. So spend some time here and search and have fun connecting.

Inviting People to Follow You

Now that you're becoming a savvy social media marketer, one of the ways to grow your following is to put your Twitter handle or user name everywhere you communicate. Put it on your business card, your email signature, your website ("follow me/us on Twitter"), your letterhead, and your other social media platforms, such as Facebook and LinkedIn.

As you get into video, mention your Twitter name there, too. When you do a PowerPoint or Prezi presentation or speech, open and end your talk with, "Let's Connect on Twitter." If you write an article, always end your byline with "Let's connect on Twitter @_____." By marketing your Twitter name, tweeting some great stuff (remember infotainment), getting recommended on #followfriday, and by people retweeting you, you will get many new followers.

To Follow or Not to Follow?

One of the debates among tweeters is: Should I follow everyone who follows me? Or should I only follow people I want to follow? This debate still goes on, but here are some thoughts that might help you with your decision. If you follow everyone that follows you, the benefits are ...

- You can send each other private messages.

- The person whom you are following feels good that you are following him or her, and this generates goodwill.

- You never know when/if this person could become a strategic alliance in your business, a client, and/or a referral source.

Some tweeters feel that if someone is taking time to follow them, then they could at least give that person the same courtesy and follow him or her back. People who share this philosophy usually have close to the same number of followers as tweeps they are following.

On the other side of the debate are those who do not want to follow everyone who's following them. This rings true for many celebrities or high-profile individuals or businesses. You'll see many that have tens of thousands of followers, yet are only following 10 people. Then you have the non–high-profile people but active Twitterers who have a lot of followers, but their ratio of followers to those they follow is lower. For example, they may have 5,400 followers and are only following 900. These are people who either don't have time to go in and follow everyone (there are autofollow tools that we will discuss later), or they have decided to follow only those they want to follow. Many do this to appear a part of what is referred to as the "Twitter Elite." They have tens of thousands following them but really don't "need" to follow them back.

I follow just about everyone who follows me. However, I quickly unfollow people who are spammers (always selling) and I don't follow people who appear to be (I'll be polite) less than professional. I mention this now because there are tools that allow you to highlight your favorite tweeters and group them by category. This makes it easier to follow larger numbers of people.

What's the bottom line? Do what is most comfortable for you. This is your business and you are marketing it, and you might want as many people to know about you and your services as possible. A best practice, however, is not to automatically follow everyone, but check out their profile first. There are many spammers and porn industry sites on Twitter, and you don't want to follow them and appear on their Twitter page as one of their followers. If this happens accidentally, remember that you can always block them. Make checking out your new followers on Twitter a daily activity, then decide to follow them in return.

Creating Twitter Lists

A Twitter list is a cool feature that allows Twitter users to organize other followers into groups, or "lists." *Note:* you don't need to follow another user to add him to a list; if you want to read a user's tweets but not see his messages in your main twitter stream every day, lists allow you to do that. Similarly, you can follow someone else's list while not actually following all users individually in that list. Rather, you follow the list itself.

To create a new list on Twitter, follow these steps:

1. Go to the icon that's an outline of a human head on the top of your Twitter screen. Scroll down to Lists. Next, click **Create Lists**. A drop-down menu will appear. Enter the person's Twitter name.

2. Once the drop-down menu appears, click **Add to list**. Then create or name your list.

3. Select **Add to list. Name it**.

4. Describe your list in greater detail. Choose whether others can see it or whether it will be private.

5. Check to see if the user you wanted to add was successfully included in that list. Click the person icon and select **Add to list**. A checkmark is added next to lists in which that user is included (shown under **Adding or Removing People**).

Creating a Twitter list by adding people.

Twittering via Mobile Service or BlackBerry

When you sign up for Twitter, you will get an initial email that asks you if you want to activate your phone. If you want to tweet via your phone, go ahead and do this. You'll then see the following.

Here's where you enter your mobile phone information on Twitter.

Enter your mobile number and click **Save**. Note that Twitter doesn't charge for this, but your carrier's standard text messaging rates usually apply. Then select the box that reads, "It's okay for Twitter to send text messages to my phone." Then click **Save**, and Twitter will supply you with a code to enter via your mobile device. They will then send you a verified message. After your mobile phone account is verified, your Devices tab contents will look a tad different.

While the focus in this book is on social media marketing and not necessarily everything mobile, it is understood that this is an important way to communicate for many people; by 2013 we will be doing more connecting via mobile than our PC or tablet. One of the best ways to get Twitter on your mobile device is to go to http://twitter.com/#!/download; it guides you to the download tools for your iPhone, BlackBerry, Android, and other mobile devices.

During the writing of this book, the mobile revolution is gearing up to make an even bigger debut. At the time of this writing, there are many tools to make your mobile experience better. A good program called Tiny Twitter (www.tinytwitter.com) is great for small screens. If you use an iPhone, there are also several applications. Do a Google search for iPhone+Twitter to get the latest updates on apps. One of the original applications, however, can still be found at www.stone.com/Twittelator.

You can Google mobile Twitter devices and see the many websites and discussion boards. Also, ask your friends or new Twitter friends what they use. Coming up, we discuss all types of Twitter applications that will enhance your Twitter social media marketing from your PC or laptop, iPad, or mobile device.

The Least You Need to Know

- When creating a Twitter profile, your user name and your bio box description are vital parts of your marketing efforts on Twitter.

- Finding a specific person on Twitter can be a challenge, but there are options for advanced searches. The #Discover button is a great place to begin.

- Think strategically about your tweets and make them easy to retweet, engaging, and a good mix of information and entertaining commentary. Be patient. It takes a while to build rapport.

- Twitter lists are a great way to keep up with the tweets of experts or Twitter friends that you don't want to miss.

- Twitter works with mobile phones and devices like the iPad, iPhone, BlackBerry, or other mobile device.

Great Marketing Applications for Twitter

Chapter 10

In This Chapter

- Managing and leveraging your Twitter experience
- Getting the basics of TweetDeck
- Uploading photos and video on Twitter
- Automating tweets and followers with apps
- Utilizing Twitter at conferences

Your Twitter experience can be made exponentially better by utilizing some terrific applications. These applications can help you network more effectively, organize tweets, and get creative with your Twitter social media marketing strategy.

In this chapter, you'll also learn about applications that make using photos and videos a snap. Okay, so let's get started. First, we talk about how to manage all those followers you have.

Managing Your Twitter Experience

When one begins using the Twitter platform, the entire universe and power of the Twitter experience isn't fully exposed. Yes, you get streaming updates from all the participants you are following, you have the ability to see Direct Messages, and you can see Trending Topics. However, this is just a small fraction of what is going on in the Twitter landscape. Some questions you might consider are:

- Who else is using Twitter?
- Where can I find more subject matter experts and specific people to follow in various industries?
- Where can I find other people in my industry?

- What are consumers talking about as they relate to my industry?

- There are certain industry leaders I want to follow, but I can't seem to find them. Is there an easier way?

- The conference I'm attending has a Twitter hashtag. How can I easily follow the stream of conversation on Twitter?

Let me pull back the Twitter curtain and show you what Twitter has to offer you and your business.

The Basics of TweetDeck

TweetDeck is a fabulous tool to add to your social media marketing business arsenal. TweetDeck is constantly upgrading their site, so your version may look slightly different from the one featured here. However, this should give you an idea of how the site works. There are many great things about TweetDeck, but let me try to narrow it down to five:

- It's a time-saver. You can view and manage all your inbound tweets and easily read all your favorite "peeps" and Direct Messages in one place. It pulls these specific tweets out of the fast-moving river and places them into a column for you to read when you are ready.

- You can categorize your incoming tweets as well as tweets of those you aren't following by industry, subject matter, or any keyword.

- You can easily send a Direct Message to someone or retweet someone's update from the TweetDeck platform with a press of a button.

- You can easily arrange it so that if anyone tweets about you or your company, the tweet is automatically sent to you (it is pulled into your @Mentions column), whether you are following the writer or not. This is great for *reputation management.*

DEFINITION

Reputation management refers to using the social media platforms to listen, see, watch, and read what people are saying about you and your business. If "bad" information is being passed along, you can now go in and address it. It's important to manage what others are saying about you or your business.

- You will feel informed and a part of the discussion, and you can learn by what and how others are tweeting.

So let's get you set up on TweetDeck. Go to www.tweetdeck.com and download the application. The software is free. You'll be asked for your Twitter user name and password. When you get in, you will see four columns: All Friends, Mentions, Direct Messages, and Trending Worldwide.

This is what you see on TweetDeck.

Following is a description of what you should see:

- **All Friends.** You will see tweets from your friends who you are following.

- **Mentions.** If anyone mentions your Twitter handle in a tweet, such as replying to a tweet you send out or just referring to you in a tweet, it will show up in this column.

- **Direct Messages.** If someone sends you a private Direct Message, it will show up here. Additionally, each time you send a Direct Message, it is listed here. *Note:* if you choose to set up an automated or auto message to any new follower, that message will show up in this column.

- **Trending Worldwide.** These are hot or popular topics that the majority of users are tweeting about.

Pretty cool, huh? Now you can see all your friends' tweets and the latest "hot topic" on Twitter. Remember, anyone you are following is a "friend."

Symbols on TweetDeck

At the bottom of each column are some symbols or icons. Again, be aware that new ones show up often because the TweetDeck staff is continuously adding new symbols and functionality.

Row of symbols is described here

Look at the row of symbols at the bottom of each column.

There is a right- and left-facing arrow symbol on each column. By pressing this, you can change the order and move your columns from left to right and put them in the order you prefer. You can always change it as you add more columns to TweetDeck (we will look at that shortly). The next symbol at the bottom of most columns is a *cloud* icon. This shows you the most popular topic or user name in each column.

DEFINITION

A Twitter **cloud** is a cluster of single words or a (visual) written description of words that you have tweeted most often.

To generate a Twitter cloud for your website or your blog, take a look at www.wordle.
net.

The next symbol, which has a downward arrow in the middle of it, is used to filter
out a column. Say you have a column on a specific topic (you learn how to create a
custom column in a minute). You want to click the filter icon. And now let's say you
just want to see recent tweets on Twitter. Take a look at the following screen.

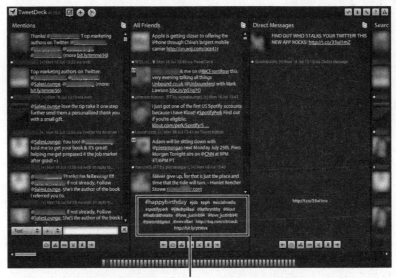

Sample of word cloud

This is an example of a tag or word cloud.

Okay, now the next symbol, which looks like an eyball pen, is used to mark your
tweets as seen. I would ignore this feature as it isn't a good use of your time. The
stream continues to move and new tweets are consistently added to the column. The
next symbol is an X, which will clear your "seen" tweets from the column. The next
symbol is the trash can, which allows you to delete all the tweets in that column.

Now let's go over the symbols across the top of your TweetDeck application. Again,
please know TweetDeck is always evolving and your version may be different from
what is here.

TRY THIS

You can delete any column by clicking the **X** in the upper-right corner of the
column. Try it, then click the search magnifying glass and create your own custom
column.

Symbols to help you navigate

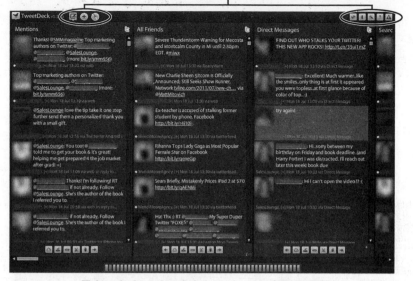

Take a look at the symbols at the top of TweetDeck.

The following list examines each one so you are knowledgeable about where to find them:

- **The first symbol looks like a dialogue square.** This is where you type your tweet directly into TweetDeck. It is like typing directly on Twitter, so click it and it will take you to "What's happening?" You can enter your 140-character-or-less tweet. To send, simply hit **Enter** on your keyboard.

- **The next symbol is a + sign.** This is where you can type in names, industries, and keywords, and see tweets mentioning them. Type in "newspaper," for example. Hit **Enter.** Watch a column pop up with every tweet in the world that mentions the word "newspaper" within it. Use this to create a customized TweetDeck to help your business excel. Also, click the word **Core** after you click the **+** sign. This will allow you to add mentions, favorites, and new followers to your TweetDeck if they are not listed.

- **The next symbol looks like a red flashlight.** This launches the TweetDeck directory, where you can search for people and tweets by subject.

- **Below this list, on the top left, you will see: from +.** When you click the + sign you will be able to add Facebook, LinkedIn, MySpace, and Foursquare. By adding these icons you will enable your tweets to be shared on Facebook, LinkedIn, MySpace, and other sites at the same time. *Note:* don't do this all the time; they are individual platforms and must be treated differently.

Refresh, Single Column, Tools, and Settings

In the upper-right corner of TweetDeck, you'll see more symbols. The first is two arrows. This refreshes your Twitter screen. Sometimes you may not be sure if your TweetDeck page is updated. If not, just click the refresh arrows. The next symbol, which looks like a "1," allows you to have a single-column view of TweetDeck open on your screen.

ONLINE CAUTION

Did you know that TweetDeck enables 200 actions per hour on its site? If you go above that, you will not be able to use TweetDeck for a certain period of time. Twitter did this to try to deter spammers. So consider yourself forewarned: don't overutilize it in one sitting. Look in the upper-right corner of TweetDeck for the number of actions you have left. It reads: Remaining API.

The wrench symbol is important to your Twitter experience. It is where you can further customize your TweetDeck settings. By now, if you are new to TweetDeck, you've probably been hearing a sound, which is supposed to be a loud chirp—but many say it sounds like a submarine! When you open the Settings, you can turn off that sound by unchecking the box next to "Play notification sound." Click **Notifications** and go through the process of turning the notifications off.

Now go through and customize your TweetDeck experience further by clicking on the other tabs across the top. You can change the colors of your text and the font, you can adjust the times that your columns are updating within the Twitter API tab, and you can add other Twitter accounts in the Account section. Go through each of these and set up what works best for you.

Here you can change your TweetDeck settings.

Customizing Your TweetDeck

Now that you know where the basics are on TweetDeck, you can make your TweetDeck platform work for your business. Here are some questions to ask yourself:

- Who do you want to follow? Search for and follow them. When you have the folks you want to follow, create a group for them (or a special column) and their tweets will be grouped together. You can always add more people to the group.

- Based on your industry, what types of people do you need to follow? Create a column or columns around your industry. Are you a motivational coach? Type in "motivation coaches" by using the Search tab. Are you a nutritionist? Type in "nutrition." An IT recruiter? Start a column for those tweets. Narrow down the industries until you get the types of tweets that you want to see in one column. You will want to have multiple columns to make this work best for you.

- Perhaps you want to create a column just for news or media, such as *The New York Times, USA Today*, and so on.

Okay, so that is TweetDeck 101. Now you are beginning to take your Twitter experience to the next level.

Third-Party Applications That Work with Twitter

In addition to TweetDeck, there are other applications that can help your experience. One is called Seesmic (www.seesmic.com). Here's what it looks like.

The Seesmic home page.

Seesmic is similar to TweetDeck in that it organizes your tweets in columns or in single rows by tweets. Some people prefer Seesmic, but others have said it's a little trickier to use than TweetDeck. As of this writing, Seesmic just launched a web-based platform (www.seesmic.com/). Again, it's similar to TweetDeck, although it does allow you to display single-line tweets. Video posts are popular with Seesmic. Figuring it out can be a bit confusing initially, but there are many loyal followers.

Another popular program is twhirl (www.twhirl.org). Twhirl runs on Windows 2000, XP, and Vista, as well as Mac OSX. It also shortens URLs and displays your new messages—the screen is just smaller. You can post images, search tweets, and use spell check. It automatically finds posts that mention your name or business name. Twhirl is also a popular application for viewing and managing tweets.

Photos and Videos on Twitter

What started out as a place to do a quick microblog or a 140-character tweet has now found new and innovative ways to keep readers engaged. One way is by posting photos and video. Remember infotainment? People like pictures because seeing is believing. And the new audience on social media is loving video. What better way to marry the two than by utilizing all three methods together on Twitter? On your TweetDeck window on the top right, you can see photo and video icons for posting.

Photos: TwitPic, Yfrog, and img.ly

There are several ways to get photos on Twitter, and one is by using TwitPic (www.twitpic.com), which enables you to share photos on Twitter from your mobile device or computer. It's free and easy to use. Yfrog (www.yfrog.com) is also easy to use. Just go to these sites, give them your Twitter user name and password, upload your photos from your computer, add your tweet, and click **Send**. Another free service that many people like is img.ly (http://img.ly). It is also good to include an interesting sentence to encourage your followers to click the picture link you are tweeting about.

Video: Twitvid, TwitLens, ZOCIAL.tv, and Twitcam

Video is everywhere, and with our cell phones and pocket-held video cams, anyone can produce or star in his or her own video. Keep in mind that, just as with all the other social media platforms and methods, the videos that you post are a reflection of your personal and professional brand. Ask yourself: How will my prospects, customers, and advocates like this? Is it informative? Does it give them a fun glance of my personal side? Is it providing infotainment, just information, or just plain fun?

Twitvid (www.twitvid.com) is like the YouTube for Twitter. It is a powerful and popular site that allows people to easily post videos and share. At the time of this writing, pop singer Britney Spears was debuting a few snippets from an upcoming video on Twitvid. TwitLens (www.twitlens.com) is a photo- and video-sharing service. You can tag your friends, post anonymously, or post from your mobile device, and upload 10 videos at a time. This is a service primarily for the Twitter audience.

ONLINE CAUTION

Before posting a video or photo, I would get written permission from anyone in the picture on a photo/video release form written by your attorney. You don't want to end up with a lawsuit on your hands or upset people who may not like that photo of themselves posted on a social site where millions can view it. You can also have people give you permission within the video to post on the sites, but I like paper in this case or have them sign with an electronic signature on your iPad.

ZOCIAL.tv (www.zocial.tv) allows you to see only the most shared videos on Twitter and Facebook. Keep in mind they are the most shared videos—but not necessarily the best quality. However, it shows you again the popularity of video among social media users.

Twitcam lets you stream (or broadcast) live through your webcam and Twitter account. Simply go to www.twitcam.livestream.com, create an account using your Twitter information, and with your webcam you can start videoing live from an event or from your office or showroom. It's that simple. The cool thing about this is you can also chat live with your viewers. They are also Twitter followers, too. Try experimenting with this and get creative.

SocialOomph and HootSuite

You might be wondering how people with a thousand, ten thousand, or even a million followers are managing it all. Well, there are two ways. They might have teams of people who manage their social media. Or they could be automating some of their tweets.

Everyday entrepreneurs and business owners can use an application called SocialOomph (www.socialoomph.com). This enables you to automate some of the process so you can get back to business. SocialOomph enables you to schedule tweets, send welcome messages to your new followers, and unfollow those who unfollow you. It's all done automatically. The jury is still out as to whether some of this functionality will win you more friends or followers (or less), but it is good to know the site is there. As you begin tweeting and following people, look at their welcome messaging, which should trigger ideas. We cover more in the next chapter what HootSuite can do, but for now, know that it is another site (hootsuite.com) that can help you market your messaging, monitor conversations, and track Twitter results (along with other social media sites).

DID YOU KNOW?

SocialOomph assists over 348,000 customers. It also enables you to "vet" someone for several days while you decide if you want to follow, ignore, or block the person.

Autofollowing

Let's talk about autofollowing. You can set it up so that your Twitter automatically follows all the people who follow you. There are two schools of thought on this. Some people feel if someone is following them, then they should return the courtesy and follow them back. Others feel that they want to be selective and not follow everyone. There is no right or wrong here. However, if you're not a public personality, and you have, for example, 4,000 people following you and you are following only two, you will appear as an elitist or Twitter snob in the Twitter culture.

The opposite is also true. If you are following 4,000 and only have two followers, you will look like a spammer, so it's a fine line. The rules are still evolving, so again, the choice is yours.

To Autotweet or Not to Autotweet?

We talked a bit earlier about automatically sending tweets, or autotweets, through an application like SocialOomph or HootSuite. Many people do it, but a lot of folks within the Twitter community (myself included) feel automated tweets take away from "social" conversations, sharing information, and networking. After all, if everyone automated their tweets, essentially no one would be reading the tweets (now that's kind of a funny thought). So think long and hard about automating your tweets. After a while, the powerful Twitter user can tell which tweets are automated and which are live from a person. Many also block autotweeters since it can become a nuisance because they aren't participating. They're just sending automessages, which can be a bore. However, check out SocialOomph or HootSuite and see if there is some functionality that will work for you and your business as your Twitter following expands.

Utilizing Twitter at Conferences

When you attend a conference, find out in advance the Twitter hashtag or hashmark. On your TweetDeck, you can create a column using that hashtag so you can connect to everyone who is tweeting at the event before, during, and after the conference. It's a great way to network, be seen, and connect. You can really stay in the know about the top takeaways and actions happening at the conference. You may see many conferences using a great tool called ParaTweet (www.paratweet.com) for live conferences and events.

Some of the powerful things about using Twitter at conferences are:

- Attendees can connect before the event.

- Speakers can interact with the audience before, during, and after the event.

- Attendees stay connected for meetups before, during, and after the event.

- Conference attendees can ask questions of each other.

- The conference can attract future potential attendees and sponsors that aren't attending the event, but participate on Twitter.

- It makes the conference appear trendy, modern, and fun, and it makes it easy for attendees to communicate.

The Least You Need to Know

- TweetDeck, Seesmic, HootSuite, and twhirl are application tools that help you manage your Twitter experience.

- Learning how to upload videos and photos on Twitter is easy because applications such as TwitPic and Yfrog are user-friendly. ZOCIAL.tv and Twitlens are additional sites that help stream videos and photos for the Twitter user.

- SocialOomph and HootSuite are tools that help you automate functions, such as scheduling tweets and welcome messaging.

- Be cautious not to overly automate, because people want to hear from real people, in real time with real responses.

- Professionals will notice Twitter's increasing presence at conferences; a conference hashtag allows attendees to communicate on a Twitter stream with a common hashtag or hashmark.

Additional Tools and Applications to Use with Twitter

In This Chapter

- Twitter applications for businesses with employees
- How to track tweets that mention your company
- Discover fun and creative Twitter applications
- Analyzing your Twitter account
- Twitter marketing checklist and sample Twitter pages

Just when you thought you knew everything about Twitter, you find out there are great applications to use with it. In this chapter, we talk about creative sites that you should explore. You'll find that some of these really do make sense for your business.

It is important to note that new Twitter applications appear daily, so keep an eye out for new options. In this chapter, I've highlighted the current popular applications that can help you with your company branding and strategy. These can help you manage the time you spend on Twitter.

Managing Multiple Twitter Users or Accounts

If you have a company that has several employees who are on Twitter for business reasons, the applications discussed in the following sections might be helpful. Maybe you're in a situation where your company uses multiple Twitter IDs? Check out the following tools that can make your life easier.

CoTweet

CoTweet (cotweet.com) is an application that helps companies with multiple Twitter users easily manage their combined Twitter experience. Each Twitterer from the company is identified by his or her initials at the end of each tweet. This works well because each writer can maintain his or her own identity, and businesses have the option of assigning different tweet types to different employees. For example the CEO may tweet one way and the receptionist another. A company could have the Marketing Director tweet along with the company intern. They all have different voices, but can tweet from the same site.

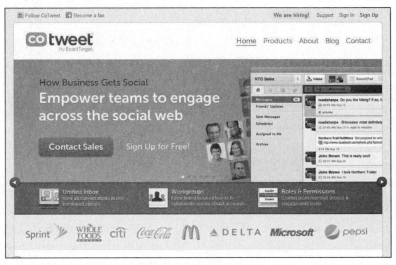

The home page of CoTweet.

GroupTweet

Do you have a team in your business that likes to communicate via Twitter? GroupTweet (www.grouptweet.com) enables the team members to be "grouped together," and they can tweet each other "privately within your company" without communications going out to the public. The tweets are privately viewed only by employees within your company. This fosters collaboration and employee communication. Trust me … your employees will like this.

This is the home page of GroupTweet.

HootSuite

This tool calls itself "the social media dashboard." Big companies such as Disney, Fox Network, Dell, and *National Geographic* use this tool, and this has added to its popularity among business owners. If you create multiple network profiles on Twitter and Facebook, HootSuite (hootsuite.com) enables you to easily manage them, preschedule tweets, and measure your progress. You can even add multiple Twitterers in your company to your business profile, and monitor their tweets and track statistics. This site is popular with marketers and entrepreneurs.

Here's the home page of HootSuite.

Splitweet

This site is recommended for heavy Twitter users who have multiple accounts, or for big corporations with multiple Twitterers or Twitter accounts. With Splitweet (en.splitweet.com), you can update and manage multiple Twitter accounts easily from one screen.

NETIQUETTE

When selecting the Twitter team that will represent your company, make sure the team members are aware their tweets will be in the search engines for days, months, and possibly years to come. They need to be aware that what they tweet is PR and that they are the digital voice of the company on Twitter. You should also look into having a social media policy for your employees.

You can also choose to send updates to one or all accounts in one step. There is also a feature that will notify you when your company is mentioned on Twitter.

Monitoring Your Name or Keywords

Do you want to know when someone mentions your name or product in a tweet? Or maybe you're interested in everything that's said about one specific topic, or a few keywords? Here are the applications that can help you track all of that.

Monitter

Monitter (monitter.com) enables users to get a live stream or real-time view of any keyword, and shows you what Twitterers are saying about it anywhere in the world. Want to know about the earthquake in Washington, D.C., type in "DC Earthquake" and Monitter tells you what folks are saying. You can also find out what a specific town is saying about you, your business, or specific keywords that you type in. Simply insert the keywords that you want to track on Monitter.

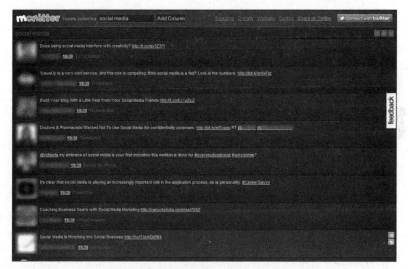

Here's an example of a search on Monitter.

TweetBeep Alerts

Savvy business owners need to keep up with what is being said or written about them online. TweetBeep (tweetbeep.com) does just that. It tracks tweets that mention your name, your business's name, or affiliated products or services. The TweetBeep alerts are conveniently sent to you via email hourly. It's Twitter's answer to Google Alerts.

Here's the home page of TweetBeep.

TwitHawk

TwitHawk (www.twithawk.com) is another monitoring tool. This marketing application helps you connect with Twitterers in your area who are tweeting about specific keywords or topics that you've chosen. For example, when someone tweets about those specific keywords within a certain demographic area (or globally), TwitHawk sends those people your prewritten custom response. For example, if you own an ice-cream store and your keyword is IceCream, and someone tweets about IceCream, TwitHawk will send them a tweet and say something like "You like Ice Cream, so do we ... visit us 24/7!" Take a long look at the site. There is a lot of strategy that must go into using it, but it might be worth a look.

Here's the home page of TwitHawk.

Getting Information About Followers and Other Twitterers

Are you getting a little overwhelmed trying to check out the people who are following you? You might want to use some of the tools in this section to help you evaluate the peeps you want to follow back—or ignore!

Checking out new followers may not seem like a big deal when you first get started, but if you start getting a hundred followers a week, you'll be glad you've got some of these applications to help you control your time and the quality of your connections.

Crowdbooster and Twitoria

Crowdbooster (www.crowdbooster.com) lets you analyze the performance of individual tweets with an interactive graph and table to quickly understand what tweets were read and which ones weren't. Users can also customize the date range to understand the impact of their Twitter campaign over a period of time. Crowdbooster can also analyze replies, retweets, and click-throughs to links. One of the new trends on Twitter is quality versus quantity when it comes to having followers. Twitoria (twitoria.com) allows you to easily find out which of your followers has not been regularly tweeting. You can then decide if you want to keep following them or not.

Digsby: Managing Tweets

Digsby (www.digsby.com) allows you to keep track of your social networks from your desktop ... and so much more. In summer of 2011, this was ranked as one of the top five Twitter application sites, with nearly 250,000 users. It is a good tool to help you leverage your Twitter, Facebook, and social media experience by looking at all of your messaging from those sites on one application called Digsby. It takes instant messaging plus email plus social media to an entirely new level. Check it out. This is great for time management as it alerts you to instant messages and email from multiple sites.

Twellow

Twellow (www.twellow.com) is the self-proclaimed Twitter yellow pages. Get your profile listed in the Twellow directory. It can't hurt; in fact it will help. You never know where your next customer will come from. This is also a great directory to search for finding out types of people within your interests to follow.

Tweet Management

You're at a conference and you're tweeting every hour with a summary of events. Wouldn't it be nice to have the luxury of more than 140 characters? Or maybe you want to make it simple for a reader to tweet your blog? Here are some applications to help you do that ... and more.

TwitThis

TwitThis (www.twitthis.com) allows visitors to your blog or website to easily post Twitter messages about you or your business. It also makes it easy for visitors to your website or blog to tweet about what you say. Post the TwitThis button to your website or blog pages by following the instructions and coding provided on their site. This is a great viral marketing tool.

Here's the home page of TwitThis.

TweetStats

Tweetstats.com is a great tool to measure your Twitter analytics. Look for more of these sites to emerge on the scene but for now TweetStats gets high marks from users. It looks at how many times you tweet per month and can even drill down to the day. It can also search for retweets and other analysis. When you are looking for research data on your tweeting, this is a good site to check out.

Other Fun and Useful Applications

Are you tired of your plain profile page and want to add a little pizzazz to it? Well, there are applications to satisfy your need for a little creativity. In this section, you'll find some fun and inventive ways to enhance your Twitter experience.

TweetMeme

TweetMeme (tweetmeme.com) can take a few minutes to understand, but there is a lot of information on this site that can be of value to you. TweetMeme aggregates all of the links on Twitter and determines which links are most popular. Then, TweetMeme is able to gather these links into categories and subcategories, making it easy for users to find the types of informational links they might be interested in and that are currently very popular.

Too Fun Not to Mention

Here is a list of powerful and fun Twitter tools you must look into for your social marketing strategy:

- www.TwitLonger.com: Allows you to send longer tweets.

- www.twistory.com: Lets you see a history of your past tweets.

- www.Mokumax.com: A popular free app to schedule tweets and brand your tweets with your company name.

- www.bitly.com: A URL or website shortener which allows you to include long links in your tweets (and elsewhere).

- www.Klout.com: Measures your real influence on Twitter. How many and who are your tweets influencing? This will show you.

- www.FollowFridayHelper.com: Really simplifies the #FollowFriday process so you can track, recommend, and thank fellow #FF peeps.

- www.SocialFlow.com: Takes your tweets and publishes to your audience at the most influential time of day or night, based on historical analytics.

- www.Triberr.com: Interesting site that will retweet just about everything in the groups you join.

- www.Twubs.com: The place to register your conference or tweetchat hashtag.

The Twitter Toolbar and TrackThis

Want instant access to Twitter? Then consider downloading the Twitter Toolbar (www.thetwittertoolbar.com). You can use the toolbar to access online Twitter tools, check your Twitter stats, post your updates, and more. Versions are available for both Firefox and Internet Explorer.

Does your company track a lot of shipping of merchandise? TrackThis (www.usetrackthis.com) enables you to track any UPS, FedEx, DHL, or USPS shipment. You can receive direct messages to your Twitter account as your shipment makes its way to a location.

BubbleTweet

BubbleTweet (www.bubbletweet.com) is a really unique and fun application, and I think we will see more like this in the future. BubbleTweet lets you post a short video message (up to 30 seconds at this writing) that bubbles up and magically appears on your Twitter page as a circular video burst when visitors land on your Twitter profile. It doesn't automatically play each time—visitors go to your Twitter profile; it creates a unique URL with the word "bubbletweet" in it. Your original Twitter profile, however, always stays in place. You will need to give your followers your BubbleTweet URL address once you have it so they can see your bubble video pop-ups. This is fun. Try it!

TRY THIS

Go to www.bubbletweet.com and enter your Twitter name. Pick the webcam or upload a short video from your handheld camera. Welcome people to your pro-file. Limit your video to no more than 30 seconds—really, the shorter the better. Give it a try! Video is extremely powerful and now your Twitter followers can see and hear the "you" behind the tweets.

You can also change your BubbleTweet daily. Participants get creative with this short video by introducing themselves or welcoming visitors to their profile.

TwitrBackgrounds and Twtpoll

TwitrBackgrounds (www.twitrbackgrounds.com) is a site that provides free themed backgrounds for you to include on your Twitter.com profile page. They also offer customized backgrounds as well for a fee. While ideally a custom background is best, prefabs from the TwitrBackgrounds are good to use to add personality and energy to your profile.

As of this writing, the company that created Twtpoll (www.twtpoll.com) says this tool ranks as its most popular Twitter application. Many businesses use Twtpoll to engage their customers, and then use the data to report back to their customers in their newsletters, marketing materials, or blogs. You can even brand your poll site to have the look and feel of your company or business.

Ruth Sherman is a media trainer to the stars. Here is her BubbleTweet page. Video is a great way to connect.

Twtvite

Over time, you are going to meet many new people on Twitter, and some of these people are in your business district or located in towns you are traveling to. As you become more connected on Twitter, you will begin to see the term "tweetup." A tweetup is a meetup or a meeting of a group of folks from Twitter. Typically, a group of people on Twitter will schedule a get-together at a specific location. Through Twtvite (www.twtvite.com), you can create your own tweetup and invite folks.

You can also search by location to find tweetups in towns to which you are traveling, and ask if you can join in. Twtvite allows you to organize and manage your tweetups, and assists you in making further strong connections. Your event can be made public so anyone can join, or you can make it private so only your list will see the event. There is even an event manager component to this site where you can track RSVPs, and provide a map and other information about your tweetup. Tweetups using Twtvite go on all over the world.

Here's the home page of Twtvite.

TwtQpon and TwtBizCard

You can get really creative with TwtQpon (twtqpon.com), which allows you to create coupons for your business services or products and share them exclusively with your Twitter followers. Many large national brands that use Twitter regularly offer discounts to their followers, and now small businesses and entrepreneurs can offer a Twitter coupon to their followers as an incentive to do more business. It could be a good way to market test your loyal following on Twitter.

It's starting to look like the day of the paper business card is over. Take a look at TwtBizCard (twtbizcard.com) for your Twitter business card. A one-time donation (of your choice) is all that is required. You can get and share Twitter business cards with your friends. Click **Create a Twitter Business Card**, then enter your business information, name, phone, email, URL, and so on, and you have a nice business card with your photo. TwtBizCard then gives you choices as to which social media networks you can send it to.

Analyzing Your Twitter Account

Alright, so now you know more than you ever thought possible about Twitter. And you've just read about the many amazing Twitter applications and sites that can support and expand upon your Twitter experience. However, how do you measure your return on investment (ROI) when it comes to the time you're spending on Twitter? How do you know if your marketing efforts are working? In this section, we'll review some sites that help you analyze your Twitter presence.

Tweet Grader

So you thought your grading days were over? Not so fast! The Tweet Grader (tweet.grader.com) will give your Twitter account, website, and Facebook pages a grade or ranking. It analyzes the number of followers, how many you are following, the number of tweets, and the quality of your followers. Then it gives you a grade from 1 to 100, with 100 being the best, of course. It will also show you how you rank among the Twitter elite in your state or town.

You simply need to register and then enter your user name and get your grade. Under the blog section on Tweet Grader, they do a great job of explaining what types of algorithms go into obtaining your grade, so be sure to read that. Tweet Grader also has some neat tools to check out under the Tools tab on the home page.

One is called TwitSnip, which is a simple tool for posting to Twitter. It lets you "quote" text on any web page. Here's what it does: when you are on a web page and there's something that you want to quote, it will look for the Twitter name or @user for the website and link it back to the source. It even shortens the URL for you.

Tweet Grader also has "graders" for your website, press releases, and Facebook page. They will rank and measure your Internet marketing efforts based on a number of factors. Go see how your sites measure up.

Tweet Grader asks you for your URL and for the URLs of your competitors. Then it provides you with a report. The team behind Tweet Grader seems to have fun because they also posted a new grader on April Fool's Day that was called the personality grader. They asked for your first and last name and then they "graded" your personality. In fact, many people thought it was for real and it caused quite a bit of commotion!

DID YOU KNOW?

You've heard of a flash mob? A new trend is to create "flash groups" and "flash trends" with a specific hashtag on Twitter. Businesses are experimenting with using this concept at conferences and special events by promoting a hashtag and having people tweet with a "specific" hashtag to win something. #Carmageddon was a hashtag that was popular in July 2011.

Tweet Grader can at least give you a feel for how you are doing compared to others and perhaps nudge you a bit to help you boost your online grade. Be sure to share your grade with your followers after you use Tweet Grader.

![Home page of Tweet Grader showing "How Influential Are You On Twitter?" with a field to enter your twitter username and a Grade button.]

Here's the home page of Tweet Grader.

Twitter Counter

I believe you will really like Twitter Counter (twittercounter.com). Enter your Twitter user name in the center of the screen where it reads "I am @_____ on Twitter. Show me my stats." A graph and stats bar will appear showing your Twitter following growth. On the right side of the graph, you will find the Twitter Counter Stats Details box, which is useful for analyzing current trends and forecasting future predictions for your Twitter account.

Another interesting feature is that you can also type in your competitors' or friends' Twitter user names and see how they are doing compared to you, which is always interesting. You might also enjoy seeing the featured users on the right side of the screen. Twitter Counter finds some really good Twitter users to feature, and you can follow them directly from this site. This site is also a good one to put into your weekly or monthly social media reporting marketing toolkit.

ONLINE CAUTION

When analyzing the number of followers compared to your competition, don't get too caught up in the numbers. Remember: it's better to have quality followers than it is to have a huge quantity of followers. This does not need to be a race. In fact, if you focus on the race, you might not win. Focus on quality tweets and followers, and engage them.

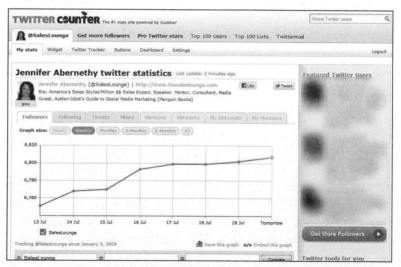

Here's the followers' graph for my Twitter name, @SalesLounge, on Twitter Counter.

Just Tweet It and PeerIndex

Just Tweet It (www.justtweetit.com) is a catalog or directory where you can list your name or find other tweeters like you. It's another place to connect and build influence by being seen with the categories of like-minded people and business experts.

PeerIndex is another popular Twitter influence measurement tool. A number above 90 means you're in the coveted 0.1 percent of Twitter influencers. PeerIndex uses your activity, authority, and audience to measure your total Twitter influence. You can search by topic, which shows just how influential you are in certain "benchmark" subjects, such as sports, politics, science, and media. Try it!

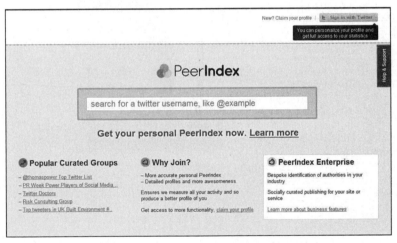

Here's the home page for PeerIndex.

Tweetburner and Qwitter

Want to know how many people are clicking on the links you share? Tweetburner (tweetburner.com) is designed to help you track your tweets that include links. With Tweetburner, you can shorten URLs and track the clicks your tweets accumulate.

We all want to know when we get more followers, but do you want to know when someone stops following you? If so, Qwitter (useqwitter.com) will tell you. This site sends you an email when someone stops following you on Twitter. It's good, though, to be aware that the opposite situation also exists; when you stop following someone, they might also have this application installed and will be notified when you stop following them.

But guess what? That's perfectly okay. There is nothing wrong with no longer following certain people or companies. If used intelligently, the data you gain from this tool can be useful. Entrepreneurs and companies can analyze the data when they lose followers. For example, you can see if you've lost followers after certain types of tweets.

Here's the home page for Qwitter.

Twitter Marketing Checklist

Are you enjoying Twitter and surprised by what it can do? Or are you feeling a bit overwhelmed? Don't worry; here is a Twitter marketing checklist to help you keep all this straight. Discuss these questions with your team and consider which tools you will start with as you begin to network, market your business, and build your following on Twitter.

- Should you use a headshot or a business logo? Twitterers love to see headshots, but if you have a company or brand that is really strongly marketed based on its name or logo, use the logo. There is no right or wrong here. Go with what feels best. You can always change your mind, you know.

- Who in your business will do the tweeting?

- Will you commit to tweeting at least daily?

- Do you have a strong bio line in your Twitter profile?

- Did you include a website or URL in your profile?

- Will you have multiple Twitterers within your business to represent your company?

- Will there be an automated welcome message to new followers? Please don't overautomate, however.

- How will you engage followers—with polls, video, sharing tips, expertise, or TwtQpons?

- Will you host your own TweetChat or tweetup?

- Will you follow everyone that follows you, or only certain people?

- What Twitter applications will you use?

- Will you have a custom background? Who will do that for you?

- Are you willing to have fun, get creative, and regularly review your Twitter stats?

The Least You Need to Know

- There are Twitter applications, such as CoTweet and GroupTweet, that are useful for the small business owner or mid- or large-size company that has more than one employee on Twitter.

- Twitter applications, such as Monitter, TweetBeep, and TwitHawk, help you monitor when people are referencing you, your company, or products on Twitter. TweetDeck, Seesmic, and other tools do this as well.

- For the power Twitterer with multiple accounts and thousands of followers, using Splitweet or HootSuite is helpful.

- There are fun Twitter applications, such as TrackThis, BubbleTweet, Twitoria, Twtpoll, Twtvite, and TwtQpon, that let you get a little creative.

- You can analyze your Twitter experience and keep track of your stats with tools such as Tweet Grader, Twitter Counter, Tweetburner, and Qwitter.

LinkedIn and Other Social Network Options

This part takes you to another level by introducing other key platforms to market your business. You'll go from the white-collar platform on LinkedIn to the funky and fun platforms of MySpace and Google+. You will easily see the differences and the opportunities to get more creative with these different sites.

Then get your camera ready as you are introduced to the world of Internet video and Internet TV. You explore how to use video and learn which sites can host your videos. Don't worry about it being too technical; this is all delivered in an easy-to-read style. When you finish this part, you should understand how to build your presence effectively on these new platforms. Who knows? When you're done with Part 4, you might be the next Internet TV star!

LinkedIn: The Cable Channel of Social Media

In This Chapter

- Why you should join LinkedIn
- How to create an amazing profile
- Finding and connecting with people
- Discovering the power of the company search feature
- Giving and getting testimonials and recommendations

Founded in 2003, many credit LinkedIn (www.linkedin.com) for getting the 35- to 65-year-old demographic of professionals comfortable with networking and sharing information online. After all, those age groups didn't grow up with MySpace and Facebook. And they certainly didn't get to use computers in elementary school.

LinkedIn is not the new social media kid on the block, but it is a widely respected networking platform for millions of professionals. Headquartered in Mountain View, California, LinkedIn operates an "online professional network," according to its website. I call this site the "Cable Channel of Social Media" because it has traditionally been vertical in its audience. Like a cable channel is vertical like ESPN is male and sports, or HGTV skews toward women and home décor. LinkedIn skews white collar professional, slightly more male then female, average age of 49, with an average income of $104,000.

Who Is Using LinkedIn?

With more than 120 million professionals representing 200 countries around the world, LinkedIn is a wonderful networking site. Here you'll find, connect, and meet professionals of all kinds.

Who exactly is using LinkedIn? You will find CEOs of large corporations, directors of associations, corporate vice presidents, entrepreneurs, and small business owners from around the globe. Furthermore, the types of industries represented are quite varied. There are 150 industries on LinkedIn, and just about every university has an alumni chapter. In 2011, there were more than 130,000 groups on LinkedIn, so one can only imagine how high that number will eventually go.

And you, as an entrepreneur or business owner, now have the ability to search for and find these people. The fact that this is all free and available from the convenience of your keyboard is a bonus. In a world where it's all about having connections, LinkedIn is a great community in which to participate.

Degrees of Separation on LinkedIn

You've heard of six degrees of separation, right? It's the theory that we can connect to anyone on the planet by connecting through no more than five other people. On LinkedIn, your network is a group of LinkedIn users who can contact you through connections of up to three degrees away.

Here's how it works: you are at the center of your network. Notice those little number icons next to the name on someone's profile? These represent degrees of separation. As you begin searching, finding, and ultimately connecting to people on LinkedIn, you will notice this number next to names. This number refers to how many people, or degrees, you are away from knowing that person directly.

Let's say you see a "1st" next to John's name. That means that you are directly connected to John. So if you click on John's profile and you scroll down a little and look on the right side of the screen, you'll see a box that reads, "How you're connected to John." For a first-degree connection, you'll see "You" and an arrow that points directly to John's name.

Those who are connected to your direct connections are your second-degree network. Let's say John is connected to Mary, but you are not. On Mary's profile, look in the "How you're connected to Mary" box, and you'll see "You" with an arrow pointing to John (and all other first-degree connections who are connected to Mary). Then you'll see an arrow that points to Mary, who is part of your second-degree network.

It's like this: you → John → Mary. And Mary's connections make up your third-degree network.

At the end of the day, as you build and build your network, you will find that we really are one to five people away from connecting to most of the people we want to meet. It truly is a small world after all—even if Walt Disney said it first.

Why You Should Use LinkedIn

By participating on the LinkedIn platform, you have the ability to market yourself, your services, and your brand. And yes, it gives you the chance to make amazing connections. In its early incarnation in 2003 and 2004, many used LinkedIn as an electronic Rolodex. You would find someone you knew (or wanted to know), ask to join their network, and make a connection. After you connected, that person's name would get listed in your profile. And, if you so desired, you would then pick up the phone and call that person to reconnect and network.

Today, LinkedIn is so much more than that. It has become a much more "sticky" site where you can post PowerPoint presentations, incorporate your blog, let people know what you are reading, and tell others where you are traveling. They now even offer a place for users to put their status updates. This lets your network connections know what you are working on. Just that in itself is another example of viral marketing and the power of a 100-million-person network. Now, will all 100+ million see your update? No, but that is not the point. Your status goes out to your network and it reminds them of what you are working on, and keeps you on the top of their minds. In the pages ahead, we'll get into all the logistics of status updates, and you'll see why this can be effective.

Another reason to join LinkedIn is that it's a great place to give and get testimonials and recommendations. You can find contractors, vendors, and strategic partners, and interact with those who may not be on the other social media networks, such as Twitter or Facebook. Think of this as another networking portal to market yourself or your business as the go-to expert. You can post questions to groups, you can answer questions in the various group forums, you can share links, and you can even start your own group. If nothing else, think of LinkedIn as an advertisement for you and your business. Remember, you never know where your next big customer or connection will come from.

Here are even more creative reasons why you should use LinkedIn:

- It's a place where your happy clients and customers can post testimonials on your behalf. And if you have a website and a business with current customers, you can place a link on your regular website under Client References that links over to your LinkedIn testimonial page.

- You can share useful information to your contacts, such as posting links to your articles or to industry resources.

- More than a million companies have LinkedIn company pages, and most list their employees. Talk about powerful information!

- You can combine LinkedIn status updates with your other accounts and further complete your social media presence.

- You can answer questions within groups or on the Q & A section to showcase your expertise without coming across as a shameless self-promoter.

- You can post your amazing PowerPoint presentations that highlight your expertise.

- You can research potential clients and prospects before you meet them, and they can reach and find you.

- You can post job listings to grow your team.

- You can write and receive valuable and authentic testimonials and recommendations that will be read by your network.

- You can import your blog and share survey and poll results with your connections.

- You can create and market your events or business promotions.

Honestly, this list could go on and on! But I think I've given enough information for you to see that LinkedIn has become much more than just an electronic Rolodex.

Creating an Amazing LinkedIn Profile

Let's begin by setting up your account. Go to www.linkedin.com and type in your information. Remember to use the name that you go by professionally. Whether it's Jeff or Jeffery, put the one most people know you by.

LinkedIn sign up

Here's the sign-up screen for LinkedIn.

Click on **Join Now,** fill out all the information, and click on **Enter LinkedIn**. You will then get directed to the following page.

Here's where you begin to create your professional profile on LinkedIn.

Continue filling out the information and click on **Create my profile**. Next they will ask you to enter friends from your data base. I suggest you skip this step for now. You want to get comfortable with LinkedIn first. Do you see across the top where it reads, **Confirm Your Email Address?** You will now need to check your email to confirm that you have set up an account.

The next step asks if you know people already on LinkedIn. Let's get your site built first, and then we can always go back and add connections from your current web and email contacts. Just like the other sites, it's not recommended that you start building your network right away. The following step will ask to add additional friends—skip this step and you will go to a page called **Choose your plan level**.

Regarding plans, you have an option to upgrade your account for a monthly fee. You can click on **Upgrade** to look at them. For our purposes here, we are going to go straight into the settings area without upgrading. You can start using LinkedIn without paying the monthly fee and just decide later if you need all the extras that come with the fee. Skip the pay step and you'll arrive at the welcome page.

Here's the welcome page on LinkedIn for our test user, Ania.

Your Profile Settings

Directly under the word Profile across the top, click on **Edit Profile**. This is your basic profile page. You can edit any of the portions in light blue by clicking on the **Add** link. Remember, you are marketing yourself and your business, so list your title—if you don't have a title, come up with something creative to put there. I've seen people use things from "World's Best Life Coach" to "Extraordinary Executive." Up next to your name, click the **Edit** button. Fill out the portion that reads Professional Headline. This, along with your photograph, are two of the most powerful marketing tools on LinkedIn. Why? Your headline will show up on everyone's profile that you connect with and in every group that you join. Get creative with the headline. Now upload your photo by clicking on the **Add Photo** icon.

Just below that, you will see **Post an update?** This is your status update on LinkedIn, so go ahead and fill that in—do this at least three times per week. Next, fill in your current position. If past positions are important to your business, please fill those in, but also know you do not need to. Education is a good one to fill in, particularly if you want to network with alumni. Later in this chapter, we will get back to recommendations and connections.

Now, your website is very important, so click on **Add Website(s)**. When you enter your website, be sure to type it as "http://www.yourwebsite.com" so you are creating a live link. Next, add your Twitter account.

Fill out all of these areas on the profile to make your profile complete.

Here's where you can add more detailed information to your LinkedIn profile.

Don't be shy! Put all of your sites here, including your website, blog, and so on. LinkedIn only allows three sites to be listed on a profile. If you don't have three sites to list, be sure to link to your Twitter page or a Facebook fan page! Again, remember to use the "http://" to make it a live link so readers can just click and go to your site.

Next, fill in your interests, and again, get creative. Just like on Facebook and Twitter, you don't have to list interests like water-skiing and golf, but you should put down some of your business skills or how your company helps clients. You can also share why you are interested in helping people or why people can work easily with you. Your groups and associations will be listed next, and if you have your own group or plans to create a group on LinkedIn, put that here as well. Then, list any honors and awards you have won. This is your place to shine, so go for it. Now click on **Save Changes**.

Your Profile Summary

Next, you arrive back on your profile page with portions filled in. Scroll down to the Summary section and click on **Add Summary**.

Here's where you can add or edit information in your Profile summary.

Professional headline

Here is my complete profile. Note the professional headline, photo, websites, and Twitter sections are filled in.

This is your opportunity to boast about what you do. LinkedIn describes this as "the place to give your elevator pitch" about you and your business. Realize that while we would like to think everyone is going to read our entire profile page word for word, typically they don't. However, they might read the summary because it is placed in a prominent place on the screen. So take some time to think about what you want to say.

In the Specialties section, list what you specialize in or what your business does to help people. Continue to go through this page, updating and adding what you like.

> **TRY THIS**
>
> If you put your website, your Twitter user name, and your phone number in the Summary section, it will make it really easy for people to follow and find you. Add spaces in between paragraphs.

At the bottom of your profile page, there is a Personal Information section. You can fill in this portion if you like, but it's not vital. You might want to put your business phone number. Just be careful not to give out too much personal information—this site is for business. LinkedIn is a bit more formal than the other sites. Readers here don't need to know about your relationship status, birthday, or how to contact you via instant messaging, unless you want them to.

DID YOU KNOW?

Just below your status update on LinkedIn (on the left side of your profile) there is a status bar. LinkedIn provides a chart on the right side of your profile page high-lighting the percentage points you gain as you complete your profile. As you give recommendations and testimonials and complete your profile, this status bar will continue to move right until you get to 100 percent. This means you are utilizing 100 percent of the profile features and your profile is complete which is good!

The next section across the top is Contacts. While they could offer more choices in this section, go ahead and see if any resonate with you. Let people know why you would like to be contacted. This is your opportunity to begin adding people, but you may want to hold off and finish this chapter before you do so.

Now click on **Profile** and look at what you've created. How does it look? Are there any typos? Does it convey what you want it to convey? Does it represent the true you? Remember, authenticity and transparency are the key buzzwords these days.

When you're satisfied with your profile, you can begin adding friends to your net-work. Click **Home**. On the right side of your screen, you will see a section that reads **People you may know**. Just click the **Invite** button. Or click on **Connections** and try it that way.

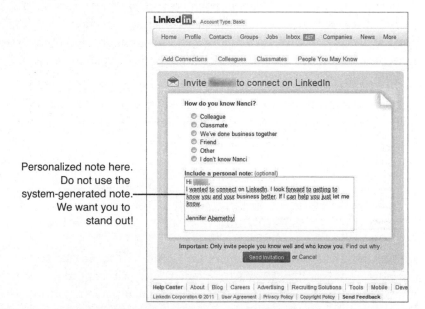

Here is a screen shot of the invitation page on LinkedIn. Always personalize your note.

You then arrive at a page that asks you to give a bit more information. On LinkedIn, you can't just connect with anyone. You need to have something in common, such as an employer, an alumni group, or a current or past business relationship.

Because the LinkedIn system suggests you might know each other, it's likely you have some sort of connection. Fill out the form, and just like on the other platforms, write a short personal note. After you write the note, hit **Send** and the recipient will most likely connect with you soon.

> **TRY THIS**
>
> When asking someone to connect, don't just use the standard text that LinkedIn provides. Stand out in the crowd by taking an additional 30 seconds and make the note personal. Sign with your name and your website and title. You will wow them!

Another way to find people on LinkedIn is by using the search bar at the top-right side of the page. Type in a name of a friend or associate and see if they pop up. You might get several thousand results for that person, particularly if their name is common. Don't panic; modify your search. Look on the left side of your screen (see the following screen shot) to see where you can narrow your search by company, school, and location to find that specific person you are looking for. Keep searching and adding some friends to begin building your LinkedIn network.

Search for people to connect with by individual name

Here's where you can search for people to connect with you on LinkedIn.

Here's where you can do an advanced search for specific people you want to know.
This is extremely powerful.

Powerful Corporate Searches and Connections

Part of the beauty of LinkedIn is that you can connect with current associates as well as past friends, business peers, and alumni.

The access on LinkedIn is often overlooked. Let's say you would really like to connect with someone who runs a powerful small business technical solutions company—let's use Network Solutions as an example. In the past, you would have to do a lot of Internet searching or even purchase a database service to get access to the names of their employees. Now, the information is literally at your fingertips. With LinkedIn, it's right here. Type "Network Solutions" in the search bar, and instead of searching for people, change it to a search for companies. Within 2 seconds, up pops information on Network Solutions—Small Business Solutions Company, including its website, live tweets, RSS feed of the company in the news, a brief bio of each employee, the location and year founded, and a powerful statistics section. If your company doesn't have a company profile, make one. This is a powerful component of LinkedIn.

Here are the company overview search results for Network Solutions.

Now, look at all the results you get when you click on the company profile. There are many ways you or your business can benefit from this information. Let's say you are a small business that makes a product or delivers a service that you feel Network Solutions could benefit from. Or, what if we wanted to consult with the CEO of Network Solutions? Well, you should be able to find your connection here, or at least find the person who can recommend the best point of contact for you.

In the middle of the page, there are several lists of their employees with job titles and a See More link to view more employees.

If you continue to scroll down on that page, you can see new hires, former employees, and more company statistical information. Click on a name and you will see the email application open.

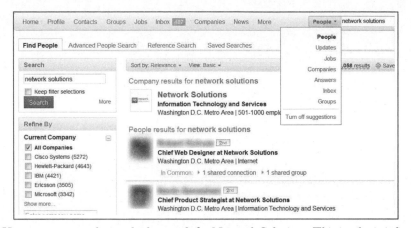

Here, you can see the people that work for Network Solutions. This is why it is key to being an open networker.

This is where you might send that person a personal note asking to be connected and giving the reason why. Lastly, you should take it to the next level and ask for a phone or video meeting using Skype or ooVoo.com. (You'll learn about those later.) All that information at your fingertips in a matter of seconds! Pretty amazing, right? You seriously are just a few clicks away from some important connections. These contacts are no longer just for an exclusive few.

Recommendations and Testimonials

Everyone likes a good pat on the back and acknowledgment for a job well done. In fact, studies show that one of the most meaningful gestures we can do is to give public accolades to people.

You should know that the best way to get a recommendation is to give one. On the top side of the navigation bar below **Profile**, scroll down and you will see the words **Received**, **Sent**, and **Requested Recommendations**. Click on **Sent Recommendations** and you will see the history of recommendations you've sent. On **Requested Recommendations** you can choose what you want to be recommended for and who you will kindly ask. This entire section is where you can keep track of your recommendations history.

Here's where you make a recommendation.

Make a recommendation and keep track of them here.

You can either recommend someone from your network of connections, or put in the person's first and last name and email address.

Here's where you can request recommendations on LinkedIn.

> **NETIQUETTE**
>
> Definitely do not begin asking for recommendations the day you log on to LinkedIn. Get your profile set up, build some connections, add some of your peers and colleagues to your network, and give some recommendations—it's important to give before you receive. And remember, customize your request for a recommendation by adding your own words and personality versus using the wording LinkedIn gives you.

Create your recommendation and a message is sent to the individual notifying him or her of your recommendation. That person will be prompted to see if he or she would like to return the favor.

The Least You Need to Know

- LinkedIn is a highly respected professional network with more than 120 million users.
- Your professional headline and photograph are two of the most powerful tools on LinkedIn because they appear everywhere. Make it work for you!
- Consider your profile to be your 30-second elevator pitch that explains why people should do business with you and how you can help them.
- Use the company search feature, and within seconds you will learn the names of the company's employees along with titles and detailed company statistics.
- The best way to get recommendations and testimonials is to give them.

Marketing Applications and Strategies for LinkedIn

Chapter 13

In This Chapter

- Learn how to further personalize your LinkedIn settings
- The power of joining and creating groups on LinkedIn
- Using the Company Search feature on LinkedIn
- The marketing capabilities of LinkedIn applications
- How to analyze and understand your LinkedIn network

After creating your stellar profile on LinkedIn, connecting to some friends and colleagues, and updating your status, you might be asking, "How do I do all that other stuff?" Many LinkedIn users are just now discovering the many wonderful applications on LinkedIn and how to incorporate those into their overall social media marketing strategy, so there's no need to feel left behind. This chapter gives you plenty of ideas and shows you how to find the many applications you can use to continue to grow your connections through the LinkedIn social media network.

Personalize Your LinkedIn Account Settings

Let's get your account settings set up first, and then we will get into some of the marketing applications and strategies.

Log in to LinkedIn, and at the top-right side of the page look for **Settings** by hovering just over your name. This is the page where you can personalize your settings and make your LinkedIn experience a bit more to your liking. Go through each of these areas and adjust your settings. Don't worry—if you are not sure about something, you can always go back and change it. I've highlighted a few here for you to examine.

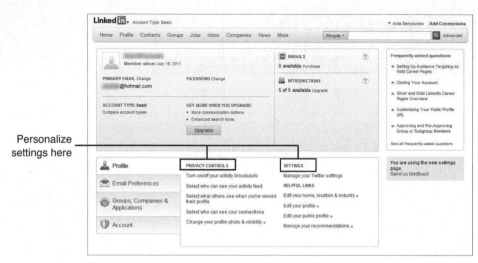

Personalize settings here

Here's where you can really personalize your LinkedIn settings.

Some key settings to review are located in the Profile section. Click **Privacy Controls**. This first box allows you to notify people when you change your profile, make recommendations, or follow companies. My recommendation is to not check this box. Because your friends will get so much email from you every time you make a change to your page and they will get annoyed. Next, click **Who can see your activity feed**. I recommend checking **Everyone** for this, but again it's a personal preference. Options are displayed to show your status to your connections only, your network, or anyone on LinkedIn. You decide, but just remember that the more people you get in front of, the wider you cast your net.

Click here to open

Here's where you choose who gets to see your activities on LinkedIn updates.

Next, click **Select what others see when you've viewed their profile**. This one is important because sometimes you may want to simply surf around LinkedIn, but you don't want the person knowing necessarily that you are looking at their profile. If you do not want people seeing that you've been to their page, click **You will be totally anonymous** and save changes.

This is what you click if you want to surf and view LinkedIn profiles anonymously.

Select **Who can see your connections**. Do you want your connections to see your connections? If not, click **Select who can see your connections** and click **Only you**. If you want to stay open, click **Your connections** and only your connections will see your contact list.

Here is the screen shot to determine if your connections can see your connections.

The next section allows you to change your profile photo. Now go over and click **Manage your Twitter Settings**. Here you can add your Twitter account. It only takes a minute. The other tabs in this section are self-explanatory.

Now go over to the right and click **Email Preferences**. If you want to manage what comes into *your* email box from LinkedIn, you'll want to tweak these settings. First, click **Types of messages you are willing to receive**. Here is what that looks like:

Here is a screen shot helping you determine the types of messages you want to receive.

Next you will see a section called **Frequency of emails**. Open that up and select accordingly using the drop-down menu.

Here is the Frequency of emails screen that you can adjust to your liking.

Next you can go through who can send you invitations. Personally, I would ignore this one unless you truly get spam from LinkedIn. Next, click **Set the frequency of group emails notifications or emails you receive**. As you join more groups, you will get a lot of updates from the groups. You will most likely want to go into this section and adjust it to daily, weekly, or no email updates. On the right side of this section are three tabs from LinkedIn where you can choose whether you want to receive emails from them or participate in their research. This is your decision.

Here is a screen shot of the Frequency of group digest emails.

The Groups, Companies and Applications section allows you to customize your group/company and applications experience. With the first option, you select the order you want your groups to display on your page. This is a great feature for a strategic social marketer, because you can list them in any order you want and therefore market to the world the groups you are in—which says a lot about who you are and the types of people you associate with.

Company Search is also a great feature to view more information on companies. Say you are going on a business trip to Washington, D.C. You go to the People search bar open the drop-down menu and click **Companies**. Type in Washington, D.C., and then narrow the search down by company type; at this point you can start listing companies and people in Washington, D.C. (because now you can get their names). Click **View companies that you are following**, then click **Company search** for a more detailed search.

Companies you may want to follow

Here is what you see when you click on Companies Home section. It also shows you companies you may want to follow.

Under **View Your Applications**, you will automatically see three applications: Events, Reading List by Amazon, and Polls. You *can* use Events to market happenings to your LinkedIn followers. Reading List is especially attractive to authors—you can upload a photo of your book from Amazon and put it on your electronic bookshelf. And with Polls, you can run surveys, which audiences tend to really like—and you can get some great data.

Applications

Here is what you see on the Applications menu.

Applications for Marketing on LinkedIn

Now that you have a great profile, know how to add friends, have joined a few groups, and have adjusted your profile settings, let's get you looking like a real social marketing pro by taking you to the next level on LinkedIn. You do this by adding some applications to your LinkedIn profile. There are 20-plus valuable applications on LinkedIn and LinkedIn Mobile. Some of these are discussed in the next few sections.

Reading List by Amazon

This is a fun and interesting application. To find it, go to **More** on the top menu and scroll down to **Reading List by Amazon**. Click it, and then click **Update Settings**. Now type in the name of your favorite book and add it to your list. On LinkedIn, you can look at your industry and see what people are reading using this application. You can also scroll down and see your network's books: to the right of a person's name, you will see a gold box that reads **Watch [name] list**. You can be alerted when that person adds a new book to his or her list. Likewise, people might begin following you if you regularly recommend books. There's wonderful potential for great viral marketing here, particularly if you are:

- An author.

- In a speaker bureau.

- A retail merchant with books.

- A book club member.

- A business consultant.

- A coach.

Actually, the opportunities are endless!

Click Select to list book on your profile.
Try it. List this one!

Here's where you can list the books that you're reading.

Events

This is a wonderful tool, not only to promote your own events, but also to find great networking and professional development programs. Go to the top menu and click **Events**.

Here's what you can do using this application:

- Browse Events within your connections.

- Find specific events by name or subject.

- Find the most popular events.

- See what events your network is attending.

- Add and create your own event by clicking the **Add an Event** tab.

TRY THIS

If you are traveling to another location, look under Events on LinkedIn and do an advanced search. Type in the location you are traveling to and see if there is an event you would like to attend. This is a great opportunity to network!

The Add an Event page is straightforward to use. Give the event a title, put in the date, and add the venue name, the location, and the time.

Add your website address or the website for the event. Check that you are attending and organizing. Add more details if you like. Preview the event online and then publish the event. And you did it!

Here's where you can browse and look for events.

On this screen, you can add the details of your event.

LinkedIn Polls

Everyone likes a good poll. So how about creating one for your business? If you want to try something new, test it out with your connections on LinkedIn. Get their responses to your idea. Click the **Applications** icon and find LinkedIn Polls. It's a great place to gauge what the business community is looking for or responding to.

This is the page you will see to create a LinkedIn poll. You can also share it on Facebook and Twitter.

The cool thing about this is you can literally create and distribute the poll in 5 minutes. Just click **Create Poll**, and it will walk you through the process. You can target the poll to your network or to specific professionals—for example, sales professionals or coaches, or people in specific regions of the country. And, yes, it's free. After you get the results back, you can analyze the data and share it with your network.

SlideShare Presentations, Webinars, and Videos

This application is worth checking out. As your network gets bigger, you will see more and more information being shared. This application lets you upload and share your PowerPoint presentations and Word documents and videos—if you add audio, it's essentially a webinar.

First you must create a SlideShare account at www.slideshare.net and sync it to the LinkedIn SlideShare page.

Once you open SlideShare, click **Home** to see all of the featured presentations. Next, click **Explore** and see the most-viewed presentations or webinars.

SlideShare is the world's largest community for sharing presentations. Its website lists some of the things you can do with this application. If you sync it with LinkedIn, you should be able to do all of this as well, so make sure you click the **+ Sync Your SlideShare Account** bar to merge the two. You will see this tab on the top-right side of the page just below the search bar.

Here are a few things you can do with SlideShare:

- Embed slide shows into your own blog or website (or now on your LinkedIn page).

- Share slide shows publicly or privately.

- Market your own event.

- Upload your presentation and distribute it to Facebook, Twitter, and other platforms through the www.slideshare.net site.

As I mentioned, you will see a + Sync button on the top-right side of the page, and after you open the SlideShare application, you can click the **Explore** tab to see what others have done. This is yet another way to market yourself, your business, and your brand.

Click on Explore to view

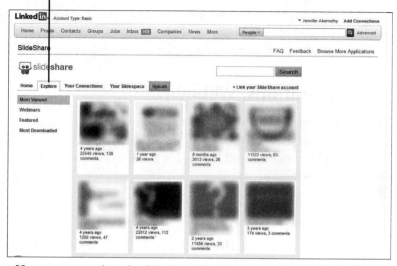

Here you can explore the slide shows that others have done on LinkedIn.

Tweets

With this application you can have your tweets show up on your LinkedIn page, and why not? You never know who may see your expertise and say to themselves, "I want to hire that person!" You will see three tabs: **Overview**, **Connections**, and **My Tweets** and **Settings**. The Overview is self-explanatory, but the Connections tab is pretty cool. You can now see all of your LinkedIn connections that are on Twitter and follow them from here. You can also create a Twitter list directly from this Connections page of your LinkedIn followers. Under the **My Tweets** tab you will see all of your tweets. Under **My Settings** on the Tweet application, you will want to check whether or not you want your tweets to display on your LinkedIn page.

Here is a screen shot from My Connections tab within the Tweets application.

Here you can decide to display your tweets on your LinkedIn profile or only tweets that you end in #in from Twitter.

TRY THIS

I would suggest that you have your tweets display on your LinkedIn page for additional branding and marketing. Again, go to **My Tweets**, then **Settings** tab. Remember: Always be marketing yourself and connecting. Show your influence.

Projects and Teamspaces by Manymoon

This is an interesting new application for people who work with teams. The description page mentions that it is a valuable tool for those in real estate, recruiting, and sales, but I believe small businesses with virtual teams also can utilize Manymoon. You can work on projects, upload documents, create project calendars, assign tasks to team members (they must have a LinkedIn profile), add attachments from Google Docs, and read team members' comments associated with each task. There are many sharing options that you can view to see which work best with your LinkedIn connections. You can also link events and time sheets and create an additional administrative dashboard by registering for Free with Manymoon on the LinkedIn application page for additional features.

Here is the Create Project page within the Projects and Teamspaces application.

Company Buzz, Box.net, and My Travel

Wonder what people are saying or what the buzz is about your company? The Company Buzz application on LinkedIn shows you what the "Twittersphere" is saying about your business. You can view keywords, trends, and tweets (the latter, of course, requires a Twitter account). This is a great application to have for company reputation management.

The Box.net application enables you to "box" a document or documents into a file that certain people can see. It truly makes file sharing simple. You can also use this application for sharing videos and photos among colleagues, clients, or even friends.

It's a great site—and it's free! Entrepreneur tip: post a one-sheet PDF about you and your business to get you hired.

The My Travel application is for you business and personal travelers out there. You can see what cities your network is traveling to, and let them know where you are heading. The thought here is if you are in the same city, you might be able to connect in person. You can display your current world location and upcoming trips to share with your network. Bon voyage!

WordPress and Blog Link

Do you have a blog that you've created using WordPress? Now you can have that blog feed into your LinkedIn profile. Simply go to the **Applications** tab again on the left navigation bar. Click it and look for **WordPress**. Open it and enter your blog's URL. Then you simply choose to display either all your blog posts, or only those that you tag with the word LinkedIn. Press **Save** and you are ready to go! Now your network will be notified when you post something new to your blog on WordPress.com or self-hosted WordPress.org. This is a great way to expand your blog's readership and attract new viewers.

The Blog Link application is similar to the WordPress application. However, you can use this one if you have created your blog using blog services from any number of providers:

- WordPress
- TypePad
- Vox
- Blogger
- Live Journal

As you enter a blog post, your connections will see your latest entry as soon as you update it. This service is powered by TypePad technology, which is a well-respected blogging service.

Google Presentation

Are you a fan of Google? Do you use Google Docs? If so, this application is yet another way to introduce your work and your expertise to your LinkedIn connections by creating a virtual presentation of you and your work. You can upload a PowerPoint presentation or a file to your LinkedIn profile through Google Presentations. If you are not familiar with Google Docs, simply add the Google Docs application (docs. google.com) and you'll see the free templates, documents, and presentation templates. Create a three-page slide presentation sharing what you do on LinkedIn.

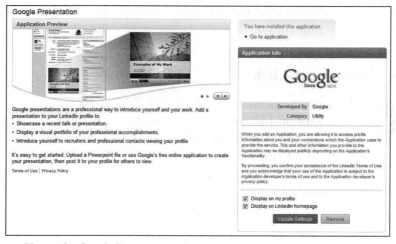

Here's the Google Presentation that you can use to showcase your work.

DID YOU KNOW?

You can export your contacts on LinkedIn. Click **Contacts**, scroll down to **My Connections** at the bottom of that page, and you'll see an **Export Connections** link. You can export your contacts as either a .csv file or a .vcf file, which you can easily load into most address book applications. (LinkedIn provides instructions on how to load your contacts for commonly used apps.) You can also save your profile as a PDF by clicking the PDF icon on your profile page. This is great to do if you are worried about losing your contact information.

The Power of Groups on LinkedIn

There are more than 100,000 groups on LinkedIn, including alumni groups, corporate groups, industry groups, and professional groups. In fact, you name a topic, and there is most likely a group for it. Power LinkedIn users strategically join groups that will help their business by expanding their connections and reach. So think about what types of groups you want to belong to, whether it's an alumni group or a professional networking group. Also keep in mind what other types of groups could benefit from having you as a member. Who needs your services? See if they have a group. In 2008, LinkedIn added a great group directory search feature that makes it so easy to find groups. Let's give it a try.

You can find groups in many ways, but the easiest way is to go to your profile page and click **Groups** at the top of the page. Try typing in a name of a school, company, or association and click **Find a Group**.

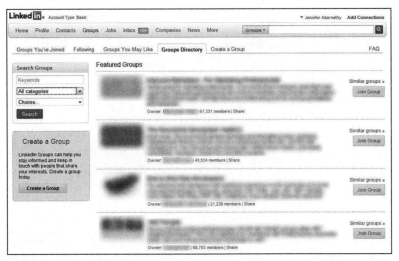

You can see your LinkedIn groups and search for new groups from this page.

Now look on the right side and click **All Categories**. You will see alumni, corporate, conference, networking, nonprofit, and professional groups. There are so many groups! Go through and find some that appeal to you and your business. I suggest that you look at the types of people who are members and view some of the discussion headers to see if they appeal to you. Then, join them!

You can search for groups by category from this page.

To join a group, pick a category and open it. Now find a group and click **Join this group**. The group manager will get back to you and let you know if you are accepted into the group.

Making the Most Out of Joining Groups

Many LinkedIn users, after they join a group, aren't quite sure what to do next ... so they do nothing. Yes, it's neat that the group name now appears on their profile, but they really aren't getting any value out of it. We want to ensure you get your best value out of being a part of a group.

Member List

After you join a group, the first thing to do is look at the member list. How do you do this? Click the **More** tab and you will see **Members**—click, and a list of names and titles appears. Welcome to another new network that you have just created for yourself. If you see people you know or want to know, click on their name, look at their profile, and invite them to connect. That is a powerful way to begin utilizing the group for your business. Remember, this is social networking—you want to make connections.

Here's how you get to the group member list.

Participating in Group Discussions

Now we want to take it to the next level. Click the **Discussions** tab. You should see an array of discussions taking place in your group. Do you see something that you can comment on? If so, go ahead and click **Add comment**, and start typing. Your name, photo, and title will automatically appear to the left of your comment. By participating in discussions, your name gets out there, your expertise is on display, and you might just make a new connection.

You can start your own discussions, too. Click the **Discussions** tab and on the right side, you see **Start a Discussion**.

Here's where you can start your own discussion.

Think strategically here. If you are within a group that could use your services, what types of questions can you ask or what type of discussion should you start? Look at the types of questions others are posting and get some ideas. Another idea is to share an article or link with the group. A great place to do that is within the News tab within each group. By sharing articles and resources, you're seen as a strong contributor to the group. You will also be seen as an expert, so keep contributing when it makes sense. This gives you great viral visibility because not only does your name and website get posted within the Discussion or News section, but the information that you posted something will also go in your news feed to everyone in your network!

Creating Your Own Group

Creating your own group is another way to build credibility and market your brand to people who may not be on Facebook.

Think about why you are creating a group on LinkedIn. Is it to make more connections? Is it to share information? Is it because eventually you want to invite members to a conference or a tweetup? Talk to your staff or mentors and think strategically. Who will manage the group? Who will you not allow in the group? Take time with your decisions. Just think of the contacts you will make and the creativity you can apply. You can make this group into anything you want it to be.

It is easy to create a group. Simply click the **Groups** icon in the top navigation bar. Click **Create a Group**. Next a list of steps will appear on the same screen, from uploading your logo, to naming your group, to summarizing what your groups mission is. You will then enter your business website and you are done.

Here you can create your own group on LinkedIn.

On the Access section, you can indicate if you want it to be an open group where anyone can join without approval, or if people will have to request to join. If you decide that incoming members need to be approved, you will designate someone to approve them and allow them access to the group. Also, don't forget to check the boxes to have your group in the display directory and to have all members display your group logo on their profile pages. Doing this will create more great visibility and viral marketing for your business.

After you create a group on LinkedIn, market it everywhere. Have it on your website, talk about it on Twitter, and put it on your Facebook page. And don't forget to mention it in places such as your business cards and your email signature.

Analyzing Your Connections on LinkedIn

As you continue to use LinkedIn, add connections, and join groups, your network is going to quickly grow. Wouldn't it be neat if you could take a demographic snapshot of your network? It'd be great to learn where your network connections are located or what their industries are, right? Well, you can! Go to the top navigation bar and click **Contacts**, and then click **Network Statistics**.

You will see how many users you could potentially contact through an introduction. The number may astound you. Review the top locations of your network and the most popular industries of your connections. This is good information to know, and if it doesn't quite match where you are heading, you can adjust accordingly. It's another strategic way to analyze your social media sphere of influence.

Here's where you review your LinkedIn network statistics.

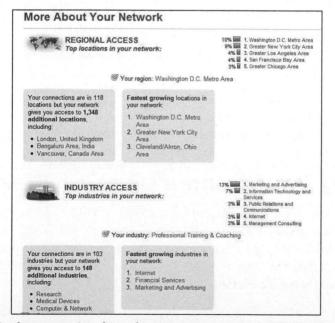

Here's where you review the top locations in your regional and industry access.

LinkedIn Mobile

Always on the go? Want to tap into LinkedIn from your mobile device? There's good news, because you can! At the bottom of your profile page, click **Mobile**. *Note:* when you sign off of LinkedIn, it will also take you to the Mobile page.

Step-by-step instructions follow for linking LinkedIn to your iPhone, Palm Pre, Android, BlackBerry, or any *WAP*-enabled phone. You can download the application for an iPhone, access the application catalogue for the Palm Pre, or go to m.linkedin. com for your BlackBerry.

> **DEFINITION**
>
> **WAP** stands for wireless application protocol, which allows users to access information via handheld wireless devices, such as cell phones.

This is the LinkedIn Mobile page that will help you upload LinkedIn to your mobile device.

The Least You Need to Know

- LinkedIn is much more than an electronic Rolodex—when the applications are used effectively.
- Joining and participating in discussions in LinkedIn groups is a great way to gain additional visibility.
- Events build viral visibility for your business, whether it's your own event or someone else's that you are attending.
- There are many LinkedIn applications you can use to help with your marketing, including tweets, WordPress for blogs, and SlideShare for webinars and video.
- You can analyze your network by viewing the Network Statistics section on your LinkedIn profile.

The New MySpace, Google+, and Other Cutting-Edge Trends

In This Chapter

- Why MySpace still matters
- Google+ QR Codes and Foursquare
- Exploring Justin.tv, lifecasting, and lifestreaming
- Combining and streaming your content
- Creating your own Internet radio show
- Social shopping sites taking the consumer by storm

When reading the chapter's title, you may have thought you'd been transported to the year 2050. And if you haven't been involved with social media marketing, you may be scratching your head wondering about this futuristic language that is emerging with these social networking platforms.

In this chapter, we explore several popular sites and tools and discuss marketing methods. Ready to be a part of the future? Okay, let's review MySpace, Google+, QR codes, and so much more!

What's Happening on MySpace?

Launched in August 2003 and headquartered in Beverly Hills, California, MySpace is a "social entertainment" media platform many should not ignore. It calls itself a "technology company connecting people through expression, content, and culture." MySpace's traffic plummeted in 2010 and into 2011, but in the summer of 2011, MySpace was sold to an advertising network called Specific Media. It's been rumored that future plans will focus the site specifically on the music industry. It is important to note there are still tens of millions of people using the platform.

This self-described "place for friends" already underwent a redo in 2008 with newly designed pages that included status updates and applications. MySpace hosts the world's largest music community and will continue to focus its efforts on that niche. Since they now call themselves the "social entertainment site," the focus seems to be on music, videos, and gaming. MySpace has been a very successful platform for those in the entertainment industry, and also for those who *want* to be in the entertainment industry. When browsing through the site, you will see a lot of the top music artists, but also many garage bands hoping to make it big. Many bands credit MySpace with helping them to develop quite a following.

MySpace isn't bland; it's a colorful display of video. There's also sound, and all this seems to draw a younger viewing audience who eagerly participate. When looking through the site, you will also find sections on videos and gaming along with what's hot in entertainment and movies. There is even a retrogaming section; in July 2011, the original Pac-Man game was getting four million "plays" a day on MySpace. While some may discount MySpace, if you are in the music business or entertainment industry MySpace is still a site to look at and consider using.

At the time of this writing, updated figures are hard to come by because MySpace is revamping the site, but if you want to reach people who love music and/or if you are in the music/entertainment industry, this is still a site to consider.

Here's the home page for MySpace.

DID YOU KNOW?

Even though it's hard to tell the exact demographics on MySpace, there are ways to target your audience. For example, do you want to reach the Latino market? There's the MySpace Latino site at latino.myspace.com. It's the same website, but written in Spanish!

Google+

Google+ is the newcomer to the social networking scene. The Google+ site is gaining popularity quickly and new users are liking many of its unique components. Interestingly, with Google+, many of its first users are male and could be labeled as "tech geeks." Comparatively, when Facebook first launched, it was popular with the female college market. Google's biggest advantage thus far seems to be its ease of use, ease of sharing, and more control for users. Google+ has three distinct features: circles, sparks, and hangouts.

Here is the sign-up page for Google+.

Circles

Remember the old "groups" on Facebook? Well, Google+ circles are like that, but much more versatile. You customize your circles with specific friends and you can cross-connect circles so you can have some friends in two or more of your circles. One great thing about this feature is that you don't have to have two separate pages for business and personal connections. You can have one page and put those you label as family in one circle so they won't see what you are posting to your business circle, and vice versa. You can send your updates to all circles or just one. Another cool feature is that you can include people who are not on Google+ but are on your email list in your circle.

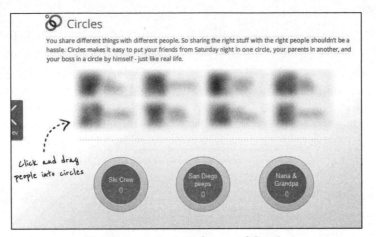

Here is a sample circle feature of Google+.

Hangouts

Google+ has created a place in the platform where you can chat with one person or to many people at the same time who are within one of your circles. You can chat via audio or video—do keep that hair looking good and put that smile on, because the video wave is expected to be a big component. As of this writing, groups as large as 20 have set up planned "hangout sessions" on Google+, but I'd put money that that group number will get bigger. You can also create what I call "on-the-spot" hangouts that aren't necessarily planned but rather offer spontaneous networking or gathering.

Google+ hangouts.

Sparks

This feature allows you to build customized information feeds that you can design and control. Perhaps they are feeds of your blog, or favorite blogs written by others, or news channels and info sites. You can easily share these feeds with your circles and allow others to opt in to your feed. This is not popular with everyone so you can now delete sparks by clicking **Settings** at the top-right corner, then **Google+** within the Settings option. Then choose **Profile and Privacy** and delete or hide.

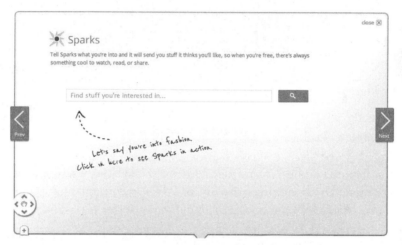

Here is the page describing sparks.

QR Codes

In 2011, QR codes began taking the market by storm, and their potential is unlimited. You've probably seen them on your airline pass or cereal box, but if you're not familiar, here is a quick review.

QR codes stand for quick response codes. Think of them like a retail bar code that you see on items from the store. But QR codes store a lot more information. Here is how they work: a QR code is a pixel barcode that is scanned by a smartphone's camera (think about when you are at the grocery store and they scan the label—it's the same type of concept). To read a QR code now, you will need to install a QR code application on your smartphone first, because you will use your smartphone to read the QR code, and then information will get transferred to you. Depending on the type of code, the viewer might see a video, a website, or contact information—the viewer could see anything really by reading the QR code.

Here is a picture of a QR code of Jennifer Abernethy, the author of this book, with a message to you.

Here are some ways your business can utilize a QR code:

- Record a welcome message via video with a special offer.

- Link to your Facebook or Twitter page or YouTube channel.

- Offer directions to your business.

- Produce a customer feedback or testimonial form.

- Directly "ring" to your office if you like. What a way to get those phones ringing.

The possibilities are endless. Put a QR code on the back of your laptop so when you are at a conference or at the airport working, someone might walk up and scan your code. You can put a QR code on a pair of cufflinks, a tie, a T-shirt.

In the very near future, QR codes are going to be able to store even more information, so keep up-to-date with the technology.

TRY THIS

Likify.net generates a QR code that allows people to "like" something on Facebook. Two other QR code generator sites are http://qrcode.kaywa.com and www.qrstuff.com.

Foursquare

What used to be only known as the game played in grammar school is now one of the most popular mobile social applications around. It is known as a "location-based" social application.

Foursquare basically rewards people for checking into places like airports, retail stores, restaurants, and nearly any location. The Foursquare website boasts that with Foursquare, one can

- Attract and retain customers.

- Connect with followers of your brand.

It really allows your customers to have fun with your business by saying that they stopped by or purchased your products and/or services. As of April 2011, Foursquare had more than 10 million users and 3 million check-ins per day. Do you have a retail location? This is worth checking out. If you don't, you should still use Foursquare, as many locations offer specials only to their Foursquare audience.

Here is the website for Foursquare.

DEFINITION

NFC, or **Near Field Communication,** allows for transactions to happen by Bluetooth or other short-range communications without the exchange of cash or credit cards. NFC mobile payments were launched not too long ago to allow people to pay for items via a mobile device. Experts predict that it will be 2014 before this type of transaction becomes mainstream throughout the United States.

Streaming Social Media

Some are saying that streaming (also known as lifecasting or streaming social) is the next big favorite on social media. But what is it exactly? It is basically a record of a person's current online and offline activities. This record can be shared via video or blog posts, or just with photos. Lifestreaming permits you to take any or all of the social media technology and give readers or viewers a snapshot of what is happening in your life.

The following sections discuss some great sites to get you started with streaming or lifecasting.

Lifecasting and Justin.tv

Keeping with the video and entertainment theme, a relatively new form of social media marketing is called lifecasting. Lifecasting is a video blog of sorts where a person does a continual broadcast of events or of a situation through video or digital media.

For example, a songwriter may have a camera running as he is composing. An artist may have the camera running as she is sketching. A retail owner may have the camera in his store window or at the cash register. Perhaps you are a radio broadcaster; you could have a camera running during a typical morning while you are broadcasting your radio show. Some use it just to talk and have people observe their life as they are just living it. It's an interesting concept, so keep an open mind about how you could use lifecasting in your business.

Justin.tv is a popular lifecasting website and live video website. Their website boasts over hundreds of thousands of channels broadcasting live video, including the Producers channel, which has Xbox lifecasting. Other channels include Educational, Animals, News & Events, Sports, and more. For lifecasting from your office or place of business, this may be the solution you are looking for.

NETIQUETTE

With lifecasting, you want to be yourself. Be real, authentic, and transparent. You didn't put on makeup? Don't worry. Didn't brush your hair? That's okay, too. Make it what you want to make it. It's okay to start a new trend, even if that involves not prepping yourself before going live. Just remember that what you put online stays online, even if it's sitting on a server somewhere, it will be on the Internet.

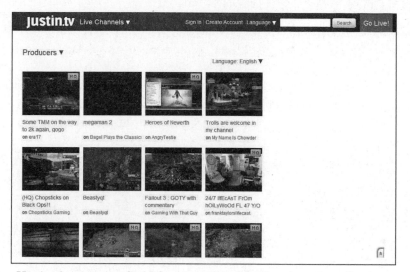

Here's where you can find lifecasting plus many other channels on Justin.tv.

Lifestreaming

Another term you may soon hear more about is lifestreaming. This is similar to lifecasting, but with a twist. Lifestreaming is an online record, if you will, of a person's activities. That record can be made via live blog entries, tweets, Facebook status updates, or with a stream of live chronological photographs. You then "stream" or send this information out in chronological order to your social media sites. There are many sites that can help you stream, and some of them are listed in the following sections.

FriendFeed

FriendFeed (friendfeed.com) is one of the sites that can help you feed and stream your information. Known as an aggregator of social media sites, FriendFeed (which was acquired by Facebook in 2009) is a website that enables you to feed all of your collected social networking services at once. It does this by providing a singular stream of updates from you to many of your social media sources. Once you create an account on FriendFeed, it will let your friends know when you share an update, video, photo, and so on. It also works across many of the blogging services, so your blog updates can feed to wherever you direct them to among your social networks.

Tumblr

Tumblr (www.tumblr.com) is another site that lets you "effortlessly" share or stream just about anything. Tumblr gets literally hundreds of thousands of posts through its blogging tool each day. Let's say you have videos on YouTube and photos on another site; Tumblr will combine them and put them in one easy place to view, or stream it for you. It does this by combining the information and sending it to your friends from one place.

Tumblr is another site that makes it easy to share just about anything with your friends.

Internet Radio

You've heard of the days when our relatives and ancestors gathered around the big radio to be entertained and informed by the outside world. Now we can do the entertaining and inform the world with our very own radio show. And we can do it all from the convenience of our home.

Creating your own Internet radio program as part of your social networking strategy will set you apart as the go-to expert in your industry, not to mention that it will give you and your business more national and international exposure. After recording, you can advertise and promote your program on all of your social media sites and even stream it to some of your sites live.

Live365.com

Live365.com (www.live365.com) reaches millions of people worldwide and features hundreds of genres of music. There are thousands of stations from a combined 150 countries. Live365.com is self-described as music programming by "real people with a deep passion for music." If your business wants to start a radio program, Live365.com attracts millions of listeners each month. You can listen from your iPad, iPhone, Android and Android tablets, and, of course, your PC. Live365.com provides broadcasting software, tracking and reporting, licensing support, and more.

BlogTalkRadio

Do you love to talk on the phone or with your customers? Ready to host your own radio show and partake in live interactive discussions? Now you can. All you need is a telephone and a computer and you are live—on the air—with an Internet radio show on BlogTalkRadio (www.blogtalkradio.com).

If you want to have your own Internet radio show, you should try BlogTalkRadio.

Not sure how you would make it work? Perhaps you are a life or business coach who wants to talk with other subject matter experts who your audience will find value in hearing from. Perhaps you are a recruiter who wants to talk about the job market and interviewing skills. Maybe you are a tax accountant and want to host a show on tax practices, or have a call-in show for answers to tax questions. Just about anyone can have a radio show.

People want to hear from you. With millions of listeners each month, BlogTalkRadio is an amazing tool for Internet radio marketing of your expertise and viral marketing for your business. Once you complete the online host form, two dedicated telephone numbers will be assigned to you. One is for the callers and the other is for the show host. For the free service, up to five callers can phone in at a time. As an added bonus, there is easy integration with all of the big social networks like Twitter, Facebook, and Ning, so not only can you easily share with your social followers, but your show guests can share with their social media followers as well.

You can upgrade to other levels to get more premium services. With the upgraded editions, you can broadcast up to two shows a day and have an optional text chat for each program so that you can have even more interaction with your callers. The site does a lot to help its host create a successful program, but one cool thing is that you can archive your show or stream it live. BlogTalkRadio also has a service that provides a simple cut, copy, and paste coding so that the hosts or the guests can place promotional "badges" (a new word for ads) on their own social media sites like Facebook, MySpace, Twitter, and their own blogs. Move over, Larry King and Ryan Seacrest, because here comes the next amazing radio host. Could it be you?

Social Buying Sites Taking the Consumer by Storm

You may be familiar with sites like LivingSocial or Groupon. The term "social buying" allows today's businesses to offer their best deals on sites that are shared around the social web via digital coupons. The model so far is proving successful—after all, where are people spending their time? Online. Let's review some (though not by any means all) of the current top social buying sites. It may trigger an idea for you and your business to use these tools or models to market your business and brand.

Groupon

Groupon (www.groupon.com) was the first to market a social buying site where users subscribe to daily deals and see everything from cooking lessons to wine tours and charity offerings. It offers a popular deal of the day, and is the biggest social buying site, with over 35 million registered users. Subscribers then can let their friends know about the deal via Facebook, Twitter, or LinkedIn.

Here is the website for Groupon.

LivingSocial

LivingSocial (livingsocial.com) is Groupon's biggest competitor. Amazon has invested a significant amount of money into the company, which offers daily deals, instant deals, past deals, deals for families, and adventures. More deal categories are emerging very quickly, so go to the site for the latest.

Here is the website for LivingSocial.

Bloomspot

Bloomspot.com is for high-end deals, like a B&B in Napa Valley, a high-end day spa, or a Michelin-rated restaurant. Whatever your liking, Bloomspot has that "quality" product approach for the discriminating experience shopper. Its site boasts that its members get access to countless opportunities to peerless luxury and exciting, exclusive experiences.

GoodTwo

GoodTwo (goodtwo.com) makes it simple and fun for nonprofits, schools, and individuals to raise money for a cause. Here's how it works. GoodTwo allows the fundraising company to run a campaign in partnership with a local or national business. Every time a consumer buys the deal, the fundraising company keeps 50 percent of the profits. The business that partnered with the fundraiser benefits from people becoming aware of its product or service. Three groups benefit: the fundraiser, the business service or product, and the consumer. Now that's a good deal.

Deals for Deeds

Deals for Deeds (www.dealsfordeeds.com) reinvests in local communities. With each purchase a buyer makes on the site, a percentage goes to a local nonprofit. Their slogan: "We bring you the deal and you do a good deed." Check it out.

The Least You Need to Know

- MySpace is still a key player in the "social entertainment" world, particularly for the music and entertainment industry.
- Google+ is quickly becoming popular with the tech community; Circles, sparks, and hangouts make Google+ easy to use and control.
- QR codes are going to continue to evolve and become mainstream for the business owner and for the consumer. Location based services like Foursquare are also going to continue to evolve.
- Creating your own Internet radio show or being a guest is a great way to add visibility and exposure to your business.
- Social buying sites will continue to be popular. They benefit the business, the consumer, and in some cases a local or national cause.

Chapter 15

Lights! Camera! Sell!

In This Chapter

- Understanding the new and popular video marketing
- Getting started in online video
- Expanding your Internet video presence
- Creating your own Internet TV show
- Integrating video with the other major social media

We all know the old saying "a picture is worth a thousand words." Well, today a good marketing video can be worth thousands of dollars—to your business, that is.

With faster-running laptops, wireless mobile technology, and amazing recording devices, video nowadays looks and sounds better online than ever before. In this chapter, you learn why video marketing needs to be strongly considered an essential part of your social media marketing identity. Terms like "web personality" are beginning to appear as business owners and entrepreneurs build a following using video. So tear down the walls to your business and let people see inside a day in the life of you. Ready to continue your journey toward becoming a social media superstar? Let's get started.

The New Video Marketing

The new video marketing is fun, authentic, and real. You no longer need big lights, studios, and production teams to get your video produced. Today, it's as simple as getting a handheld video camera—like the Sony Bloggie, Kodak Playtouch or EasyShare—to take video on the go. Take some time to practice pointing and aiming, and you're ready to go live!

Today, anyone can potentially become the next Internet TV star. The playing field is leveling out, and this is great news for the entrepreneur or small business owner. Today's entrepreneur can create an unlimited array of videos that will help with marketing and branding his or her business to the world.

Some popular examples include welcome messages to new customers when they first visit a company's website and "how can we help you?" videos aimed at new prospects. Also, many people are using video to record testimonials of happy customers. Gone are the days of only having a written testimonial. Today, seeing and hearing testimonials is what audiences are responding to. Video brings these testimonials to life.

NETIQUETTE

Always get written permission from people to broadcast their image in your online videos. Usually, they will verbally agree when they are filmed, but a best practice is to get a video release form signed. For ideas on wording, search online for video release form samples or contact your business attorney for assistance.

Television was designed as one medium for many viewers. Online video is crafted as one on one (or at least to feel that way). Today, corporations, small businesses, and entrepreneurs are using online video and mobile products to seemingly speak one to one to their customers, prospects, and Internet audience through video.

By appearing onscreen within your customers' and prospects' computers, an interesting psychological transition begins to take place. Viewers begin to feel that they "know" you. They grow (hopefully!) to like you. And if you provide good information, they grow to respect what you do. Here are some examples of how entrepreneurs and small business owners are using online video:

- A tip of the day or tip of the week.

- Auto dealers showing a maintenance tip of the week.

- Success coaches giving a motivational thought.

- Real estate agents sharing neighborhood reports via video or house and neighborhood walkthroughs.

- Sales experts sharing online sales tips or features of their product or service.

- Entrepreneurs recording from their home office or other creative locations, such as from a local café, park, restaurant, or museum.

- Marketing an upcoming workshop, product, book, or opening.

And the list goes on and on. But the difference today is that these videos are conversational and authentic. That's what people are responding to on social media sites.

> **DID YOU KNOW?**
>
> The .tv domain is becoming a popular top-level domain that is becoming a popular website extension. Savvy professionals are thinking ahead and buying this domain for their business. Get yours today, even before you get into online video. Go to http://www.watch.tv/.

Who Is Watching Online Video?

In February 2011, the social media resource Mashable reported that YouTube has 490 million unique users worldwide per month, who rack up an estimated 92 billion page views each month. We spend around 2.9 billion hours on YouTube in a month—over 325,000 years. And those stats are just for the main YouTube website—they don't incorporate embedded videos or video watched on mobile devices or other video sites. The number by now has obviously gone up tenfold.

The point is that these numbers are forecasted to continue to increase. Video is hot, hot, hot! So let's get your business "camera ready" and part of the online video revolution.

What You Need to Get Started

You need a good camera. Aside from the Sony Bloggie, Kodak Playtouch, and Kodak EasyShare, there are many other good ones out there with more launching, it seems, each month. They can be found easily and they are not expensive. The high-definition editions are recommended so you get the crisp, clear image on the screen. However, there are many other video cameras that will work. Cell phones with video are convenient, but the quality isn't quite as good as a digital video camera. Cell phones are good, though, to catch something on the fly. However, if you are serious about making video an integral part of your social media marketing, invest in a camera. There are plenty of cameras on the market that aren't expensive.

In addition, many computers come with built-in web cameras (webcams), and that is a fine place to become familiar with video. If you use a webcam, you will also want to consider investing in a good microphone because you can also use this for webinars. The EYEBALL, by Blue Microphone, is a combination webcam and microphone.

Order it online or find at select stores. (We will get into webinars in Chapter 17.) You should also get a tripod for your small handheld or DV camcorder.

What else do you need? Just like I said earlier in the book, you need a great mind-set. Talk to your audience. Pretend your ideal client is on the other side of that camera. What would you say to him or her? Lastly, come up with a plan. What would your audience like to see? Bring them into your business by letting them get to know you, your products, and services better. Don't be shy … just be yourself!

The more you do video, the better you will get at it. Social web audiences react well to conversational tones, so be yourself and have fun. The most important thing to know is that if you want to be findable, you need video. Most people under the age of 35 use YouTube as their primary search engine for research, so you need to be found there.

YouTube: The Leader of All Things Video

Founded in February 2005, YouTube is the definitive leader in online video. Today, it gets a staggering three billion views per day. In fact, more video is uploaded to YouTube in a month than the three major TV networks created in 60 years!

YouTube makes it easy to upload and share your videos. You can post your videos on YouTube and even create your own video channel. If you haven't done so yet, go ahead and create a YouTube account. Go to www.youtube.com and click **Create Account** at the top-right side of the screen. It's easy to do.

Here's where you create your account on YouTube.

DID YOU KNOW?

YouTube was created by Chad Hurley, Steve Chen, and Jawed Karim in 2005. The three founders knew each other from working together at another Internet startup, PayPal. In fact, according to Mashable, Hurley designed the PayPal logo after reading a *Wired* article about the online payment company and emailing the startup in search of a job. YouTube was initially funded by bonuses received following the eBay buyout of PayPal. You could argue that if there was no PayPal, there would be no YouTube.

After you get your account set up, enter a topic into the search bar and look at all of the content. You can subscribe to video channels, search videos, and more. Imagine seeing your channel on here, too! It's good to know in advance that viewers cannot download your video from YouTube; however, you will be given an option to allow viewers to *embed* your video when you upload your video file. There is a site called KeepVid (keepvid.com), which allows you to download videos from YouTube. Savevid.com also allows you to download.

DEFINITION

Embed means to make something an integral part. This is a common term used when referring to putting a video onto your website or blog.

For great social media marketing, you should upload videos to YouTube. But how do you do that? First, ensure your video is no longer than 15 minutes in length or no larger than 2 GB—in fact, the shorter the better. Viewers truly like video that is 1 to 3 minutes in length. Ten minutes is the maximum time that YouTube allows. Next, sign in to YouTube and look for the Upload link along the top of your screen. You can upload your video from here or record from your webcam. Click the yellow **Upload video** button and select your video file from your computer.

Now you need a title for your video. Think of words that your customers would search for. For example, if I did a video with sales tips, I may title it, "The Sales Lounge with Jennifer Abernethy gives 10 powerful business startup sales tips." This way, if people are searching for me or my company, I will be found. Also, if they are searching for business startup or sales tips without knowing me in advance, the video will be found and they'll discover my business anyway.

The next step is to describe the video. Assign your *tags*. Then choose broadcast options: public (with the world) or private (up to 50 people) or unlisted. Use unlisted if you want to upload a video and send it to a single person or group, not the entire Internet audience. To upload or select another one, click **Upload Video**.

DEFINITION

Tags are keywords that describe the content of your video. They are also search words that people use to find content. When selecting tags, think about what keywords viewers would use to find your video and surround each tag word with quote marks (like "this").

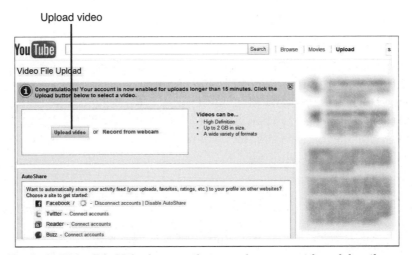

Here's the Video File Upload screen where you choose your title and describe your video.

Next, click **Go to My Videos**, where you can play the video editor and your video.

DID YOU KNOW?

The AudioSwap feature on YouTube allows you to add royalty-free music or permission-free music on top of your video. You can pick the genre of music and publish it to your video. You cannot just use any music or you will be fined. Stick with royalty-free … always.

Now click **Edit**. Go through all of the areas on the left side of the screen. They ask you about online broadcast options, such as if you want to allow comments, if you want people to vote on a video, and more. You can even add a map for where you recorded the video. You can add annotations or wording on the screen and promote the video. After you've finished, save your responses.

Congratulations, you have a video on YouTube!

This is the final screen that enables you to name and describe your video and add tags.

Editing buttons here

Drop and drag video

This screen enables you to make choices about editing your video and adding music and wording on the screen.

To create your own channel on YouTube, click **My Account** at the top of the page. Name your channel and describe it. You have the ability to let people add comments to your channel and check the option that lets others find your channel. After you enable these options, click **Update**. Click **Channel** on the far right and then select **Settings** to name your channel, etc. Then click **Themes and Colors**. Now select your theme and colors for your channel. Click **Upload** to load a video. *Note:* there are also video tutorials on this on YouTube.

This screen enables you to make choices about your YouTube channel branding.

Other Sites to Market and Share Video

YouTube is the biggest and most popular site for videos, but there are other very popular sites that you should know about. Video is the future, and the future is now. Be on the lookout for new sites and new ways to incorporate video into your marketing. Next, we discuss some of the smaller—yet still powerful—sites that you might find useful.

Skype

Skype (www.skype.com) isn't just for calling anymore. In fact, many savvy marketers (myself included) have begun recording video on Skype. It's very easy and powerful because you can record just yourself, you can interview someone and have them on a split screen, or you can both broadcast and record your own webisode with a video partner on the other side of the world.

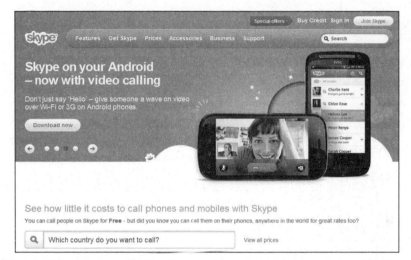

Here is the home page to Skype. Get creative and use this to market your business.

MailVU

I discovered this great tool, mailVU (www.mailvu.com), on Twitter. MailVU is simple to use and is great for emailing video greetings. Video email—or Vmail, as I like to call it—is such a powerful way to expand your influence and branding. For example, if you are a coach, you can use mailVU to send your client a video telling them you are eagerly looking forward to working with them, or send them some follow-up tips. If you own a restaurant and a client just had a large private party, you can send the client a thank-you video. The possibilities are endless.

Simply click Record and now you are on your way to wowing your clients.

This is the home page to mailVU.

Vimeo

Vimeo (vimeo.com) is a clean and professional site where members gather to post and share videos. Vimeo was created by filmmakers and video creators who wanted to share their creative work, along with intimate personal moments of their everyday life. As time went on, a community arose of like-minded people creating a wide range of high-quality videos. Vimeo's video player has extraordinary quality. You can join groups on Vimeo, create your own group, or even create your own channel. There are tens of thousands of groups and channels on Vimeo. Basic membership is free, but a Vimeo Plus membership will cost you $59.95 per year.

After you create your account, there is a profile page to fill out before you can begin uploading and sharing videos with your friends and networks. It's another place to market your videos and your brand, and to network with others by joining like-minded groups.

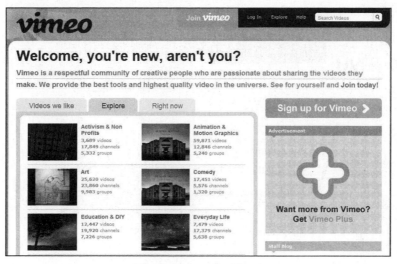

The home page for Vimeo.

Blip.tv

Blip.tv began in 2005 and now boasts tens of thousands of independently produced web shows. It claims to be the largest independently owned video network in the world, reaching more than 22 million people. A unique component of Blip.tv is that advertisers share revenues 50/50 with the show creators. When you sign up, you have the option of allowing advertising (which you can make some money from). You still own your own work, but I recommend reading the terms on their site for more information about this. This is great for those who want to create episodic Internet TV shows. Blip.tv provides a nice, user-friendly web page, which helps users quickly upload video and produce away. Everything is on Blip.tv, from independent film trailers to video shows from entrepreneurs.

Here's the home page for Blip.tv.

Viddler

Viddler (www.viddler.com) is a fun site that enables you to share and optimize your videos for further marketing. The component that makes Viddler so cool is that you can brand your videos with your logo, frame them with your color scheme, and even have the videos link back to your website. What great marketing! You can also post comments and *tags* at specific points in your video and even share your videos with iTunes or via an RSS feed.

DEFINITION

Tags in this instance are singular words used to describe what is being discussed in the video. Tags help draw viewers to your video if they are interested in the subject words of the tags that they read.

For business use, however, there are monthly fees. But with the fees there are many perks, including dedicated support, so it's definitely worth a look. When you create your account, you'll see the many membership offerings.

The home page of Viddler.

Viddler also has a feature that enables viewers to easily interact with your video by posting comments within the video. The site says it's even possible for viewers to record a video comment. Viddler is hip and popular among savvy Internet marketers—it's certainly a site to check out.

Click Learn More to explore the functionality

The Learn More tab on Viddler.

Creating Your Own Internet TV Show

Internet TV is quickly becoming popular among savvy marketers and celebrities. In a medium where people want to see, hear, experience, and engage with the show host or expert, Internet TV with interactivity is becoming the place to be seen.

Ustream

Founded in 2007 as a way to connect U.S. military soldiers with their families back home, Ustream (www.ustream.tv) has turned into something with even broader appeal. This site is for anyone and anything that wants to have a live streaming Internet TV show. It provides an interactive video broadcast platform where anyone with a camera and Internet connection can easily broadcast to the world. This site's system encourages two-way communication between on-air talent and viewers. It also offers unlimited possibilities for the entrepreneur and small business owner.

You will see what seems to be every genre represented, from pets to ponds to politics to people. Yes, it's the one place where people, places, politics, plants, puppies, and even hamsters have their own streaming show. And if you are wondering about plants having their own show, well, there are live streaming shows of gardens.

Search for live-streaming video on Ustream.

Some creative ideas for you about live video streaming:

- A pet store runs a live feed from the store window showcasing homeless pets.

- A retail store can broadcast live.

- A book retailer or book club could stream live book reviews.

- A coach could stream a live coaching session.

- A fitness coach could stream a weekly exercise regimen.

- A sales trainer could stream a weekly class in sales calls.

- Set up a live broadcast from an event and record from a booth or table.

- Host a call-in show and talk about your industry.

- An artist could stream while painting or designing a piece.

- A performance group could stream their rehearsals.

Again, the possibilities are endless. Both creativity and reality are what's attracting people to brands and businesses.

NETIQUETTE

A best practice is not to rant on your Internet TV show. You never know whose eyes will land upon the video. Keep it viewer focused, share value, and entertain (or infotain) people with your knowledge.

BlogTV

You've heard of a blog and you're reading about Internet TV, so let me introduce you to BlogTV (www.blogtv.com). Want to continue to build your fan base and share your expertise and your business story? You can do it live on BlogTV. The site exclaims, "You bring the webcam, we bring the stage." Founded in May 2006, this is a site where you can broadcast your own shows from your webcam and blog. You can chat with viewers and get live feedback while you are recording your show. You can share your show with friends and post it to your blog. You can also upload photos, create events, upload music, and share it with just friends or make it public.

BlogTV also provides a Junior Channel for the 13- to 15-year-old age group so they can create their own TV shows. Once you sign up for the account, you will receive an email confirmation. You can then name your show, gather your audience (send an email to your friends), send an update to your Twitter account, send info directly to your blog, add a custom background to your show page, and more. There is also a pro version for a nominal annual fee that gives you more upgrades, bandwidth, and priority. You may just become the next Internet TV star! If you don't want to see advertising on your screen, you can subscribe to the Pro version, but there is an annual fee.

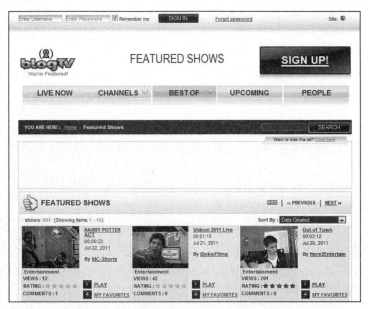

The featured shows on the home page on BlogTV.

TubeMogul

TubeMogul (tubemogul.com) describes its service as an online video solution for marketers where video is made "actionable." TubeMogul has a solution for users that distributes or syndicates your video to a number of sites, and also provides you with some light user analytics.

A cool feature is that as soon as your video goes live, you can send it directly to Twitter and Facebook. The dynamic thing about the TubeMogul solution is that they make your video actionable—they can incorporate the video description, title, and so on. They can also brand your video display screen.

For example, if you're in the video and the viewer of the video puts the cursor on your face, an information pop-up box will launch that describes who you are. They also provide a dynamic video analytics dashboard of your videos so you can see where your videos are viewed from geographically, as well as how often. The rich analytics seem to be a true strength with this solution, along with the actionable links and information that they install into the video.

Instead of uploading your video to all kinds of sites yourself, let TubeMogul distribute it. If you are looking to promote a video campaign or web series with a wide distribution, TubeMogul can help you by delivering a "guaranteed television-sized audience that is specifically targeted to your business demographic" (on a cost-per-view basis). TubeMogul provides you reports on viewership so you can really determine who is watching from where. It's worth taking a look for your big video online and mobile campaign and distribution.

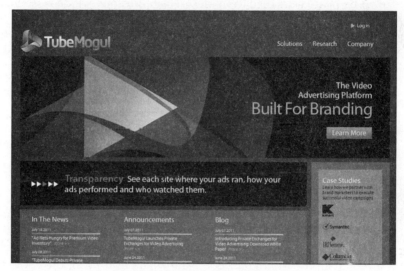

Here's the home page for TubeMogul.

Dailymotion

Dailymotion (www.dailymotion.com) is another site that gets your video distributed. According to its website, Dailymotion attracts 60 million unique monthly visitors worldwide.

The site is about helping you find new ways to see, share, and engage your audience through the power of online video. Aside from uploading your own videos, you can also find videos centered on your interests. Check out Dailymotion to …

- Share your videos publicly with the world or privately with friends.

- Discover new videos through channels or keywords (tags).

- Get feedback on your video clips.

- Push your videos across the web by posting them to your blog, website, or other social network profiles.

Metacafe

The Metacafe website (www.metacafe.com) is one of the world's largest video sites, attracting millions of unique viewers each month (per comScore/Metrix). Know, however, that Metacafe is not a video-sharing and -hosting site that enables any and every video to be posted. Instead, how the website promotes videos is what makes it different.

- Metacafe specializes in short-form videos averaging approximately 90 seconds long.

- The focus is on entertainment, so you won't find hard-news stories.

- The experience is audience driven and the videos are user generated, user reviewed, and user selected.

There's also a community panel composed of 80,000 volunteers that reviews and ranks videos daily.

Veoh.com

Veoh (www.veoh.com) boasts that "Veoh is now part of Qlipso, the revolutionary social content sharing company. Over the coming months, users and business partners will start to see more and more social features coming to one of the world's top video sites."

This is a site to look out for. Once you register, you can:

- Get started fast with Facebook or Twitter IDs.

- Watch videos longer than 30 minutes.

- Download high-quality videos.

- Upload videos of any length.

- Share videos with friends, family, and clients.

- Create your own groups and build a community.

- Send and receive messages with other members.

- Create and organize playlists of videos.

This is the opening page for Veoh.com.

The Least You Need to Know

- Video marketing continues to grow in popularity, and anyone with a camera and a computer and a business must get into online video.

- The new video marketing requires being real, authentic, informative, and entertaining. Think "infotainment" or "edutainment."

- There are many websites to host and deliver your video at no charge, but some sites offer upgrades for a nominal fee.

- Sites like BlogTV, Viddler, Blip.tv, Ustream, Vimeo, and Skype are fun and easy to use.

- There are many sites, such as TubeMogul, that help you push your video to many platforms and gather site analytics and viewership.

Blogs: The Hub of Your Social Media Marketing

In This Chapter

- Why you should consider having a blog
- How to keep your readers reading
- The top blogging service providers
- Ways to promote your blog
- Applications to help you blog from abroad

With all of the excitement and newness of social media, is it still important to have your own blog? Absolutely! Blogs are very much alive and doing better than ever. After reading this chapter, you'll understand that your blog is not only an integral part of your social media marketing strategy, but it is, perhaps, the most influential part.

In this chapter, we discuss what blogs are, how popular they are, how to set them up, what makes them successful, and how to tie them into your other social media sites. This chapter puts it all together so you know all the essentials to make your mark on the blogging word.

What's a Blog?

A blog is short for web log. A blog is sort of a log or a personal writing that's accessible to the world on a web page. The act of sharing one's personal thoughts on the Internet can be traced back to one blogger, Justin Hall, in 1994. Things have evolved since then. Gone are the days of the blog with just text, text, and more text. Today's blog can be just as dynamic and engaging as some of the social media platforms that we've already talked about.

If you want a place to write about your expertise, gear it to your target clients, and package it so it can be easily found via search engines, a blog is the perfect platform to do just that.

Why Should You Consider a Blog?

Blogging is here to stay, and participation by writers and by readers is on the rise. In June 2011, Mashable reported that there were over 40 million blogs between Tumblr and WordPress alone. Technorati.com stated that, as of April 2011, there were 133 million blogs indexed with them since 2002 and the number goes up daily.

> **DEFINITION**
>
> **Blogosphere** refers to the blogging universe in general. If you blog, you are part of the collective blogosphere.

There are many reasons why you should consider writing a blog. In fact, many would argue that it's essential for someone promoting a business or product. Here's a short list of reasons that might inspire you to start blogging:

- You can't control what is going to happen to all of the other social media platforms as they continue to evolve, but you can control your blog. It's your platform to do whatever you want to do with it.

- It's a great place to share your expertise, so you'll be seen as a subject matter expert and your readers will begin to see you as an industry leader.

- Blogs are a great way to attract clients. Once they find you and follow your blog, they'll learn to respect your expertise and trust your brand. You will also become a better writer by practicing the craft regularly.

- You can guide your other social media followers from Facebook, LinkedIn, and Twitter to your blog to learn more about you or the subject matter you write about.

- You can invite guest bloggers to post on your blog, which is a great networking and strategic marketing tool for you.

- It will give your followers, fans, and prospects a place to leave detailed comments about your blogging posts, and thus become more engaged with you.

- You can now add video to your blog, which readers love.

- The Internet search engines love blogs. This makes you easier to find for clients, prospects, and strategic partners.

- A good blog can give you great credibility among your clients, prospects, and potential strategic partners.

- Most bloggers agree that having a blog helps you to become a better writer and that it also helps you to clearly define your passions, business direction, and focus.

- For some entrepreneurs, their blog is so alive with information—such as video, Twitter, and other social media links—it actually replaces their websites.

Getting Started

When getting ready to get into the world of blogging you really want to consider your "Why?" As a business owner, think about who you want to read your blog. But before you jump into the *blogosphere*, answer the following questions to focus and do a better job of crafting your blog:

- Are your readers male, female, or both?

- What age are they?

- What's their income level?

- Are they stay-at-home moms, writers, or entrepreneurs?

- What do readers need to know?

- Why would people want to read my blog?

- Why am I writing my blog?

- What problems am I solving for my readers?

- Where can I find these people on the web?

- What should I name the blog?

And here's one more very important question to ask yourself: Are you willing to commit to regularly updating your blog? The first 60 days are crucial to success and building credibility.

ONLINE CAUTION

Don't start your blog with one entry and not go back to it. As you can imagine, this does not look good. Get three to five posts going and then start promoting it. Experts agree that there is nothing worse than finding a blog that hasn't been updated in 3 months.

Blogging experts say one post per week is the absolute minimum. Ideally, you want to update your blog two to three times per week to keep things fresh and current and to maintain readers' interest. This may sound like a lot of time, but once you start, you must be dedicated to writing new posts and putting new content on your blog.

Tips for Writing Your Blog

A common writing tip given by the popular bloggers is that you need to enjoy, love, and have a passion for what you are writing about. It will come across in your writing and that will attract followers and prospects. Here are a few more basic tips:

- Along with having a passion for your topic, lists are good to incorporate into your blog. We'd like to think that people are going to read your blog word for word each time, but people do skim. Lists are great for skimmers.

- Shake things up a little now and then. Using the same format month after month can get a little stale. So in some weeks, incorporate a list of items. In another week, use a video or have a guest blogger write a post.

- Your blog is your domain to keep people informed, build rapport, and—here's that word again—infotain them. Be sure your posts are informative and entertaining.

- Use catchy titles, or headlines, for each entry. Great headlines will attract readers and give them an idea of what your post is about. You can also put these headlines in your other social media sites like Facebook, Twitter, and LinkedIn. Be sure to include a link to take readers directly to your blog.

- When writing, you can put your posts into categories. You can use as many categories as you like, but a best practice is to keep the categories in sync with your subject matter expertise. In other words, if you stray too far off your topic, first-time viewers might get confused because they are going to see a variety of topics and categories that don't have a central theme of your blog.

- Make sure you spell-check your blog and, if you're not a strong writer, have someone else proof your blog post for typos.

- Don't forget to have fun. Your blog isn't a doctoral thesis. It's supposed to be a bit more informal in tone. You don't have to get it perfect, just keep evolving and listening to your readers. Keep posts short and engaging. If you are having fun writing, chances are your readers will have fun reading it.

> **NETIQUETTE**
>
> Even with your own blog, shameless self-promotion is a turn-off to readers. Sure, if you have an event, product, or service offering, you can promote it. But your blog should be highly content driven and it should showcase your expertise.

Blog Service Providers

Your blog acts as the hub for your company and is the definitive "talking source" for your business. You want to choose your blog service provider carefully. Let's take a look at the providers that are currently most popular. By the time this book is published, there might be even more options—check the Internet for any new providers on the horizon.

WordPress.com and WordPress.org

There are hundreds of thousands, if not millions, of users publishing their blogs on WordPress. It's a highly respected platform. But there are two WordPress platforms, WordPress.com and WordPress.org, and this can be confusing. You can choose to start a free blog at WordPress.com, or pay for hosting and start your blog on WordPress.org. WordPress.com is also easier to set up than WordPress.org.

I'll briefly highlight the differences between the platforms, but for a more comprehensive explanation, please visit www.support.wordpress.com/com-vs-org. The highlights of that web page are listed here. A few tidbits about WordPress.com:

- Upgrades and security are handled for you.

- The site gives directions for setting up your blog.

- There's no software to download, and the platform provides very social media–friendly apps.

- WordPress.com has hundreds of hosting servers, so it's unlikely to go down.

- WordPress.com backs up your posts automatically.

- You might get extra site traffic from blogs of the day and tags.

- Note that you cannot upload *plugins* or run your own custom-themed blog. They provide the themes, which you can modify to varying degrees.

Get started!

Here's what you see when you land on the home page for WordPress.com.

DEFINITION

Plugins are software applications that can be added to blogs to increase the functionality or provide added features. For example: Twitter has a plugin on WordPress that allows you to install your Twitter "stream" onto our blog. It will update your tweets on your blog automatically as you add new tweets.

With WordPress.org, you can upload custom themes and plugins. Here are some tidbits about WordPress.org:

- You'll be part of a great, supportive community.

- If you are technical, you have complete control to change the HTML code.

- You can monetize your blog and run advertisements.

- You pay for your own web hosting.

- You must download the software to get your blog set up and running.

- You are responsible for stopping spam and backing up your blog.

- If you get a big increase in traffic to your site, your blog may go down unless you have a robust hosting setup solution.

With this platform, you have a lot of control, and it's a very powerful solution for your blogging needs. However, it also means you need to back up your blog and beware of traffic issues.

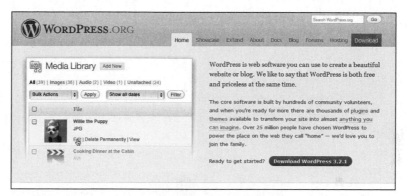

Here's what you see when you land on the home page for WordPress.org.

Do some research and think about which platform meets your needs. The WordPress folks suggest setting up a free practice blog on another topic (say, a hobby of yours) on WordPress.com. This gives you a chance to check out the features. Then you can decide if you want to stay with that or shift over to the more powerful WordPress.org.

TypePad

TypePad (www.typepad.com) is a service provider that charges a minimal fee, but offers the capability to customize the look and feel of your blog. TypePad has several different subscriber levels of engagement and you can easily upgrade to other service tiers without sacrificing your blog site.

TypePad's strength is that it is easy to use, and it also incorporates easily with the other social media platforms, such as Facebook and LinkedIn.

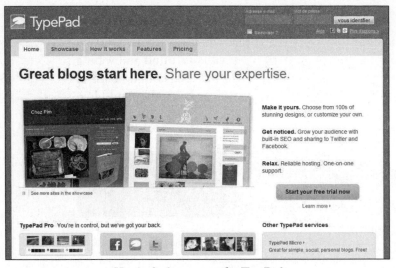

Here's the home page for TypePad.

Movable Type

Movable Type (movabletype.com) has a fairly sophisticated blogging service, as the graphics and templates are elaborately designed and colorful. In fact, it refers to itself as "your all-in-one social publishing platform." Brought to you by the folks who created TypePad, this solution is one of the more expensive options, but if you want to use the same provider as celebs such as Britney Spears, leaders such as Obama and Biden, or schools such as Harvard, then Movable Type is for you.

Squarespace

Mentioned in both the *Wall Street Journal* and *Business Week*, Squarespace (www.squarespace.com) is a site worth checking out for your blog. Priding itself on beautiful nontemplate design and reliability, Squarespace also provides great viewing stats for the business blogger. Reports show you where people are coming to your blog from and what keywords they are entering to find you. The monthly fee is affordable and runs across the board from as low as $12 per month ($36 per month for their business edition). Applications for iPhones and integration to other social media platforms are available.

Blogger

Blogger (blogger.com) is a free site offered by Google that can help you get a blog up in minutes. A nice feature is that when you create your blog, you can choose an available URL and later, if you change your mind and want another URL, you can easily make the change. Blogger also has a custom domain option and will host your blog for free. Other features include team blogging and blogging on the go from your mobile.

Here's the home page for Blogger.

Promoting Your Blog

So you've named your blog, you are clear on your target audience, and you have selected your blog service provider. You've got your page set up and you have entered a couple of posts. Congratulations! Now it's time to start promoting your blog to the world.

One of the first things to do is to go back and list your blog on all of your summary or informational pages on Facebook, LinkedIn, and MySpace. You can also list it in your bio line on Twitter or put it in the background template on your Twitter page. Then list your blog everywhere else: your business cards, your email signature, your website. If you are a speaker or writer, be sure you list your blog in your bio box or signature.

Another way to promote your blog is through the many online communities that offer a place to list your blog. And consider going to blogging conferences. BlogHer (www.blogher.com, a blogging community for women) holds an annual conference, and BlogWorld Expo also has an annual conference and a new media tradeshow worth checking out. You will also want to begin keeping your eye out for strategic partners so you can link your blogs on each others' websites and/or blogs. For many, self-promotion can be uncomfortable. But remember, if you don't promote your business (particularly in the beginning), no one will.

Here are some other ideas:

- Get listed with the blog directories or catalogs. BlogCatalog (www. blogcatalog.com) and Technorati (technorati.com) are two very popular ones. BlogExplosion (www.blogexplosion.com) and Blogged (blogged.com) are other all-around directories to take a look at. If you Google blog directories, you will find more.

- Try to find blog directories in your industry. For example, if you are a writer, check out Red Room (redroom.com). If you are a mom blogger, look at Real Savvy Moms (www.realsavvymoms.com).

- Record a short video clip announcing your blog and put it on Facebook, Twitter, YouTube, and LinkedIn.

- Do you publish a newsletter or e-zine? In the next issue, write about your blog and tell everyone about it.

- Incorporate your blog into Facebook and LinkedIn. Use the blog applications to feed it directly into Facebook and LinkedIn.

- Look for interesting people to write a guest post on your blog. Ask your guest blogger to promote it to his or her network.

- Comment on other blogs. While I don't recommend spamming or making inauthentic comments just to get publicity, strategically comment on certain blogs that interest you and that may also interest your readers. You never know who may find your comment and check you (and your blog) out.

- Write an article. At the end of your article give your name, business name, and blog information.

- When people leave comments on your blog, respond to them. Remember, people want to feel connected.

- Be patient. Building a large following is going to take time. Just know that if you post good content, people are going to find you. Content is king and it will help you build your credibility. The first 90 days are crucial because it will feel as if no one is reading. Keep writing—50 percent of blogs stop within the first 90 days because of this reason.

Applications for Your Blog

One of the methods for distributing blogs to others on a regular basis is a web feed. People sign up for a subscription to your blog to get it "fed" or sent to them automatically. You should encourage readers to subscribe to feeds so you can build your readership fan base. Let's review some of the websites that allow you to feed your blog to millions.

FeedBurner and FeedBlitz

FeedBurner (feedburner.com) is a news feed management tool brought to you by Google. If you already have a blog feed, you can run your feed through FeedBurner and get access to stats that will help you understand your readers.

FeedBlitz (feedblitz.com) is also a popular site to feed your blog directly to folks who want to receive it. Some people would like to get your blog via email versus RSS. Here's how it works: you sign up for FeedBlitz, which provides you with a "widget" to place on your blog or website. This widget gives readers an opportunity to sign up for an email to see all of your latest posts and the post headlines. Start looking at the popular blogs and noticing if they use FeedBlitz.

Here's the home page for FeedBlitz.

Widgetbox.com

Speaking of widgets, if you still aren't clear about what they are, go check out Widgetbox (www.widgetbox.com). This is a great site that enables you to create and import widgets that link to specific sites. These are kind of fun and you may find some that you want to put on your blog.

CoverItLive

One day, you may get known as a serious blogger and you may be asked to live blog at an event. CoverItLive (www.coveritlive.com) is used by thousands of bloggers to engage millions of readers each month. This software delivers what you need to blog from any event live with your laptop. If you don't feel like bringing your laptop to the event, you can still cover it using your iPhone through the software. Get the app and you'll be able to launch and run live events, publish live commentary and photos, run audio and video, email event links, and more. They offer free basic service and a premium option. Serious bloggers should check this out!

Here's the home page for CoverItLive.

Technorati

According to their site, Technorati (technorati.com) "collects, organizes, and distributes the global online conversation." Is there any doubt that you need to get your blog listed with Technorati? Their website says they are the third-largest blog media property and the sixth-largest social media property.

Simply join their site, "claim" your blog, and include a personal profile so readers from around the world will be able to find you. Did I mention their site is free? Well, it is!

We see the term *RSS feed* all the time, but what does it mean? Basically, this is a method that allows for really easy distribution of your online content, called a web feed. The technology that enables the feed is called an RSS.

> **DEFINITION**
>
> **RSS** stands for Real Simple Syndication or Rich Site Summary; an RSS feed enables you to "feed" your blog automatically to other sites after you've completed your blog update.

Bloglines

Bloglines (www.bloglines.com) is a news aggregator that collects the RSS feeds from online content. Bloglines then makes this content available to you online at its site for free. First you'll create an account, and then you'll decide on your blog subscriptions and news feeds. You can then sign up and get your favorite Bloglines sent directly to your email inbox. Check it out, because this is one site that is gaining in popularity.

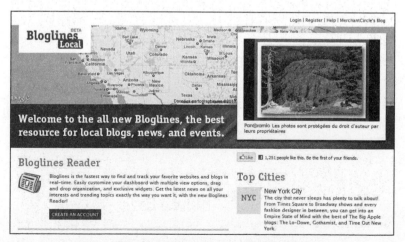

Here's the home page for Bloglines.

AddThis

AddThis (www.addthis.com) is something you simply must have for your blog. You may have noticed that a lot of blogs have a share link at the bottom. (If you don't see one on your favorite blog, tell the writer … he or she will love you for the suggestion. One of the most powerful things you can do is to add a sharing tool to your blog.) This link may have other social media site icons listed on it. How do they do that? Go to www.addthis.com. According to their site, this feature is served billions of times per month. And that number has only gone up. So run (don't walk) to AddThis for a share link, which will help your readers share your blog with other platforms and networks. Readers simply click on the Share button, select where they want to share it (Facebook, Twitter, LinkedIn, etc.), and boom … it's been sent.

Here's the home page for AddThis.

Alexa

Alexa (alexa.com) offers many powerful tools, but one that I've noticed on a lot of blogs is Traffic Rank. This is Amazon's search engine and it ranks every website according to the amount of traffic (or views) it receives. If you want to tell the world your traffic rank, sign up with Alexa.

Applications That Help You Blog from Your iPhone

Bloggers today are on the go, but there are several iPhone apps that allow them to write entire posts, add videos and photos, and otherwise stay connected with their readers.

Evernote

This website (www.evernote.com) is like your memory on steroids: it helps you remember sights, sounds, locations, and everything else so you can refer to them in your blog. Not only can you capture information, but you can also organize it on Evernote and find it fast when you need it.

Here is a screen shot of the Evernote page.

Pixelpipe

This site (pixelpipe.com) allows you to upload photos, audio files, and video files through the Pixelpipe Media Gateway. In turn, it will distribute the content to your blog (and 100 other social networks, too). This is where Pixelpipe comes in by utilizing "cloud" technology. Cloud technology allows users to use one BIG application instead of purchasing multiple app products. The cloud provides an overall service.

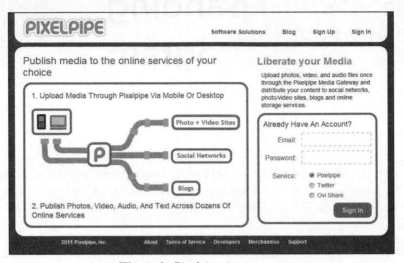

This is the Pixelpipe sign-up page.

The Least You Need to Know

- Your blog can be one of the most powerful tools of your social media marketing strategy.

- Your blog is your own branding platform, and you can link it to the other social media platforms.

- Before you start a blog, know the who, what, where, how often, and why of your blog.

- There are many applications to help market your blog, such as RSS feeds or using sites like FeedBurner, FeedBlitz, and AddThis.

- No excuses anymore. You can now blog from anywhere, including your smartphone.

Streamlining and Expanding Your Program

New social media sites and tools are introduced each week, and it can be overwhelming to learn how to manage it all. This part shows you some shortcuts to take so that you can effectively handle all of your social media.

Additionally, you are introduced to other tools and sites to help you further expand your marketing efforts online. From the simple to the more creatively complex, this part will have you imagining new and even more savvy ways to connect, reconnect, and share information with your clients, prospects, and business referral partners. As you are reading, try to imagine how you could use these products to support your business. Have fun exploring!

Using Social Media for Meetings and Presentations

In This Chapter

- Discover the new world of webinars and teleseminars
- Get tips for hosting webinars and teleseminars
- How to promote your events using social media
- Learn about webinar/teleseminar service providers
- Get introduced to podcasting and 3-D animation technology

How do you drive people to you and your business and how does all this technology impact how you have meetings? Well, if you haven't participated in an online meeting lately, this chapter should open your eyes to new possibilities. Webinars, teleseminars, podcasting, and 3-D animation sites are all great tools to combine with your social media marketing.

Today, you can meet in your office with a group of 2 to 10 employees, but online you can meet with a group of 2 to 2,000 people from around the world. Come and explore the new world of online meetings to network, collaborate, and grow your business and brand.

Webinars and Teleseminars

The term "webinar" was derived when someone had the idea to give a seminar over the web. These days, with the cost and inconvenience of air travel, webinars are not only an increasingly popular way to do a presentation, but you can also chat with a loyal following or announce a new product offering to your prospects, clients, and fans. Today's webinars are different than 5 years ago, and there are some great sites to take a look at. Entrepreneurs and small business owners are saving time and money by delivering webinars to their clients and prospects.

Teleseminars are similar to webinars, but without the computer. A teleseminar takes a phone plus a seminar (or discussion). Participants are given a number to dial in to and the facilitator leads the call. The audience is typically muted so the facilitator can speak without interruption. No business is too small to host a teleseminar. You can even have one with no one on the line but still reach hundreds (if not thousands) of people.

> **TRY THIS**
>
> Are you an entrepreneur? Host a webinar or teleseminar about the state of your industry. Share the top three things your target audience needs to know about your industry and how it affects them.

Let me explain. I know many people who have done teleseminars with no one on the receiving end by prerecording it, and then posting it on a website or blog, or emailing it out to intended recipients. You can also turn it into a product, but that's for another book. For teleseminars, you will still need to plan in advance, but you can promote the same way you do webinars. For topics, you can pretty much host a teleseminar on just about anything. People like teleseminars because they are easy to participate in—you just need a phone. They typically are free or for little cost, and participants can still get a lot of information without investing a lot in travel time driving to and from the event.

Think you need to be a large corporation to host a webinar or teleseminar? Think again. Today's entrepreneur and small business owner are successfully using today's amazing technology to talk with prospects and clients and educate fans on what they do. It's another way to stay connected with people and share your expertise. Still not convinced how you could use a webinar or teleseminar?

Here are some ideas for webinars and teleseminars:

- You want to announce a new product line at an upcoming conference. Have a webinar so you can show slides and talk about the event. A teleseminar can do the same thing, but without the slides or video.

- Participants love to hear from the owner or from the business itself because they hear your energy and enthusiasm. Host a "meet the CEO" webinar.

- Webinars are a great way to show some statistics or pictures of a new product. In teleseminars, you can talk about the statistics and invite listeners (who are your prospects) to a website to see pictures.

- With many of the new webinar platforms, you can give clients or prospects control of the screen so they can collaborate and share from their end. Teleseminars are good, too, particularly when you don't necessarily need the visual.

- Are you an artist and have an upcoming show? Host a webinar/teleseminar and talk about where, when, and why you are doing the event.

- Are you a charity or an association? Have a webinar to talk about your organization. Show photos with statistics. Remember, people want to feel connected. Teleseminars can actually have the same effect because you can simply send your audience an email document afterward with photos and information.

- Do you own a winery? Or are you a photographer? Host a webinar/teleseminar showcasing your vineyard and upcoming events. Photographers can talk about upcoming specials, or what companies and entrepreneurs need to know about how photography can really impact marketing.

- Are you a real estate agent or broker? Host a monthly webinar/teleseminar on, say, "Seven Things First-Time Homebuyers Need to Know." Or do a quarterly webinar on the state of the market in your region of the country. Share statistics and show photos.

- Are you a speaker or an author? Speakers can hold a webinar/teleseminar talking about their expertise and how someone can go about hiring them. Authors can talk about their background and discuss three takeaways readers will get from reading their book. You can do a webinar shout out before a conference you will be speaking at or a book signing.

Tips for Hosting a Webinar or Teleseminar

When hosting a webinar or teleseminar, you must first be prepared. Know how much time you have to speak. Have a timer or clock in front of you and make sure you don't go over the time. Everyone now wants succinct, to-the-point events. If targeting a variety of time zones, ensure you are specific about which one is being used (for example, 9 P.M. Eastern Standard Time). However, do list all time zones and state what time the meeting starts in each one.

Other points to consider:

- Make sure you have the ability and know how to mute the phone so listeners can't hear, um, distracting noises. The sounds of dishwashers, phones, talking, and, yes, toilets flushing will ruin your call.

- Have a slide on the screen (if it's a webinar) when they arrive. If it's a teleseminar, have some music playing.

- Be enthusiastic (or at least warm!) and smile. The listeners can tell if you are bored and don't care.

- Start on time and end on time or a few minutes early.

- Have a glass of water handy in case you need to clear your throat.

- Offer a special or incentive to participants for taking time out of their schedule to attend the webinar or teleseminar.

- If you can, record the event. Most services today have that option. This gives you the option to replay the teleseminar later or send it as an *MP3 file*. (*Note:* if you record a webinar with video or slides, it will be saved as an *MP4 file*.)

- Take the opportunity to promote your other social media sites. Ask participants to follow you on Twitter. Connect on LinkedIn and Facebook and let them know about your blog. You should consider creating a hashtag around your webinar.

DEFINITION

An **MP3 file** is a computer file that uses compression technology. The files are small and often used to make digital audio computer files that can be easily transferred over the Internet.

An **MP4 file** stores digital video and digital audio streams along with images that can be easily transferred over the Internet.

Promoting Your Webinar or Teleseminar

After you decide that you are ready to do some webinars and teleseminars to grow your business, you need to go back and promote them on all your social media sites. There are arguments for how much time in advance you need to promote, and the bigger your webinar/teleseminar, the more advance notice you need to give. Let's say your target audience is less than 100 people on a webinar/teleseminar; you will want to start promoting it about 2½ weeks in advance. Avoid holiday weeks or weekends.

The best times will vary, depending on your audience and industry. Webinars can be done first thing in the morning, at noon, in the afternoon, and even during evening hours. Know your audience and what time they will respond. You might have to experiment or offer a few different times, or give people a survey to see what time works best. A lot of webinar and teleseminar companies offer the capability to record your webinar so people can play it back at their own convenience.

Promoting It on Twitter, LinkedIn, and Facebook

Even though I don't advocate constant 24/7 self-promotion on Twitter, you can certainly promote your webinar or teleseminar there because your followers will benefit by attending. Typically, participants are going to learn something that is going to help them in life or in business. So promote your webinar on Twitter by providing a link to sign up for the webinar in a tweet. Ask staff members, your PR person, or your clients if they would promote the webinar or teleseminar. Typically, if you are connected to them via Twitter, they will retweet your tweet and spread the news to their network.

You can also promote your webinar/teleseminar in the Events area on LinkedIn. If you are in groups on LinkedIn, let your groups know, and also promote your webinar in your status update section. You can even create an event on LinkedIn promoting your webinar/teleseminar.

To promote your webinar/teleseminar on Facebook simply put it in your status update or post an Animoto video about your event on Facebook.

Promoting Webinars/Teleseminars in Other Ways

Here are a few more ideas to get the word out:

- Promote it at the top or bottom of your blog a few weeks out. Add a link where people can RSVP.
- Mention the webinar/teleseminar in your email signature.
- Promote it on your voicemail and website for a week or two prior to the event.
- If you are at a speaking engagement, promote it there.
- If you are at a networking event, ask the host in advance if you can leave flyers about your webinar/teleseminar on a table.
- Highlight it on your website, newsletter, or e-zine, and on area event calendars.

Webinar and Web/Video Conferencing Service Sites

Here are just a few companies that can help you host a webinar; if you do a search on the Internet, you'll find plenty of others.

> **DID YOU KNOW?**
>
> The difference between a webinar and a video conference is that on the video conference participants can see you and the team of speakers live on the screen, movements and all. On most webinars, the audience may see a still photo in a slide and hear your voice, but not live video.

GoToMeeting and WebEx

I like GoToMeeting (www.gotomeeting.com) because it's easy to set up. It offers service for phone/web meetings of up to 15 people. It also offers the GoToWebinar for those who need more space (up to 1,000 people), and an even larger solution for large corporations. There are monthly fees, so check their sites for a variety of programs.

WebEx (www.webex.com) is very popular within the corporate world for large formal presentations, but it still can be used by the entrepreneur or small business owner for groups of up to 25. It has a few more bells and whistles and there's a bit more technology involved. WebEx also has a video conferencing service online.

InstantPresenter and ReadyTalk

A webinar, web, and video conferencing site, InstantPresenter (www.instantpresenter.com) is neat because of its video collaboration component. Say you begin talking and then want to introduce someone else, such as a strategic partner, collaborator, vendor, or another employee. The attendees to your webinar will enjoy seeing who is talking. You can also share screens and chat live (via text) on the site. There is also on-demand recording and site branding.

InstantPresenter has a video collaboration option.

ReadyTalk (www.readytalk.com) has web conferencing, audio conferencing, and webinar and recording services. It prides itself on quality performance and customer service excellence.

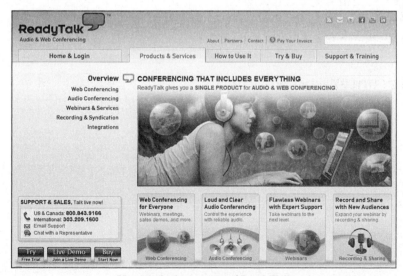

Here is the home page of ReadyTalk.

ooVoo

Another great video chat and video conferencing site for your webinar or video conference is ooVoo (www.oovoo.com). Let's say you want to have a web meeting with your team or with a prospective client. With ooVoo, a webcam, and a computer microphone or headset, you would all be able to see and hear each other and have a great conversation while saving travel time. The display is very professional, with the names of the conference attendees appearing above their heads.

Here's the home page for ooVoo.

MegaMeeting

MegaMeeting (www.megameeting.com) is a web and video meeting tool that allows you to share documents as well as control others' computers to show them a live demonstration. You can have hundreds of participants and up to 16 video screens simultaneously. The site gets high ratings.

Here's the home page of MegaMeeting.

Teleseminar Providers

When starting out on your first teleseminar, know in advance it can be a little awkward. You will be talking and not hearing anyone responding back to you. Even simply getting used to talking without a live person in front of you is a bit uncomfortable.

There are many teleseminar companies to choose from, so first ask yourself what you can afford. Then ask friends and associates what they have used. Ask your Twitter or Facebook friends which services they recommend.

After you find one, see if you can do a trial run. An important question to ask yourself is if you just want to speak or if you want to open up the lines to get others talking. This is important because if you want to open up the lines and ask questions, you might need specific types of providers. Also, determine if you want to record the teleseminar and learn how to do this in advance. You don't want to end the call and then realize somehow it didn't get recorded. The recording functionality is also important to know in advance when selecting a provider, because some offer it with their service, but for some it's an extra charge.

Next, get comfortable with the teleseminar setup and features. Learn how to mute callers. Again, do this so you don't hear unflattering noises in the background. Before you do your first one, log in at least 15 minutes early to get it set up and going. Just before you begin, send out a tweet (if it's a public teleseminar) and invite folks to join in. Have fun!

DID YOU KNOW?

Telegathering, teleseminar, and teleconference are interchangeable words—all imply that you are gathering a group of people together via phone.

Here are just a few teleseminar service providers:

- **MaestroConference** (maestroconference.com) is a really neat conferencing service for your teleseminar. It gives you the ability to put your teleconference listeners in individual chat rooms so they can talk among themselves or brainstorm about a project. This keeps your audience members more engaged.

- **FreeConferenceCall.com** (www.freeconferencecall.com) takes minutes to set up. It provides you with a conference bridge and pass code so all participants can dial in. You can record as well. I also like www.FreeConferencePro.com which allows you to create customized welcome messaging.

- **Instant Teleseminar** (instantteleseminar.com) lets you create an opening page for your teleseminar and a reminder page so participants can listen through a stream on their computer or by dialing in. You can also record to replay the teleseminar at other times.

- **Toll Free Conferencing** (www.tollfreeconferencing.com) has reservationless conferencing, operator-assisted conference calls, and much more.

Podcasting

If you haven't done a podcast before, it can seem a little daunting. Don't despair; after you've done it a few times, it's not so bad. The word "podcast" combines the words "broadcast" and "iPod." However, you do not need an iPod to produce a podcast. What you will need is a microphone and computer audio editing software, an RSS feed, and a website or hosting service that you can upload your podcast to.

When you create a podcast, you will want people to get it delivered to them automatically via an RSS feed. When you download a podcast, it's in the form of an MP3 file.

Podbean.com is a great site to help get you started. As of September 2011, the site boasted 400,853 podcasters—with 174,351,161 downloads alone on September 30.

Another option is to use an audio editing program such as Audacity, which has a free audio editing program (audacity.sourceforge.net) that works with both Macs and PCs. To learn how to create a podcast using Audacity, view an easy-to-understand video on YouTube (search for "creating a podcast with audacity") to actually see how it's done. When you have created your podcast, you can upload it to the Internet using Podcast Alley (www.podcastalley.com) or PodOmatic (www.podomatic.com). To create your podcast on other sites, you can go to www.blogtalkradio.com and your radio show can be used as a podcast.

Podcast.com is a hosting provider that can help you create a distribution format. If you have a WordPress account, use Podpress.org.

After you complete your podcast, remember to market it and upload it onto your social media sites. Facebook has the My Band application, so you can upload it there. Also, put it on your blog and on your website.

3-D Animation Technologies

This is not your Saturday morning cartoon or the sci-fi 3-D movie with the red-and-blue glasses that you remember as a kid. With the emergence of all this new technology, people are meeting, mingling, networking, and teaching in virtual worlds. If you haven't participated in a meeting this way, you must try it. You will not only meet amazing people from around the world, but you just might decide this is something you want to try for your business.

Large Fortune 100 companies are using and experimenting with 3-D technology for collaborative meetings and some of their training. Instead of having employees fly in, they can go to these virtual sites, meet with co-workers, and learn and collaborate there. You can make your meetings as imaginative as you desire. A headset and a high-speed Internet connection with a relatively new computer is all you need. *Note:* a computer that's older than 5 years might not have the speed or memory to use this technology.

To experience virtual environments from your computer involves your Internet connection, your video card, and the correct processor speed. If your video card is older, you can upgrade it or add an additional card. Most computers made after 2005, however, have processors and video cards made for video gaming, which is perfect for video environments.

Second Life

Many people call this site another type of social media marketing, but with a twist. Second Life (secondlife.com) calls itself "the Internet's largest user-related, 3-D virtual world community." Why do you need to be aware of 3-D animation, you ask? Because as time goes on, more and more often we are going to see virtual world invites to seminars, conferences, and networking events on sites like Second Life. Secondly, with this social media revolution, it is highly important to keep an open mind about all new emerging technology.

One downside is that Second Life can be a bit technical, but there are several folks out there who give Second Life tours and orientation sessions on how to get started.

Even more than Twitter and Facebook, the social communities found in virtual worlds like Second Life become very close and supportive. These are not just gaming or dating sites. There's a whole lot of learning, networking, and training taking place on Second Life.

A unique bonding seems to take place when you meet in virtual worlds; this bonding is tough to explain. One of the outcomes when engaging on this type of platform is that the professionals in Second Life are a supportive community, and as a result, participants are getting answers to their questions about all kinds of business tools, trends, and applications.

> **NETIQUETTE**
>
> Even though you are in a virtual world, this shouldn't give you permission to be someone you are not. There are highly educated professionals on these sites and you still want to leave a good impression. Try to get creative and think about how your company can utilize Second Life.

These types of environments are especially great for busy entrepreneurs and professionals, because they can attend conferences and seminars and grow their skill set directly from their home office or business location—or even from a mobile location, for that matter. Where else can you practice your elevator speech in a virtual elevator, talk about your business goals while riding an elephant, or practice your negotiation skills at a car dealership? In Second Life, that's where. This is the new world of networking, learning, and branding within 3-D animation sites.

Here is a virtual meeting on Second Life.

This technology enables you to engage just as if you were at a regular networking event—it's just virtual instead of in person. All you need is a Second Life account, a headset/microphone, and a short tutorial, and you're ready to go.

Some other virtual world platforms include TelePlace (formerly Qwaq), Protosphere, Open Sim, and Olive. Like any of today's hottest technology tools, there are new virtual environments popping up all the time.

The Least You Need to Know

- Webinars and teleseminars are amazing ways to connect to individuals or groups of people around business.
- Today's technology lets you see, hear, and chat with people from around the world.
- Webinars, teleseminars, and podcasts can all be tied into one's social media marketing strategy.
- Podcasting is relatively easy to do and it's another marketing tool to get the word out about your expertise and brand.
- 3-D animation sites such as Second Life are worth investigating.

Social Media: Tying It All Together

In This Chapter

- Gaining basic networking skills that help you effectively grow your list
- Examine today's new business card, as well as the virtual business card
- The importance of your email signature and how it helps you market your social media sites
- Time-saving sites that distribute your status updates to your social networks
- Learn about a news aggregator that collects it all in one place
- Creative ways to market your social media user names or sites

By now, you should be social media savvy. You've read about all the platforms, sites, and services. However, how does this all tie together? There are many ways to cross-promote your social media presence, and they've been mentioned throughout the previous chapters.

In this chapter, we go into a bit more detail about how you can create a fluid social media marketing campaign that will make you more findable, more visible, and make your life a bit easier. After all, what good is a great blog, Facebook, LinkedIn, Google+, and Twitter page—not to mention all those wonderful videos—if no one knows how or where to find you?

Networking in Person

We talked about how social media marketing is a networking tool. You can meet other people around the world and get to know them, and they, in turn, will get to know you. However, let's step back just a little bit. Now that you are setting up your sites and deciding which ones to start with, you also need to begin doing one more key thing: network in person.

Yes, in-person networking is not dead. You still need to get out there, particularly now that you are building your following and connections online. (In fact, while I'm writing this, I'm returning from a networking event I flew to in Utah with a group that I met through Twitter.) So while this isn't an in-person networking book, it does play a crucial role in your social media strategy. Let me share a few networking tips.

Survey your current customers, clients, and prospects. Where are they networking? What social media sites do they use? Start attending some of those events (even if it's every other month). After all, if you simply had all your clients following you on Twitter, that would not be so bad. It's a great way to communicate with them.

More importantly, you want to start finding out where the people that you want to target are online. You might hear that they have a blog. Or you might find out they are all on LinkedIn, and that's great. Now you have more information than you did before. And chances are, if your clients are using these sites, then most likely your prospects are as well.

When networking in person, know it's just as uncomfortable for other people in the room as it is for you, so stay outwardly focused. When engaging in conversation, keep the focus on the person you are talking to versus worrying about what you are going to say next. Ask questions and learn how you can possibly help them in the near future. Try not to start with "so what do you do?" Comment on their outfit, ask them if they are a member, comment on a current event. Don't offer a business card until they ask. If you really want to get their information, ask if you may have one of their cards. They, in turn, may ask you for yours.

 ONLINE CAUTION

Be careful about putting exact details of where you are going, how long you will be out of town, and where you are staying on your social media status updates. Do you want the world to know you are away from your home for days or weeks on end? Experts predict that would-be criminals will soon begin scouring the status updates to look for those who are not home or who are traveling to specific locations.

Ask people what social media sites they are using. Start getting a feel for what is working for others, but also know at the same time that what works for one person might or might not work for you. At least you will start getting a general sense of what folks in your network are doing.

Here are some additional networking tips:

- Be early. Some of the best prospecting and conversations usually happen before the event starts.

- Bring plenty of business cards and carry them in a business card holder or place you can easily access them.

- Bring your BlackBerry, iPhone, Android, or "smart device" and tweet from the event.

- Have your smartphone camera or digital video camera handy for spur-of-the-moment video clips.

- Carry a digital camera. Remember, you now have a blog and several social media profiles that you can upload information on.

- Wear your name badge (if they give you one) on your right side. This way, when you shake hands, the recipient's eye goes directly to your name tag.

- If at a large convention or conference, ask if there is a Twitter hashtag for the event so you can put that in all of your tweets. Some people are now wearing shirts with their Twitter user name on it preceded by the @ symbol.

- See if you can view a guest list ahead of time and try to meet one to three people intentionally. Be the first to say hello—it will leave a good impression.

- When you exchange information with people, ask how they prefer to be contacted (text, phone, email, and so on).

- Remember, you are there to network, not sit. Eat beforehand so you don't gorge on food. You are there to make an impression. Be yourself, be authentic, and listen.

Your Business Cards

Okay, so you've got a basic primer on networking. Now let's move on to that all-important business card. The etiquette around business cards is changing quickly, depending on your generation. For the paper business card user, the new business card should include, obviously, your name, phone, and email.

Next, be sure to list your Twitter user name; you can ask people to "follow me on Twitter @yourtwittername," or you could simply include your Twitter user name. Also put your Facebook information and other social media platforms on there. Have a blog? Put the name of your blog on your card. Remember, we are trying to tie all of this together. Have a Facebook fan page, YouTube channel, or LinkedIn group? Put it on your card. Now people are even putting a QR code on the card with a personal video greeting!

You don't want your card to be too wordy, though, so use your best judgment. Perhaps you just want to mention your fan page on Facebook, your blog, or your Twitter name. Start paying attention to the business cards you get and see what others are doing. If you are a retailer, have your cards at the checkout counter with all of your social media addresses on it. You could have a sign above that reads: "Follow us on these sites and we'll follow you back."

This will start the engagement and the conversation between you and your followers. There is a great debate about whether to include information on the back of your card. Some say leave it blank so people can write notes, others say that is valuable marketing "real estate," so use it. I say use it—more people don't write on the back than do. On the back you could remind folks of the best way to reach you, explain in a line or two how you can help them, ask a question that addresses a certain business or personal pain that you can help with, or invite them to subscribe to your blog or e-zine.

Honestly, there is no right or wrong answer. However, many people feel it's important to put information on the back of the card because more times than not, people do not write on your cards. The back can be valuable marketing space where you can further communicate how you can help professionals. Another trend is to round the corners of your card, while this isn't vital the most important thing is not to skimp on the quality of the paper. Your card needs to "speak" that you are a professional.

DID YOU KNOW?

There is a trend now among busy entrepreneurs to not put their direct dial information on their business card. They are putting an email address or a number to their virtual assistant or personal assistant. Also many Gen Xers and Gen Yers prefer not to use the phone anyway, so this could also be the reason why this trend is catching on. The point is: learn how your prospects and customers want to be reached. Make a habit of looking at the new business cards you receive for new trends.

Now for the other type of business card: the electronic business card. The day has arrived when many people, particularly the Gen Xers, do not carry business cards. They will carry their smartphone, likely an Android, BlackBerry, or iPhone, and put your information directly into their database as soon as they connect with you. A popular smartphone app, Bump, enables you to literally "bump" your phone to another person's phone and share contact information. This tool is making the hand-shake seem old school.

This is the screen shot of the Bump application.

Another site, www.contxts.com, lets you easily send your contact information via *SMS*, which is built into every mobile phone device. As Contxts claims, "Business cards are so 2007," so they've created the virtual Rolodex.

Basically, with this site you can use your mobile phone to easily distribute your contact information to another phone. I believe we'll see a lot more of this in the future, but if you are a heavy mobile user now, check out Contxts.

DEFINITION

SMS, the acronym for Short Message Service, is the connection between the phenomenon of text messaging and the underlying technology. In some parts of the world, SMS is used as a synonym for a text message or even for the act of sending a text message (even when a different protocol is actually being used).

Your Email Signature

How many emails do you send out each day? Did you ever think of your email as a marketing tool? Well, it is. In fact, your email signature (the text at the bottom of an email below your name) is the perfect place to list the social media sites you belong to. Savvy social media marketers utilize the email signature as a place to give the recipients more ways to reach you. By putting these links in your email signature, the recipient can click on them and learn more about you.

The most common links that you see are Twitter, Facebook, LinkedIn, and blogs. However, also look out for Skype, YouTube, Second Life, and links to online videos. Think about where you want to drive your readers. You can also put a live link to a client testimonial or a link to your book on Amazon.com. Or you can promote a special event.

Obviously, you don't want it to get too busy looking, but take advantage of this prime "real estate" for your social media marketing. You've done all the work creating these amazing profiles, so now you want to drive as many people to them as possible. This way, you can stay connected with them, build stronger relationships, and continue to share your expertise.

Many sites offer buttons to put on your email signature (buttons are the logo or icon from popular social media sites). Simply Google "social media buttons" and you will see many sites that provide downloadable buttons.

One site I want to bring your attention to is WiseStamp (www.wisestamp.com). The only downside to this site is it works only with the web browsers Firefox, Safari, and Chrome.

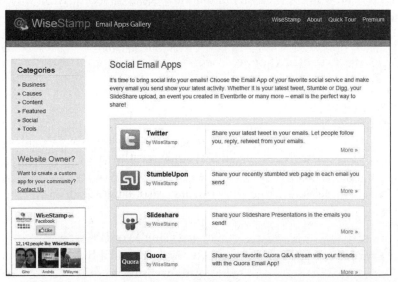

Here's a screen shot from the Social Email Apps Gallery on WiseStamp.

This site lets you easily share and add the logos and links to your email signature for all the major social media platforms. It even has fun additions, such as adding a motivational or inspirational quote to your signature. It will also automatically include the title of your latest blog post in your email signature. All you have to do is add your blog feed site to your WiseStamp feed account. You can share your latest status updates in your email signature, too, and so much more.

I hope you are seeing a common theme throughout the book. Email signatures can be a highly personal choice. Use your own style and be creative. There is no box you have to stay in any longer. There are amazing tools and services that are available to you for free to help you become much more findable and visible and marketable to the world.

Another service that provides interesting email signature templates is Email Ideas. This site (emailideas.com) allows you to create your own personalized email signature (called a Bojo) with clickable tabs, a texting feature, your headshot, and contact information. It also provides many already designed templates for a variety of industries like real estate, automotive, corporate, broadcasting, education, and modeling, to name a few. Email Ideas also offers a custom development template program.

TRY THIS

Begin looking at email signatures that you receive each day. Start examining what you like and what appeals to you. Think about what you can incorporate into your email signature that will showcase your brand and identity and make you more findable and visible to others. Now try it on your signature.

Your Website

On your website, you need to have all your social media marketing sites either listed with an icon or with a link. Many people put the links for Facebook, Twitter, LinkedIn, and RSS feed logos across the top or bottom of their home page, so people can click and directly follow their companies. Also, have a link to your blog so people can start getting that as well.

A trend recently is that many businesses are using WordPress.org to create their websites, with WordPress serving as both a website and a blog with live feeds from Twitter and Facebook. Start looking at other websites to see how they market their social media marketing sites.

Ping.fm

How do people seem to update all their sites so easily? Many of them use a free service called Ping.fm. Ping.fm allows you to update all of your social media sites through one entry point. Sign up and simply type in your status, check which sites you want to update, click on **Ping it!**, and you have updated your networks.

Here's the home page for Ping.fm.

At this writing, Ping.fm has nearly 32 social networking sites and 83 apps that you can send your status update to, but they are always adding more. Ping.fm now works well with mobile devices and has over 83 apps to add to your experience.

ONLINE CAUTION

Ping.fm is a great tool to use, but strongly consider how often you want to use it. Many feel if you put the same updates on Twitter, Facebook, and LinkedIn all the time, why should people follow you on all three places? Good food for thought. Each social media site has its own culture and personality. It's good to chime in live more often than not.

You don't want to lose followers. People seem to like to know that you are "there" on the other side of the site. Even if it's automated or done by an assistant, they like to feel you are really there and not just sending automatic pings to every site every day. So although Ping.fm is a great way to tie it all together and save time, my advice is don't ping to all your sites 100 percent of the time.

One recent update is the Ping.fm toolbar, enabling you to "ping" your updates more easily directly from your workspace.

Click here to select the social sites you want your message to go to!   Enter your message here!

Here's the Dashboard for Ping.fm.

As you can see from the previous figure, after you create your account, you can select which networks you will be sending updates to. In the message box, you can see the words, "This is where you type your status update!" At the bottom-right corner of the box, you see the words **Ping it!** Click on that and it will send your message to all of your sites. Hint: the first time you try it, go to your selected social media sites to verify that your message was sent there. If not, you'll need to go through the process again. Make sure to save your changes.

Netvibes

Netvibes is an amazing site that claims to save you 30 minutes a day in Internet time. And I believe it's true. Go to www.netvibes.com and create an account. After you do that, you will have a blank landing page. You will want to perhaps make this your home page. With Netvibes, you can have your Facebook status updates stream into this site, along with your Twitter and LinkedIn feeds, along with your news, local weather, and so much more.

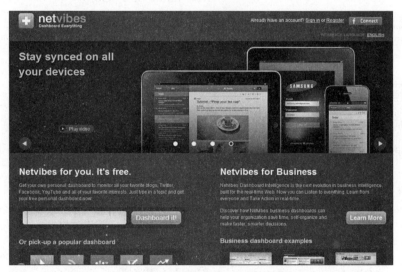

Here's the welcome page for Netvibes.

You can include your current to-do list, news feeds from online industry magazines or newspapers, and blogs that you subscribe to within your industry. It's a custom page with all of your social media and news feeds coming directly to you.

Netvibes calls itself a "news aggregator," enabling users to aggregate their desired information into one place. This is another place where you can tie it all together.

Clever Ways to Market Your Social Media Sites

What is beginning to happen is that people are networking, socializing, and growing their business and branding nationally by connecting to people on sites such as Twitter and Facebook. They're creating new and different ways to communicate their brand.

Here are a few more ideas to put in your social media marketing toolbox:

- Have a shirt created with your Twitter user name (@_____) on it. Then ask your staff to wear the shirts at events or at your retail location. If you're an entrepreneur and don't have employees, wear the shirt yourself and/ or have your family wear it.

- Have pens made with your Twitter name or a "Connect with me on Facebook" message.

- Have coffee mugs made with a quote and your Twitter name and/or blog name. Send them to clients and prospects. Another idea: have an open house with coffee and give out the mugs.

- Have custom Christmas or holiday cards made that have all of your social media contact information on the back.

- Do a video of the month (or week), and remember at the end to ask viewers to follow you on Twitter, Facebook, and so on.

- Send your top clients, prospects, or business champions a great book, and include custom bookmarks that have your social media information attached.

- Change your answering machine so that you mention your social media platforms during your message ("follow us on Twitter, join our fan page on LinkedIn, and view our channel on YouTube").

- Put your Twitter name and other social media links in your newsletter and/or e-zine.

- In all of your publicity, whether it's an article, a seminar promotion, or phone interview, ensure that at the end you mention one or several of your social media sites. Blogs and newsletters are the number one things to mention because you want to begin capturing names and email addresses.

- Check out fiverr.com. You can hire someone to do anything on this site for $5, including having someone stand on the Eiffel Tower and hold a sign with your Twitter name on it and snap a picture. You can have someone make a video for you and you can have someone retweet your message to their network for, yes … $5.

Here is the screen shot of the fiverr.com page.

A last but important tip: from this point forward, start connecting with fellow Twitterers, Facebook friends, and LinkedIn connections and see if you can do some strategic cross-promotion. Here are some examples: be a guest blogger, be a guest on each other's teleseminars or webinars, or do a seminar together. In other words, make a pact to promote each other's social media sites. It's networking at its finest.

The Least You Need to Know

- In-person networking is not dead and is, in fact, a great way to grow your visibility and build social media connections.
- Products such as Contxts allow us to electronically share contact information.
- Be sure to include your social media sites information in your email signature.
- There are timesaving sites like Ping.fm that enable you to update your status to Facebook, Twitter, LinkedIn, and other sites.
- There are many creative ways to market your social media sites, including T-shirts, pens, and e-zines.

More Ways to Wow Your Audience

In This Chapter

- Join other social networks on a particular topic to meet and network with like-minded people
- Create your own social network … with a little help
- How social networks are becoming more customized
- Using great social networking platforms
- Creative ways to engage your audience

Are you feeling like a social media marketer yet? No doubt you are familiar with and have most likely joined several social media networks, such as LinkedIn, Facebook, Twitter, and YouTube, just to name a few.

In this chapter, we explore other ways to impact your audience and look at the tools and websites that can help you do that. If you have ever thought about creating your own social network and weren't quite sure how to do that, this next section is for you.

There are many additional ways to impact your audience, so let's continue on. Who knows? Perhaps your own social media network could be the next one to have millions of members.

Creating Your Own Social Network

You might not have realized until now that you can have your own social network—literally within a few minutes. If you have a lot of customers or clients and are looking for one portal where you can post questions and share information, then you might want to create your own social network.

Think about it. If you can create a place to listen to your customers, view discussion boards, and read what's on their mind, this would empower you and get you better connected. There are several sites out there that make it easy to create your own social networking platform. Let's look at two of them: Ning and SocialGO.

Ning

Founded in 2004, Ning (www.ning.com) claims to be "the world's largest platform for creating social websites." It is an ever-growing platform enabling anyone to create his or her own social network. As of July 2011, Ning had more than 1.8 million social networks with more than 90,000 Ning sites, with tens of millions of registered users. If you want to create a forum for your customers or create a community for your clients, followers, and fans, Ning may be for you.

With Ning, you can create your own custom social network with your own page design, name, member profiles, photos, event calendars, and more. You also have the ability to make your network public (so anyone can join) or private. You can really create a great sense of community with Ning because you can observe what discussions are taking place. When taking a glance at the Ning network, you will see a multitude of small businesses, entrepreneurs, and special-interest groups. You will see Twitter groups, mom groups, coffee groups, and entrepreneurial groups. And you'll see highly focused groups like fitness, foodies, realtors, and private entrepreneurial groups.

Here's the home page for Ning.

To get started, join the network. Give your name, email address, and other requested information. Then, like the other platforms you have registered for, you will get a confirmation email, and you are in. Ning recently announced a new paid access feature giving site owners new ways to monetize their communities with complete flexibility. In a matter of a few clicks, you can transform your Ning community into a social business.

Look at all of the different categories and try the 30-day free trial. You will see both large and small brands alike utilize this site.

> **TRY THIS**
>
> Perhaps you want to create a site for your mastermind group or for people that have the same interests as you—say opera, or cats, or hiking, or small business. It would be great networking for you and set you up as a leader. Try having a brainstorming meeting with your team or mastermind group and come up with an idea to build your own social community around, and go for it!

Here are some of the things you can do with your Ning site:

- **Branding:** You can have a branded site with your colors and logo and customized tabs.

- **Member creation:** You can have your members create their own unique member profiles. They can upload headshots, bios, and their social media information.

- **Privacy and moderation:** As a site owner you can choose to make your Ning network public or private.

- **Invite and share:** You can invite members via Twitter, through your address book, or by private invitation.

- **Real-time updates:** With this great feature you can see a real-time activity feed of everything happening across your Ning network, including status updates from members. Track activity and encourage more engagement, which members really love. Remember: everyone wants to be validated.

- **RSS feeds:** Another cool feature is that you can pull info from your network, your favorite blog, or your own blog onto the Ning page. The additions can keep your page "sticky" and dynamic as new information will consistently be flowing in.

- **Photos and videos:** Photos can make your site come to life, and with video, it will seem trendy. You can upload videos and have your members upload videos. You can also upload slide shows and presentations.

- **Chat:** You can also enable your members to see who's online and talk in real time with the chat feature. Choose to have chat appear as a persistent bar across the bottom of your Ning network or as a dedicated tab. Be careful that, as the owner of the site, you don't spend too much of your day answering questions. Set specific virtual office hours when members know you are online and may ask you questions.

Here's a sample of a site on Ning. This page is for bird enthusiasts.

Join the group, create an amazing profile, and impact this audience with your information and knowledge.

This is how strategic alliances and partnerships are born. Perhaps you want to begin speaking in your town. Find other speakers on this network who are near you. Connect with them and then arrange an in-person meeting. Perhaps you can develop a joint venture together.

That's one way to use a service like Ning. Want to do business locally and become a contractor in your area code? One social network on Ning that you should know about is Inside Area Codes, a social networking site for every area code in the country. Go to www.insideareacodes.com and click on your state (yes, they include Alaska and Hawaii) and then find your area code.

When you find your area code, click on it and you will be driven to a social networking page. Every small business owner or entrepreneur who wants to do business locally should be on local social networks like this. It's a great way to get on a social media network and meet people in your area code so you can network, get involved, and become known. Check out area code 919 and look at their site. This was amongst the first on Inside Area Codes, and they have a great network of members.

Inside Area Codes has a social networking site through Ning.

Seek out other social networks and join them. Contribute to the conversations. Share information. And consider the idea of creating your own social network.

SocialGO

SocialGO (www.socialgo.com) says it's the "social network maker." It's based in the United Kingdom. Although it is smaller than Ning, it has some of the same features as well as additional ones.

On SocialGo one of the cool features is the live video chat sidebar where you can "dial up" a member and chat live with them through the site. Another good feature is that you have the ability to "white label" your site. This means that no one would know it is a SocialGO platform because people see only your business's branding. *Note:* both of these features are available at the premium level, which requires a small monthly fee. Also, at the fee-based levels you can accept advertising and actually make money from your site. However, at the free level you can still create forums, groups, events, photo sharing, member profiles, and some branding.

Here's the home page on SocialGO.

Another interesting component of SocialGO is that participants can create their own blogs, which can be placed on a SocialGO magazine portal, where they will be displayed with other bloggers on the platform. They have multiple templates to choose from and you can fully interact with your blog readers.

CrowdVine

At CrowdVine (crowdvine.com), many entrepreneurs create their own networking group or even produce a conference. This site allows you to communicate information with your group or conference attendees through an organized portal, which is basically a social network. Founder Tony Stubblebine said his site "helps people get rid of the social anxiety of knowing beforehand who they can connect with at [a] conference."

It also helps promote your conference because would-be attendees get "social proof" of who is attending, and they want to be a part of the event. The other great feature around this site is that when you create your account, you give your Twitter, Facebook, and other social media information. When you register for a conference that is using CrowdVine, the site will tell you who in your social media communities (or even your Google Mail or your Outlook contacts) is attending the same group meeting or conference. The site is also very user-friendly. This is a must-have tool for your conference.

Here's the CrowdVine home page.

More Reasons to Create Your Own Social Network

You already probably realize that having your own social network is a great marketing tool. But just in case you need more reasons why you'd want to do this, here are a few:

- You want a private community for your clients or customers.

- You want to create a public community for your fans.

- You want to further establish yourself as an expert in your industry.

- You want to easily communicate with your clients in an organized way.

- You want to create a membership portal for your business.

- You want to use the latest technology to further market your brand.

- You want your customers to be able to communicate with each other.

- You want to expand your reach nationally or globally and combine those folks in one portal.

- You want to use a site like CrowdVine to allow your group or conference attendees to meet and socialize beforehand.

- You want to create a site that is a central hub for discussion in your industry or around your business.

Other Social Networks to Consider

You're probably quite surprised at just how many social networks there are. Well, we're not done yet! Here are some more social networks that you might find useful for your social media marketing efforts.

PerfectBusiness and StartupNation

PerfectBusiness (perfectbusiness.com) is the place to be seen for serious entrepreneurs, investors, and experts in a variety of industries. Here, you might just meet potential strategic partners, mentors, and advisors. There's a video center and a nice learning portal that provides resources for you. There are also free and additional services for a fee at upgraded levels. It's a rich and robust platform.

StartupNation (www.startupnation.com) is for new entrepreneurial startups and small businesses that want to grow and connect with others. On this site, you can connect with other entrepreneurs and learn from experts and their blogs. There are many blogs, articles, and podcasts, as well as many forums and groups for business owners to participate in.

They have a great dashboard that is easy to use. It's a very rich site with incredible tools, resources, and a community feel. Also, check out the Community tab, which is a great place to find local connections forums and even classifieds from your area.

> **NETIQUETTE**
>
> Most of the sites featured in this chapter are getting very serious about spamming. They encourage their members to report spammers and will not tolerate it. Don't lose your memberships on sites because you want to sell, sell, sell. Sales success will come naturally as you continue to participate and share. Focus on building relationships.

PartnerUp and Meetup

There are two additional social networks to examine: PartnerUp and Meetup. PartnerUp (www.partnerup.com) is for entrepreneurs and small business owners who are searching for specific business resources. You can find commercial real estate for your next big move and find both professional service providers and vendors who will help keep your business on track. Just like on the other sites, you'll also find a personal profile page, forums, and a place to ask and answer questions.

Are you looking for new ways to meet people to network with and grow your business and connections? Or do you want to create your own live group or "meetup"? Meetup (www.meetup.com) does just that. No longer will you have the excuse that you can't seem to find networking groups to attend or that you can't afford them. Many on Meetup are free. Claimed to be the "largest network of local groups," Meetup has thousands of meetups based on hundreds of topics, all happening all the time.

With 6 million monthly visitors, 7.2 million members, and 80,000 meetup groups, you are bound to find something of interest. Whether you're a book lover, wine enthusiast, or entrepreneur, at Meetup there is something for you. Consider going to meetups that are not in your industry. You might meet interesting people this way. Sure, an entrepreneurial or small business marketing meetup is great and good to attend, but also consider a sports car meetup, a movie enthusiast meetup, or a book lover meetup. Again, you never know where your next business partner, client, or business supporter will come from.

Another creative way to use Meetup for your business is to create your own meetup. By creating your own, you set yourself up as a leader, and you will start to become a power networker.

Here's the home page for Meetup.

Entertaining Ways to Engage Your Audience

The world of social media gives you unique opportunities to be creative with the ways you engage your clients, customers, or followers. You're only limited by your imagination. Take a look at the following sites and you'll probably get some new ideas.

Creating a Channel on iTunes

Yes, iTunes is not just for rock stars anymore. Did you know many experts, coaches, and consultants have their own channel on iTunes? It's another great way not only to reach new potential clients, but to be seen and heard. There are literally thousands of "shows," and you can have one, too! First you go to the iTunes page. Then go to the bottom of the page and find the iTunes Store section. Then scroll down and click on **Browse iTunes store**. The iTunes Preview page will pop up. Next click **Podcasts** and see all of the categories. Let's click on the business category. From here you will see a list of hundreds of shows ranked by popularity or by alphabetical order.

Search your category. This is the Business channel.

Here is a screen shot of the business channels on iTunes.

UserVoice

UserVoice (uservoice.com) allows you to really monitor and listen to what your customers are saying. You can get them to vote on ideas, share, and give new ideas. And you can respond to all of them in one "uservoice," or forum. You can integrate this product into your website by installing one of the widgets (by copying and pasting code into your website). If you need to have your webmaster install it, that's okay, too. You can now capture feedback and ideas directly from your clients.

Remember that people want to feel connected, so this might be another tool to consider when trying to engage and listen to your audience. Note that prices range from free to upper-tier, so be sure to read about the pricing structures and consider the costs and benefits.

Here's the home page for UserVoice.

FireText

Text messaging entertainment is a new buzzword you may be hearing. As you know, adults and teens are using texting along with social media. It was just a matter of time before businesses developed a way to use texting for entertainment and advertising. FireText (firetext.com) is used by everyone from speakers and churches, to conferences and night clubs. It allows customers and audiences to interact via text at the venue and actually makes the event more social. It also allows venues to instantly interact and/or alert audiences with updated information.

For instance, if you are speaking, the "Tweet to Screen" feature allows shy audience members to "text" the speaker a question to appear on a large screen. If you have a sponsor at your meeting or event, you can place the sponsor's hashtag in the software.

While you are speaking, any tweet from around the globe that mentions the sponsor will stream in live. The sponsor will love it (assuming they are all good tweets, but usually they are). FireText is always updating its software, so be on the lookout for the latest features. One other great benefit is that with texting, you can begin to build a database of phone numbers.

Here's a sample screen shot from FireText.

Using Social Media for Contests

Contests involve fun interaction. Here are additional ways to engage your audience on a variety of social media platforms:

- Create a link that promotes a sale or a special promotion. Tell your Twitter followers that the first 30 people who retweet that link will get a coupon or a prize.

- Have people send in a video (with their digital camera) as to why people should use your product or service. The top video gets a great prize from your business.

- Tell friends and followers that the next 10 new clients will be featured in your blog.

- Have an Internet radio show? Tell your audience that your next big referral partner or next new business client will get 20 minutes of airtime on your next radio show to talk about his or her own business.

- Have a dental office or restaurant or photo studio? Get out your digital camera and take pictures of your clients and patrons and ask them to do a funny pose. Have a photo contest encouraging the social media audience to vote for their favorite picture. Post it on video sites, Twitter, Facebook, and LinkedIn. (*Note:* if you're a dentist, make sure the patient's mouth isn't still numb!)

- Work with teens or tweens? Have them do an online video as to why they like your business. Post it to your social media sites. (Remember, if they're under 18, you need parental permission.)

- Post a status update on Facebook and ask a question. Tell them the first 20 people who reply will get placed in a drawing for a free certificate to try out your service.

- Are you an author who just published your first book? Ask readers to send in a video or comment on your blog as to what they got out of the book or why they liked it. Take your best testimonials and interview them as part of your blog, radio show, or e-zine. Ask them to tweet about your book.

- Create a meetup and the first 10 people who arrive get a coffee gift certificate, a prize, or a discount on your fees. Or even feature them as guest bloggers on your blog.

You've gotten some great ideas in this chapter, and I'll bet you come up with some creative ones on your own. Have fun with it!

The Least You Need to Know

- Social networks are becoming more individual and industry-specific to their audiences.

- Many social networking companies enable you to both join individual social networks and create your own.

- Many social networking sites are rich with content for the entrepreneur or small business owner. The more you can build community around your business, the better it will be.

- Your followers, fans, and clients want to be entertained, so get creative with the social media sites by using contests, iTunes channels, and your own social network.

Writing and Marketing Your Articles, E-Zines, and Books

In This Chapter

- How to build an "expert" mind-set
- Learn that published articles, whether online or in print, are one of the best ways to build instant credibility
- Ideas on how to begin your first article
- Companies that can help you with your electronic email/newsletter marketing
- Ten creative ways to build your e-zine subscriber list

One of the best ways to build credibility for your business is to begin writing so your customers and prospects can begin reading about you and finding you online. I often tell my clients that one of the first things people will do when they consider working with you is Google your name. What pops up on the screen? Are there articles, stories, and newsletters you've written? If not, read on and you will discover easy and effective ways to get yourself published online.

You, the Expert Author

Most people don't necessarily think of themselves as an expert, but as a business owner, you need to begin believing that you are. You are an expert in your industry. You are the expert in what you do, whether you are an architect, Realtor, coach, actor, financial planner, artist, speaker, chef, mom, lawyer, interior designer, consultant, or car salesperson.

People want someone they can rely on, and that is why they will pay you for what you do. More importantly, from a business development standpoint, the more people read about your expertise, the more they'll be attracted to your business. This leads to your website, subscribing to your blog or newsletter, and then, perhaps, ultimately hiring you.

One way to build instant credibility is to get an article or two published. If you write an article, it could potentially be read by hundreds, if not thousands, of readers. And it's easier than you might think.

If you are not sure what you could write about for your first few articles, let's do a little brainstorming. Ask yourself the following questions:

- What three tips can you share about your industry?

- What three things can you share with people to help them avoid a certain pain in their life? Can you help them with a financial, job, health, home, car, travel, legal, business, or real estate problem?

- What three questions should people consider before hiring someone like you? In other words, what are prospects looking for? Are they interested in credentials, testimonials, or examples of your work?

- What are the latest trends in your industry?

- What are the five biggest mistakes people make when hiring the wrong _____ (fill in the blank with your industry/title)?

- What experience have you had that would benefit others if you shared it? Share a big learning experience and be relatable.

- Five ways to _____ (you fill in the blank). Examples: five ways to change your home, five ways to have better fitness, five ways to a better job, five ways to a better vacation, five ways to upgrade your home for under $1,000, and so on.

These are just some examples of what you can write about to highlight your expertise in your subject or industry. Smaller articles of 300 to 600 words are easy for readers to quickly digest, so that might be a good starting point.

Okay, let's get your article online. This way, when people Google your name, your article will pop up as an "expert author" in your industry. One site I'd like to direct you to that will do this for you is EzineArticles (ezinearticles.com). Through their website, you can submit up to 10 articles for free; after that, you can upgrade to a platinum member status for a fee.

To create your account, go to www.ezinearticles.com and click on **Join**. You can click on the audio links to get detailed instructions. After you're done, you will get a confirmation email. If you have questions, review the editorial guidelines. They also have a good video tutorial and provide newsletters to assist you.

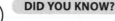

Here's the home page for EzineArticles.

Be sure you select a category that is closest to your article content versus your business. The title is key, so make the first three words in your article title very strong. Search engines love the first three words and the keywords. Your article content is where you share and give information. There's no selling here.

After your article has been accepted (and it will only be accepted if you are giving information to help people, not shamelessly self-promoting), try to submit another. Remember, you have up to 10 to submit before you can be upgraded to a platinum member. Over time, I encourage you to go back into the site, click on your article stats, and see how many people viewed your article and how many people clicked on your website.

Another way to get an article published online is to be a guest contributor to another person's blog or newsletter. This is a great marketing strategy. Let's say you own a dog-walking business. You could approach a local veterinarian and see if he or she has a newsletter; if so, ask if you can be a contributing writer. Chances are the answer will be yes.

Another option is to check with a neighborhood newsletter or even a small-town magazine. In exchange for submitting an article, ask if you can put your name, website, and email address at the end of the article. Oh, and don't forget to add your Twitter user name, too.

Newsletters, E-Newsletters, and E-Zines

There was a time when print newsletters were all the rage. Now it seems everything has gone online. But the counter viewpoint is also true. Because there's so much online, if you did mail a newsletter, chances are pretty high that it will at least get looked at ... and maybe even be read.

What many entrepreneurs are doing now is publishing their own print newsletter quarterly to save a bit of money. If you can do one monthly, that is great. But printing a newsletter and mailing it can get expensive, so let's examine some additional options.

E-Newsletters and E-Zines

An e-newsletter is an electronic or digital newsletter. An e-zine is really the same thing. The "e" stands for electronic and the "zine" is the last syllable of magazine.

Many define it as an electronic magazine because an e-zine should have a more visual component, such as color, art, and photographs. In contrast, an e-newsletter is more like a newspaper with more words and fewer graphics. The line can be easily blurred for some, but it's important to know the two terms and how they differ. We examine the e-zine in the next few sections.

As you get into social media marketing, you might get asked if you have an e-zine or e-newsletter. Earlier in the book, I mentioned several times that building your list is important. One of the reasons is that you will want to stay in touch with your customers, clients, and fans from your social media sites by publishing a regular e-zine.

By regularly communicating with your followers, you continue to build credibility by sharing your expertise. Another big bonus is that if your e-zine is good and you truly give great information, over time you are not only building credibility but you are creating loyalty. There is nothing like a loyal fan of your business—they'll stick with you.

When you offer a 30-percent-off special or a two-for-one promotion, or want to promote your book, chances are loyal readers of your e-zine will either buy it, or at least tell everyone in their network that they should buy it. It's better for you to keep your name in front of people and stay on the top of their minds—better you than your competition.

> **DID YOU KNOW?**
>
> Sending out an e-newsletter or e-zine is also referred to as email marketing. To find additional service providers to help you distribute your e-newsletter or e-zine, you might want to look under email marketing solutions. If someone asks if you participate in email marketing, you now know what that is. The best way to have a successful e-zine is to include quality content and distribute it weekly.

Resources to Help You Create Your E-Zine

There are many reputable email marketing solution providers who can help distribute your e-zine or e-newsletter. Most will also provide you with amazing analytics so you can see how many people opened the email, how many opted out, how many forwarded your e-zine, and so on.

Constant Contact and VerticalResponse

Constant Contact (www.constantcontact.com) provides great templates, wonderful training, and powerful customer service. Free customer support is another benefit that comes with this site.

VerticalResponse (www.verticalresponse.com) is another popular newsletter tool. Members get the first 500 distributed copies for free through the email. Once over 500 you pay by number of copies that you distribute to. It also has a great tracking component to its system.

MailChimp and iContact

With over 30,000 new users per month and more than 400,000 users as of this writing, MailChimp (mailchimp.com) is popular and has a lot of good features. This tool has great email design templates, Facebook integration, and smartphone integration. It also uses something called Social States, which makes it easy for users to integrate their campaigns with social networks and find out who's tweeting about your newsletter. Another interesting feature with its reports is that you can find out not only who received your email (as you most likely will not know personally everyone who is receiving your newsletter), but where the recipient is located geographically which is powerful information.

iContact (www.icontact.com) is a powerhouse. It is regularly used with small business owners as well as Fortune 500 companies. It has hundreds of template designs for you to choose from. This site is worth a look.

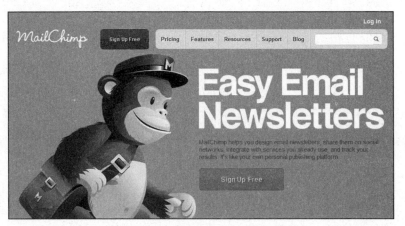

This is the home page for MailChimp.

1ShoppingCart and Infusionsoft

1ShoppingCart (www.1shoppingcart.com) not only allows you to integrate your direct marketing, but provides a whole host of other service offerings. It has email broadcasting, autoresponder email services, ad tracking tools, shopping cart links, online payments, affiliate program tracking (for those of you who want affiliates to resell your services), and so much more. 1ShoppingCart is one of the top-rated total solutions for Internet marketers.

Infusionsoft's (www.infusionsoft.com) claim is to "help your marketing happen automatically." How do they do all this? By automating your follow-ups, managing your contacts, and helping you send targeted emails with powerful reporting.

Infusionsoft supports tens of thousands of users. This is a sophisticated and robust email marketing system with CRM, email marketing, and e-commerce. It integrates these features into one system.

Tips for a Successful E-Zine

Keep the tone of the e-zine conversational and write as if you were talking. How often you want to send your e-zine to people is up to you. Some people send e-zines quarterly, monthly, bimonthly, or weekly. I deliver mine weekly. It builds loyalty and people look forward to it. And maintaining a weekly schedule keeps me on my toes because every week I need to communicate good information that will help businesses grow.

> **DID YOU KNOW?**
>
> An International Standard Serial Number, known as an ISSN, is an eight-digit code or series of numbers that provides an identifying mark for your publication. An ISSN is not vital for your e-zine or e-newsletter, but it is an idea worth considering. Having an ISSN can lend credibility to your publication. The best way to obtain an ISSN in the United States is at the Library of Congress site (lcweb.loc.gov/issn).

An e-zine, whether weekly or monthly, allows you another forum in which to communicate with your friends, fans, and followers. While this is not a general Internet marketing book, I will review just a few of the many pointers that will help you produce a successful e-zine:

- Promote it everywhere—in your email signature, blog, website, letters, and business cards. The point of the e-zine is to build your list or subscriber base.

- Whichever service you use to deliver your e-zine, make sure you have a good thank-you message that is automatically sent to subscribers when they sign up.

- Write as if you are speaking to your audience. Keep it conversational, less formal, and use real-world scenarios. Include photos and color, if you can. Put a copyright notice at the end of each issue.

- More and more e-zines are including video—consider it for yours. Infotain your readers, give them information in an entertaining way.

- Look at your stats. How many are opening your e-zine? How many are forwarding it? What you can analyze, though, will depend on the service you're using. If possible, find out if people are subscribing to your newsletter regularly. Are they unsubscribing? You should be getting new readers each week.

- Put your social media links and sites in your e-zine, asking readers to follow you on Twitter, connect with you on LinkedIn, join your group on Facebook, and so on. Remember, everything is circling back around to each other.

- Look at other e-zines that you receive. What do you like most about them? Dislike? Try to deliver something you would read, and the followers will come.

- Have a great subject line in your email so recipients will open it. Keep it short yet strong. Hint: Look at magazine headlines for ideas!

- End your e-zine with an author's box describing who you are. Include the name of your business and a short bio.

One cardinal rule about sending your e-zine: it should be sent only to people who subscribe. You should not be a *spammer* and send your e-zine to people who have not asked for it. Send it to people who want the e-zine, not to those whom you happen to sign up only because you have their business card.

And one more tip: take a look at e-zine directories. Early in this chapter, it was mentioned that you should get your e-zine placed into certain directories. This will help you become more findable on the Internet. A great website that provides a top-20 list of directories is www.ezines.nettop20.com.

> **DEFINITION**
>
> A **spammer** is one who sends unsolicited email to people.

Ways to Build Your E-Zine List

Now that you have a terrific e-zine, you want to get it out there and grow your subscriber list. Here are a few ideas:

- Put your e-zine/e-newsletter sign-up box at the top of your website and Facebook business page.

- When first starting out, ask colleagues and friends to subscribe. Ask them if they'd like to forward to people they think will benefit from reading it.

- Tell all of your new customers and clients that they will get a complimentary subscription to your e-zine.

- Offer new subscribers a free gift such as a CD of tips, a discount on one of your products, a free report of some kind, advanced news on new releases or products, and so on.

- Look at online forums where people who are similar to your subscriber base hang out. Participate in the forum and list your website and e-zine information.

- If you are an independent professional, put your e-zine info on everything. Put it on cards, invoices, and promo material. Example: "For weekly (your industry) tips, get my content-rich e-zine."

- Get with other business alliance partners and agree to cross-promote each other's e-zines. You can recommend their e-zines in your e-zine, and then they can return the favor.

- If you do any speaking, offer a giveaway when you are done speaking. Tell everyone in the audience who submits their business card for the giveaway that they will also get a complimentary subscription to your e-zine.

- If you have a reception area or checkout counter, put a bowl or a booklet out that reads, "We want to stay in touch with you. Sign up for our monthly e-zine for specials and great information."

- Mention it in your blog and YouTube videos, and tweet about it from time to time. Also, remember your Facebook page? Remind people about your e-zine in that box below your photo or in your information summary page. Invite people to become subscribers on your LinkedIn page as well.

ONLINE CAUTION

Make sure your e-zine or e-newsletter is readable on mobile apps. Soon there will be more people viewing your e-zine on their mobile device than on a computer. By 2013 more people will be reading on a mobile device than on a computer as the laptops will begin to disappear and more people will want to access info with handheld or pocket devices.

Self-Publishing a Book

Want to take your writing to another level? How about considering self-publishing or creating an e-book? Of course, if the big publishing houses come calling along with an interested literary agent, that's great. However, many entrepreneurs don't know that they can still get a book published without an agent or signing a six-figure book deal.

You can self-publish your own book. This means that you write it and get it published or printed on your own and then market it yourself. There are many publishing resources out there to help you. Although this isn't a book on becoming an author,

I thought this might be good to mention because writing is a big part of social media marketing. And if you have a book, you can promote it on all of your social media sites.

Imagine, now that you have all of these great vehicles to share your expertise, what it would be like to capture your expertise in your very own book. By self-publishing a book, chances are you will gain expert status in the eyes of your clients and prospects. And you will also establish greater credibility and generate a lot of publicity for yourself and your business.

You might be thinking that you could never write a book. Well, did you ever think you could write a blog? What many self-published authors are doing is taking their blog posts and turning them into chapters in their self-published book. Another idea is to take articles that are in your e-zine or newsletter and use those as chapter guides for your book.

If you are a dentist, doctor, lawyer, artist, fitness coach, chef, business coach, speaker, photographer, or decorator, how great would it be to hand your book to new or prospective clients who are looking to work with you? For example, one time I visited a new dermatologist, and as part of the welcome kit, I received a copy of her book. I was very impressed, because not only was it a great book, but no other doctor had ever given me a book as part of a welcome package.

Book coach Sam Horn (www.samhorn.com), who's also the 17-time Maui-Hawaii Writers Conference emcee and author, has helped thousands of entrepreneurs become authors. She's fond of saying, "I have never met any authors who were sorry they wrote their book. I've only met authors who were sorry they didn't write it … *sooner!*"

Donna Kozik, who helps professionals write and self-publish their first books (www. mybigbusinesscard.com), says, "Self-publishing a book is a great way to capitalize on your message and business or life philosophy." And it's one of the best business cards you will ever have. So consider self-publishing. There are many businesses that will help you get your book published.

The Least You Need to Know

- Writing articles on sites like EzineArticles will help establish you as an expert author in your industry.
- If writing articles seems daunting at first, try simply writing about three to five things that people need to know about your industry.

- There are many email service providers that make it easy to help you electronically gather email addresses and deliver your e-zine/e-newsletter to subscribers.

- Your electronic newsletter or e-zine should be professional, conversational in tone, and include links to your other social media sites. It helps you build a relationship with your readers.

- You, too, can be an author. You can self-publish a book and it will give your business and brand a professional boost.

Time Strategies to Get It All Done

In This Chapter

- Gain better mind-set strategies
- Learn about time-saving tools and ideas
- Manage your social media time
- Discover the world of virtual assistants

Okay, so now you're on your way to becoming an expert on social media marketing. You've learned a great deal and now you're probably wondering, "How do I manage my time on so many different social media networking sites?" Well, this chapter is here to show you how. Keep in mind that it is important to make time, because this is where your clients and prospects are spending their time.

Mind-Set Strategies

Let me just say this: don't panic. You may feel you have to do it all and know it all today, but you don't. You have this book and now you are in the know. You might be thinking, "I've got to get a headshot, video camera, set up a Twitter account, consider a Facebook fan page, produce videos, and, oh yeah, determine my strategy."

Just step back and take a deep breath. Think about what you want to get out of social media. Ask yourself, "What is your why?" Start with one site, get comfortable, and then try another. Remember that we talked about mind-set in previous chapters. Well, having the right mind-set as you become involved in social media is key. Stay focused, but don't worry about the number of friends you have online or the number of followers you get the first week. This isn't a race, it's your business. But you must become social because your competitors are, and they are gaining market share.

Focus on Sending Out High-Quality Messages

Remember, people don't necessarily care about what you had for breakfast. Share tips and tell them what you're working on (without giving away your trade secrets). Give them a glance inside your business. You'll be amazed over time what that will do. And don't forget to share useful links and highly relevant updates. Be interesting and interested. If you continue to send out high-quality messaging, you will build credibility with your followers which will ultimately lead to more business.

Ask yourself before hitting the send button, "Is this something that people might want to hear? Will they pass it along and will they find it valuable?" If the answer is yes, then you are on the right track. Remember, all of your updates will be online … forever. It gets tempting to vent or express what you are feeling at the moment, but if you focus on quality relevant updates, you will have nothing to worry about.

Watch Your Time

Be selective about how you spend your time. Many people put a timer next to their computer so they don't get drawn in. Sometimes, before you know it, an hour has gone by. After you have your social media sites set up, log on to Twitter, post an update, and check your Direct Messages.

Then, log on to Facebook and post a status update and check your inbox. Next, log in to LinkedIn and post a status update and check your inbox. Time spent so far? About 15 minutes.

If you are really in a pinch, you can save time by using Ping.fm to shoot out the same message to all of your sites. Check into Ping.fm in the morning and again at night.

Have Realistic Expectations

Many people set up accounts on these platforms and expect the cash register to begin ringing within the first 30 days. It doesn't really happen like that. It takes time to build trust and credibility. The first 120 days are critical to building rapport so it's important to show up.

Review your experience either monthly or quarterly. Think about which social media sites you are getting the most value from, but give it time initially. Look at your web stats from your website hosting provider to see where people are coming from, but don't give up any of them yet. Give it a good six months to see where you are achieving success and feeling confident. You might be comfortable with one form of social networking, or you might feel at ease on several.

For example, you might find that having a blog is working well for you; however, you are not quite ready for video yet. And that's okay. Be realistic and take it slow if you need to.

Learn to Skim

After you have TweetDeck, Facebook, and LinkedIn running (and you are participating in groups and business pages), you just can't read it all or it will turn into a full-time job for you. Over time, you will know your favorites and the people that you want to follow. These are the sites or the people who provide you great value. Focus on them.

Don't feel you need to read it all. The same advice goes for videos. Over time, you will begin getting a lot of videos. After a while, you will start to learn which videos from certain people provide value to you. Focus on these videos and don't worry about the rest.

Reach Out

Some amazing alliances will be formed, but you will need to reach out. Reach out to people you seem to enjoy following, those you have something in common with, or those you just want to get to know better. That's what a lot of this is about. You're expanding your network of influence.

Arrange a time to speak on the phone with one of the followers you feel comfortable with. Ask questions about this person's business and where he or she is trying to take it.

Time-Saving Tools and Ideas

With all of these Internet tools to help you market your business and expand your networks, you might find that you are busier and more overwhelmed than ever. Here's a tip for you: the more you can consolidate or leverage your time, the better focused you will be.

> **TRY THIS**
>
> Sign up for a bit.ly account. This is a URL shortening service that tracks all of the links you create, as well as shortening long links. It also saves all the short links you create to save you time in the future. Try it! The website is http://bit.ly. *Note:* while this is a great tool, there is a trend now toward opening links that spell out the URL because of all the viruses online.

Here is a list of ideas to help you manage your social media marketing time:

- When scheduling a meeting, think about whether it makes sense to meet in person or if it would be more efficient to schedule a web meeting or teleconference. If you're a home-based business owner, don't be a hermit. At least get out one time per week for a networking event or an in-person meeting.

- As mentioned previously, when you want to update your social media networks quickly, use Ping.fm. Another site that simultaneously updates social networks is Hellotxt (hellotxt.com). Try not to overuse this feature though. There is a trend to not overautomate or autopost.

- Use news aggregators, such as Netvibes, to combine all your feeds and news into one landing page. Make it your home page. This way you can easily scan the news, your incoming blogs, and your social media messages.

- If it is possible, check your voicemail only three times per day: morning, noon, and evening. This will allow you to focus on your business. Use a tool called Onebox (www.new.onebox.com) to help with your call management.

- Update your Twitter, Facebook, and LinkedIn sites in the morning and at the end of the day—20 minutes in the morning and 20 minutes in the evening, and a little less—perhaps 10 to 15 minutes—around noontime.

- If you must automate your welcome message on Twitter for all new followers, use SocialOomph. But don't automate too much, as you will lose credibility for being too impersonal.

- Make three appointments with yourself each week to post on your blog. Or write three blog entries at one time and then post them on three different days.

- Get an intern to help you with posting information, answering new friend requests, and uploading videos. But remember, young interns are not as business savvy as you are. It's your business. Stay on top of it.

- Write a week's worth of blog posts and updates at one time if that's your style. Tweet about the topics with a link to your blog. Post a link on Facebook and LinkedIn as well.

- Get a *virtual assistant* to help you with your social media marketing. While the tone and the wording should come from you, an assistant can help you implement your strategies. An assistant can also provide you with weekly reports, such as how many new followers you have, the number of retweets, how many joined your fan page, and so on. We'll talk more about this later in this chapter.

DEFINITION

A **virtual assistant**, known as a VA, is a person who provides professional support to assist their clients. A VA is usually someone who works from home for an entrepreneur or a small business owner and can provide many services, such as social media marketing and web development.

DID YOU KNOW?

Do you like those little yellow Post-It notes? Do you have them on your desk or computer right now? Well, they've gone virtual as well. Check out Zhorn Software (www.zhornsoftware.co.uk/stickies). It's a cute time-saving utility tool that allows you to post notes on your computer screen. You can pick the color and size. After trying this, you can say you've gone green.

NudgeMail

This tool sends an email reminder to your mobile phone or inbox. If you organize your life through email, go to www.nudgemail.com for a great application.

This is the home page of NudgeMail.

Tungle.Me

Make your calendar a digital calendar. How many times do you go back and forth with someone, leaving voicemails, sending emails, playing phone tag, just to come up with a date and time to connect? Tungle.me helps alleviate this. The tool allows clients and prospects access to your calendar with times that *only you* allow them to see. The client then schedules the time automatically via digital calendaring through email or mobile access. You then get the information, give a thumbs-up, and you've got a business date!

Here is the website for Tungle.me.

TimeTrade

TimeTrade (www.timetrade.com) is another time-saving tool. The appointment scheduling software has a fee, but it is worth it if you are in the business of scheduling a lot of appointments (say, for a salon, a dental office, or a bridal salon).

This is the home page of TimeTrade.com.

TrafficGeyser

You've worked hard to start your business, and you may offer the best service and most unique product that everyone should have their hands on. You want to get the word out quickly to a lot of people. Obviously, by now you know social media marketing can truly help you get the word out, and there are many products that can help you accelerate that.

We know now that the more findable you are and the easier you make it for people to get to know you, the greater the chance your business has of being successful. That said, it takes a lot of effort and time to manually distribute your information on the Internet, and we've mentioned several sites throughout this book that will automate the process for you.

TrafficGeyser (trafficgeyser.com) is a service that seems to solve the distribution issue. It charges monthly fees, but there are a variety of affordable price levels to choose from. This solution helps entrepreneurs and small business owners save time by helping them distribute many of their social media marketing products to various online channels.

Onebox

Onebox (www.new.onebox.com) is a terrific phone management tool. It makes your small business appear bigger, with multiple lines and an auto attendant, professional greeting, call routing, and, most importantly, easy voice message organizing and streamlining. One of the great features is that it will send a voicemail message to your inbox, so all your voicemails can go to your email or turn your voicemail into text. No more spending time listening to all of your messages—now you can read them and save time.

This is the home page of Onebox.

Sample Social Media Marketing Timeline

By no means is this the only way to manage your social media marketing when you are first starting out, but it's a sample timeline to give you an idea of how to organize your time. You want to get the benefit of marketing your business and brand using social media, without it taking over your entire day. One could obviously take this to higher levels, but here is a "basic" starter timeline. (Note that times will vary depending on how big your network is.)

- Monday morning: Send out a Facebook, Twitter, and LinkedIn status update. Check your inbox on Facebook and LinkedIn. Post a quick 30 second video sharing a tip. Time: 20 minutes

- Monday afternoon: Post a previously written blog update. Time: 5 minutes

- Monday evening: Check your Facebook inbox and profile page for comments. Respond to comments. Check friend requests. Check Twitter for retweets and messages. Post a new update. Time: 15 minutes

- Tuesday morning: Send out updates to all sites via Ping.fm. Check messages on Twitter, Facebook, and LinkedIn. Time: 15 minutes

- Tuesday evening: Check inbox and comments on all sites (Facebook, LinkedIn, and Twitter). Be sure to acknowledge others. Time: 15 minutes

- Wednesday morning: Send out Facebook, Twitter, and LinkedIn status updates. Check your inbox on all sites. Go onto LinkedIn and look at discussions within the groups you are a part of. Add to the discussion. Time: 10–20 minutes

- Wednesday afternoon: Write an article for your e-zine. Send it to a virtual assistant for posting.

- Wednesday evening: Check friend requests on Facebook. Look at inbox and respond to wall comments. Check direct messages on all sites. Time: 15 minutes

- Thursday morning: Update status on all sites via Ping.fm. Check Twitter direct messages. Look at blog comments. Send out your prewritten newsletter. Review and send out your e-zine. Time: 25–30 minutes

- Thursday evening: Check your inboxes on all sites. Respond to Twitter messages. Send out a tweet, look at blog comments, and check the discussions on LinkedIn. Time: 20 minutes

- Friday morning: Update your status on all sites. Get out the videocam. Record a 30-second tip. Post to Facebook, Twitter, and YouTube. Time: 20 minutes

- Friday afternoon: Post to blog (prewritten). Respond to blog comments. Send a tweet and respond to direct messages on Twitter. Log in to Facebook and LinkedIn to review comments and Messages. Run a report on your newsletter to see the open rate. Time: 30 minutes

- Friday evening: You've connected to a lot of people this week and many people are receiving your branding messages and understanding your expertise. Check direct messages and update status via Ping.fm. Time: 15 minutes

- Weekends: Post a tweet and update your status each day if you can. Stay visible. And unless you choose to write it during the week, one idea is to try to write your blog and newsletter/e-zine over the weekend so you can simply post it during the week. Time: 30 to 60 minutes

Congratulate yourself! And take note: it's good to alternate your times that you post your status updates. You will reach different people by doing so. Business success tip: Remember to pick up the phone and call people as well to ask how you can be of service to them. Watch what happens.

Virtual Assistants

Never heard of a virtual assistant? No, it's not a robot. The virtual assistant industry is still an emerging industry, but the entrepreneurs and small business owners who use them say it's one of the best investments they have ever made for themselves.

When you Google "virtual assistant," you will see virtual receptionist, virtual phone assistant, and virtual office assistant. With all of this technology available to you, it's important to know that you can have real people help you with your business. They just won't physically be in your office; they work virtually for you from their home office, whether it be 5 minutes away or 5,000 miles. There are tens of thousands of virtual assistants. I'm sure you can find one for you. Just begin searching.

A virtual assistant can help you respond to emails, post your status updates, and create your social media sites. He or she can also schedule meetings, plan events, maintain records, schedule appointments and interviews, and so much more. Many entrepreneurs have a VA do most of their administrative tasks so that they themselves can manage the social media which is an idea I like.

Some entrepreneurs ask their VA to do both administrative duties and help run the social media. Many power social media users who have tens of thousands of followers have a virtual assistant (maybe plural!) to help them manage the administrative side of their businesses behind the scenes.

To find a virtual assistant, you can check out the International Virtual Assistants Association at www.ivaa.org. You can also check out AssistU at www.assistu.org. ODesk (www.odesk.com) and VADirectory.net all have great information.

Virtual Phone Assistants

There are many of these types of services out there that help with your phone issues. As an entrepreneur or small business owner, your phone presence is key to your overall marketing, and having a virtual phone assistant should not be overlooked as another place to market to clients. For example, your voicemail greeting is very important.

In the spirit of getting it all done, you might consider a solution like this if you are a one-person show or you run a small business office. Consider a phone service that will automatically answer your calls, particularly if you travel often or are in frequent meetings. Services like this will give the caller prompts as to what the call is in regard to and then direct that call to the appropriate person (or line) based on what the caller is looking for.

While this really doesn't have much to do with social media per se, we would encourage you to make the most of your voicemail. For instance, mention one of the following: "Let's connect on Twitter @_____," "We'd love you to join our Facebook community," or "Make sure you see our blog, called _____."

Having an automated system that will track you down to deliver the call either by text or by voicemail will certainly help save time.

Password Management

Not all of us are gifted at organization. How many times have you had to ask the system to retrieve your user names and passwords to certain websites? Well, sometimes it was because you simply couldn't remember the password. Now that you're involved in social media, it can be a real problem—you have been introduced to so many social media marketing sites, and all of them require user names and passwords. It's no wonder that you might get confused. RoboForm (roboform.com) is a tool that can help you manage it all.

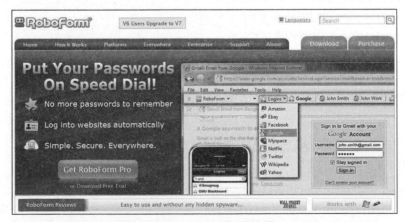

Here's the home page for RoboForm.

RoboForm helps remember your passwords for you by giving you an online "place" to put them. This password management software not only manages all of your passwords, but also fills in all those site registration forms, backs up your passwords, and more. I'm sure there are other programs out there, but this seems like a good one to at least check out.

The Least You Need to Know

- Try one social media site at a time so you don't panic or feel overwhelmed.
- Set realistic expectations for the amount of time you spend on sites and try to use timesaving shortcuts and tools to help you.
- Schedule social media in the morning and evening and write blogs over the weekend if you can.
- Consider using a virtual assistant to help you with social media or other administrative tasks.
- Reflect at the end of the week on all the new connections you made and give yourself a pat on the back!

Glossary

avatar   An image, photo, logo, or user name that represents a person online.

bit.ly   A free URL shortening service that provides viewer statistics for the links you shorten online.

blog   Created from the words "web log," blogs are usually composed of regular commentary or written entries by an individual online. Entries are kept in chronological order.

blogosphere   The blogging universe, in general. If you blog, you are part of the collective blogosphere.

BlogTalkRadio   A free web application that allows users to host and create their own online radio show.

business champions   People who always give you a great reference and are high-powered networkers who sing your praises. They can also serve as your strategic partners, so that no matter who they are talking to, when the opportunity arises, they will bring up your name.

chat   Refers to communication over the Internet. Live chat is in real time. It traditionally refers to one-on-one communication via the written word through social online applications.

collective intelligence   Knowledge that develops from a collaboration of many individuals creating ideas and decisions from a group social network.

Delicious (http//del.icio.us) A free bookmarking service found online that allows users to save website addresses publicly and privately online so they can be accessed from any devices connected to the Internet and shared among friends.

Digg A social news site that allows members to submit and vote for articles based on which articles they like best. The articles with the most votes are then seen by more users of Digg as they are ranked by popularity on the site. The more votes you have, the higher your ranking.

embed To make something an integral part, such as coding a video into your website or blog.

EventBrite A provider of online event management and ticketing services for public and private events.

Firefox A popular open-source web browser that enables users to customize their browser through the use of third-party extensions.

flash mob A term that is generally applied only to gatherings organized via social media or viral emails. It consists of large groups of people who assemble suddenly in a public place and perform unusual or entertaining acts, and then quickly disperse.

Flickr A social network built around photo sharing. This service allows users to store photos online and share them through social media sites or emails.

forum Known also as an online message board, it is an online discussion. It's the modern version of a bulletin board.

Foursquare A social network in which users share their physical locations and connect with others in close proximity. It offers digital badges to reward users who "check in" to various locations. This is common service for businesses with brick–and-mortar locations.

Google Buzz A social networking tool from Google. It is designed to integrate with Gmail (also run by Google). Users can share links, photos, videos, and messages which are visible in the user's inbox.

Google Chrome A free web browser from Google that completely integrates with its online search system.

hashtag   A tag used on a social network, such as Twitter, to annotate a message. The hashtag is a way for Twitter users to organize themselves: if everyone agrees to append a certain hashtag to tweets about a topic, it becomes easier to find that topic in search. Example #Superbowl is a hashtag for those conversing about the Super Bowl.

HootSuite   A web-based tool that allows you to manage multiple social media profiles, preschedule tweets and updates, and view metrics.

HTML (hypertext markup language)   A programming language for websites or pages. The next version of HTML will be called HTML5.

instant messaging   A form of real-time text based on communication between two or more people, conducted via video or live voice.

Joomla   A content management system that enables users to build websites and online applications.

KitDigital   An online and mobile video application that provides video hosting for live and recorded events.

lifecasting   A continual broadcast of events in a person's life, usually through digital video. Broadcasts are transmitted through the Internet—and in the near future through wearable technology.

lurker   A person online who reads posts and discussions but rarely if ever participates—only lurks.

MP3 file   A computer file that's created with compression technology. The files are small and often used to make digital audio computer files that can be easily transferred over the Internet.

ORM (online reputation management)   The process of monitoring online references to a person, brand, company, product, or service, with the objective of minimizing the damage of online negative feedback and defamation.

Pandora   A social online radio station that enables users to create their own stations based on favorite artists and music likes.

permalink   A URL or address of a particular post within a blog or website.

plugins   Software applications that can be added to blogs to increase the functionality or provide added features.

Posterous   A content syndication platform that allows users to post content from any device or computer via email.

real-time search   The method of indexing content being published online into a search engine without delay.

Reddit   A social news site with a community of users who share and comment on stories and ideas.

RSS (Real Simple Syndication)   Also known as Rich Site Summary, RSS helps create website feeds that enable you to publish frequently updated texts, such as from blogs.

Seesmic   A desktop and mobile social application which allows users to share content on social networks such as Google Buzz and Twitter from the same application.

SEO (search engine optimization)   Various techniques used to improve your website's search engine rankings.

Skype   A free program that allows for video chats and audio chats between users.

SMS (short message service)   The connection between the phenomenon of text messaging and the underlying technology. In some parts of the world, SMS is used as a synonym for a text message or even for the act of sending a text message (even when a different protocol is actually being used).

spammer   One who sends spam, or unsolicited email, to people.

status updates   Information posted on social media sites. Your status update answers the question "What are you doing right now?" or "What is on your mind?" Think of your status update as your marketing message on social media sites.

sticky   A social media site where one can easily write/post (or paste) information on the page and then replace it with something else.

StumbleUpon   A free web-browser that acts as a smart searching tool for helping you discover websites and videos on topics that may be of interest to you. You suggest topics and StumbleUpon will send you sites and articles that may be of interest.

tags   Keywords that describe the content of your video. They are also search words that people use to find content. When selecting tags, think about what keywords viewers would use to find your video.

Twitter cloud   A cluster of single words or a (visual) written description of words that you have tweeted most often.

unconference   A participant-driven conference centered on a theme or purpose that strives to be unconventional in its approach. Very popular with the social savvy crowd.

URL (uniform resource locator)   The "address" of a specific web page on the World Wide Web. My URL is www.thesaleslounge.com.

video blog   Think of this as a traditional blog, but done regularly via video only or with limited associated wording.

video status   Like a written status update, except that it is distributed via video.

viral marketing   A marketing technique that encourages users to pass a message to other users or websites, which can create an exponential growth in the number of people who see the message.

virtual assistant   A person who provides professional support to assist his or her clients. A VA is usually someone who works from home for an entrepreneur or a small business owner and can provide many services, such as social media marketing and web development.

wall   A feature found on everyone's profile page, fan page, or group page on Facebook. This is where visitors can write a message that stays on the profile page, or wall.

WAP (wireless application protocol)   Enables users to access information via handheld wireless devices, such as cell phones.

Additional Resource Directory

These following websites are great resources for your social media marketing efforts. Some are mentioned in the book, others are not. These sites offer valuable information and resources that can help you stand out in the crowd of millions online! These are some of my personal favorites.

The Sales Lounge (www.thesaleslounge.com)   Hip, fun, conversational, relevant success/sales and social media/success/sales. Mentoring, training, and success products. Learn from an award-winning sales expert and million-dollar producer. Five tiered ultra hip success club. With virtual learning, seminars, and annual success conference.

About.me   Another social networking site that features all about you. Another site to be findable and visible.

Buzzref.com   This site allows you to view your Facebook fan page analytics. A bit humbling next to the celebrities but, you can view your site and your competitors.

TweetDeck (www.tweetdeck.com)   This site is an absolute must for managing your Twitter account. Set up your TweetDeck account and then create custom columns based on your areas of interest.

BubbleTweet (www.bubbletweet.com)   Incorporate video into your tweets—it's a great way to be innovative. Change your video greetings around the holidays, around an event or company special promotion, or just before a product launch.

12seconds (12seconds.tv)   A great site to use to create 12-second video clips. Post on your blog or website, or incorporate into Twitter.

Animoto (animoto.com)   This one was not mentioned in the book, but it is great! Create MTV–style videos for your blog, Twitter, or Facebook page to promote you and your products or services.

TubeMogul (www.tubemogul.com)   Use TubeMogul to distribute your videos to sites across the web.

TweetPhoto (tweetphoto.com)   TweetPhoto is a platform that enables your photos to be discovered, published, and shared easily using the popular social media tools, and encourages viewer interaction with your photo and push marketing.

Twitalyzer 4.0   Key metrics and analytics for you to measure your Twitter ROI. There is a small fee for the report, but many say it is worth it.

Klout.com   The goal of social media is to have it work for you. Klout takes your Twitter, Facebook, and other social influence sites and measures the impact you are truly having on others. Try it!

Kurrently.com   A real-time search engine for Twitter and Facebook. You just have to try it.

CoTweet.com   A great site for businesses with one Twitter site but with multiple voices. Your team and leaders can tweet under one name but can be individually identified.

SocialFlow.com   Knowing when to post tweets and Facebook updates is always in question. This tool appears to take the guesswork out of that and retweets and reposts at optimum times for your greatest impact.

Blogsearch.google.com   Searches topics and people and content within Google but solely within blogs.

SocialBakers.com   Tout themselves as the number one social analytic tool for marketers and analysts. Very in-depth site great for brands, authors, and product marketers.

Slashtag   An easy-to-create custom search engine. It is a tool used to filter search results and helps you to search only high-quality sites, without spam or content farms. Example /bluegrass. You can search for slashtags on a site called www.blekko.com.

Wetoku.com   Create your own interview, TV show, or interactive webcast by finding a friend or source to interview, invite them to Wetoku, and you will then have a split screen broadcast ready to record. Lights. Camera. Action!

http://qrcode.kaywa.com/   A great site to generate your QR Code or Quick Response Code.

BlogTalkRadio (www.blogtalkradio.com   Thinking about an Internet radio show, or want to create podcasts? Look into BlogTalkRadio.

Viddler (www.viddler.com)   Create and share great marketing videos using this tool. There's lots of customization potential.

Ustream (www.ustream.tv)   Create your own streaming TV channel or watch many content-rich (or just plain fun) shows. Lifestreaming (or just streaming) is going to become ever increasingly popular.

Ning (www.ning.com)   Create your own social network around your industry, brand, or business. Create a custom-looking social networking site and make it private or public with just a few easy steps.

AddThis (www.addthis.com)   The number one bookmarking and sharing site. (ComScore July 2009) Place on your blog, e-zine, or newsletter. Let the world share what you have to say—it's a great way to encourage viral marketing.

ooVoo (www.oovoo.com)   Use this great timesaving tool to conduct live meetings, see each other, and collaborate. I use this tool all the time and just love it. It's free, fun, and very professional.

EzineArticles (www.ezinearticles.com)   Article marketing is here to stay. Use EzineArticles to showcase your expertise. When someone runs a search for your name on the Internet, your expert article will appear—remember, though, no selling. You'll find great information and tips and your article will get published online on their site.

Second Life (secondlife.com)   Great for virtual meetings, networking, and presentations. More and more events, meetings, and gatherings will take place using this tool, or others similar to it.

VideoTrio (www.videotrio.com)   Online video production from Hollywood insiders. This group unites professional video production expertise together with the power of online marketing and your business expertise and messaging.

bit.ly   Shorten your links, track your links, and collect a history of your links and how often they are clicked. Great tool to use to provide links in your social media marketing.

Tiny URL (tinyurl.com)   Shorten that long URL or link, and make it tiny. A must for your social media updates to make space for your content links.

Mashable (mashable.com)   A news resource site with everything dealing with social media. I mean everything. Articles, updates, and statistics, etc.

StumbleUpon (www.stumbleupon.com)   This site will help you discover great websites that are matched to your personal preferences. These are sites that have been recommended by others with similar interests as you.

Twellow directory (www.twellow.com)   Get listed in the Twellow directory. Want to reach other journalists? Type in the word "journalist" and see who pops up. This is a great way to connect and follow like-minded folks! Search based on your Twitter bio line that you fill out on Twitter.com.

ShockandAweSales.com   An extraordinary video site that allows purchasers to order customized "infotaining" videos to share on your social sites.

Pinterest.com   A relative newcomer to the social scene, but a popular one. Use it to create a following on your own virtual bulletin board.

Get Glue.com   A social entertainment site that's quickly becoming another hot site for the social sharing of all things entertainment.

Instagr.am   A popular photo-sharing site, not only for the iPhone but for Twitter and other social media sites as well.

Lockerz.com   A site that calls itself "the social site that pays." Upload photos on this site and share them on social sites to earn points toward retail discounts on popular items.

Index

C

L

M

U

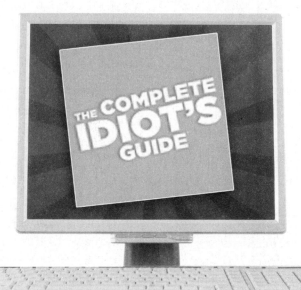